Canals, Cats and Catastrophes

Canals, Cats and Catastrophes

Margaret Awty-Jones

Books by same author:

Hardships, Warships and Feryboats

© Margaret Awty-Jones, 2014

Published by Merseyman Books
20 Bawhead Road, Earby, Barnoldswick, BB18 6PE

Tel: 01282 844902   email: merseymanbooks@gmail.com

All rights reserved. No part of this book may be reproduced, adapted, stored in a retrieval system or transmitted by any means, electronic, mechanical, photocopying, or otherwise without the prior written permission of the author.

The rights of Margaret Awty-Jones to be identified as the author of this work have been asserted in accordance with the Copyright, Designs and Patents Act 1988.

A CIP catalogue record for this book is available from the British Library.

ISBN 978-0-9569429-1-3

Illustrations by the author

Book layout by Clare Brayshaw

Prepared and printed by:

York Publishing Services Ltd
64 Hallfield Road
Layerthorpe
York YO31 7ZQ

Tel: 01904 431213

Website: www.yps-publishing.co.uk

Dedication

To Peter and all our four pawed feline family
for making this book possible

Acknowledgements

Much appreciation to Val and Brian for kindly reading through the manuscript and advising on grammatical amendments

Contents

1.	Light at the End of the Tunnel	1
2.	You Can't Sink a Rainbow	20
3.	A New Crew Member	36
4.	Cat-astrophes and Corncockes	54
5.	Man Overboard	73
6.	A Runaway and Stolen Bike	91
7.	Tragedy Strikes	106
8.	Saga of Red Bull Basin	120
9.	Bigfoot Aboard	137
10.	Jesse Goes Missing	154
11.	Another Mouth to Feed	169
12.	'Bottle Kicking' Custom	189
13.	'Run In' by the Police	209
14.	Blobs Missing	225
15.	Blizzards and Hooligans	245
16.	Snowball or Blobs	265
17.	Mission Jesse	280

Chapter One

Light at the End of the Tunnel

It all started in the late 80's with a phone call from an ex neighbour who had a somewhat unusual query and request. Had I ever been to the local 'Singles Club'? Where was it and on what evenings was it held? And, would I be prepared to take her widowed brother-in-law there, as she thought he needed to get out and meet people, socialize a bit and maybe even eventually meet up with a long term potential lady friend?

Well, it was not the sort of request you'd expect out of the blue and I was at a bit of a loss as to what to say. However, I had been to the Singles club once with a friend but had felt alienated and disappointed. I'd probably built up some romantic notion in my mind and pictured it as a sort of Cinderella-like fairy tale place where I'd glide in and immediately stare into the eyes of some Prince Charming who would be equally smitten by me. But not so, that doesn't happen in the real world. I felt nervous, completely out of place and just wished the floor would open and swallow me up. I felt more isolated and alone than when I was on my own, and although "Singles" suggested that people would be alone, the place seemed just the opposite, full of couples dancing, sitting at tables together and in groups laughing and talking, all obviously getting along famously. It was all too over powering for me at that time, so I quietly disappeared when my friend was invited up onto the dance floor. It was a relief to escape and get back home. The 'light at the end of the tunnel' that everyone kept reassuringly trying to tell me would one day be visible was still shrouded in smog and something I didn't believe I would ever see.

So, "okay" I said. I would meet the brother in law – Peter, and take him along to the 'Singles' club to help him break the ice and hope that his initial reaction wouldn't be the same as mine had been on a previous occasion when I had been there and that he would want to do 'a runner'. Anyway, hopefully, I thought that once we were there he would soon meet up with someone he liked and give me an excuse to opt out early and go home. We met at the club, blind date fashion, and after introducing ourselves decided we would go downstairs into the bar for a drink to give us both a bit of moral support. I'm sure we both needed one, or maybe even two, to calm our nerves. Well that was it, we didn't get any further than the bar stools and just sat talking and laughing a lot together. We came to the mutual decision that neither of us really wanted to venture into the 'Singles' club that night, another time maybe! At the end of our evening I felt glad that I had decided to take Peter to the club and surprised that he'd been such good company and made such a favourable impression on my emotions and wondered if we'd meet again.

However, the weeks went by and we didn't meet up again for months and I gradually pushed him out of my mind and got on with life. As it happened, life had, in different ways, dealt us both extremely painful and de-railing blows. Peter had only recently lost his wife to cancer after 40 years of marriage and I had lost my husband to another woman after 28 years of marriage. Thankfully, I had six lovely children to help and support me through those early 'breaking up' days and they were what kept my head above the water through it all, along with my sanity. It must have also been an unimaginably miserable time for them and one I wish I could have saved them from having to go through.

Although we had felt an instant chemistry between us, and we also met up again to make up a foursome at some event, Peter and I were not emotionally ready when we first met to embark on a relationship; it was too soon. They say that the milestone that eases emotional pain is in the majority of cases about 2 years. Maybe that was a true average, but even so, during those long days after the break up I did sometimes wonder where that illusive light at the end of my dark tunnel would ever appear and where it would lead me. Putting it mildly, they were 'limbo' days but time is the great healer, along with kindness, love and understanding from family and friends. Each little act of kindness, however small, acted as a stepping-stone across my turbulent river of troubled waters.

Every now and then Peter invaded my thoughts and I wondered how he was getting on and if he was happy or sad and miserable. I felt sad that he had no children of his own to comfort him in what I felt sure must be the unhappiest and loneliest time of his life. I wondered if maybe he had met someone else and was in a relationship with them. On a few occasions I rang to just see how he was keeping, but always seemed to ring when he was not there and he told me later he never knew I had phoned.

Some 18 months passed and a friend of one of my daughters invited me to her engagement party and I wondered who I could ask to go with me. I couldn't think of any one that I was enthusiastic about but half-heartedly Peter came to mind. At first I couldn't muster up the courage to ring him in case he turned down my invitation. But finally I picked up the phone. I had to know one way or the other and he could only say 'yes' or 'no'. As things stood, I had everything to gain and nothing to lose. So phone I did and much to my surprise he accepted and we were back on track and from then on, as they say today, we were very much 'an item'.

At about this particular time, when we couldn't bear to be apart for any length of time and wanted to spend every minute together, Peter had promised to take some friends and relatives on an Easter trip up the canal. He had recently bought a sea going cabin cruiser which had been some compensation to him now he was living so far away from the sea and boats something he had never experienced in his life before. The boat had put an interest back into his life and helped him to move on a bit. But canal navigation was a completely different kettle of fish to sea going stuff, as he had discovered on his first few outings up the 'cut' when batting along at – well over the limit – rates of knots; creating tsunami like bow waves that almost washed the fishermen off the canal banks and invited howls of protest from them and other boaters too. Ex Mersey Ferry boat skipper he might have been but with his novice navigation knowledge of the canal system and its 4mph speed limit, he had a lot to learn. Then again, with a boat named "IM-A-WRIGHTONE" what could you expect? This boat was like using a racehorse to plough fields.

One day, out of the blue, Peter asked me if I would like to go with him and his shipmates on this planned canal trip and my beaming face told him my very definite affirmative answer. I had secretly been hoping I would be invited along. I hadn't even seen the boat at this stage and my imagination ran amuck with visions alternating between some stately floating gin palace type Mediterranean cruiser and an old African Queen like wreck.

"It needs a good old clean up after sitting all winter moored up", Peter said. So I bunged a bundle of rags and cleaning equipment into a bag and off we went to see if she was still afloat. I knew nothing about boats or the canal but had always had a passionate interest in boats and ships so the thought of being on one was exciting and I was raring to go. We parked the car and walked a short distance to the moorings at Barrowford on the Leeds & Liverpool canal where an assortment of boats were tied up, most of which were looking a bit the worse for wear and in desperate need of some TLC after their winter sojourn.

"Here she is", announced Peter, pulling back a navy blue and green algae stained PVC cover and disappearing beneath it, leaving me to clamber aboard virtually no-handed, with bagsful of STUFF, as is usual practice for women, even though the days of 'Slave Ships' are long gone.

'Blimey, this really is IT,' I thought as my brain slipped into neutral gear, not quite knowing what was coming next. Peter was fumbling with a key which hung from a large cork ball.

"That's an odd key ring Peter" I said. Silly me! Apparently all boaters had them due to the fact that if the key fell into the water the cork floated so that the key could be safely retrieved. Peter grinned and told me about an incident many years ago when he'd been working on the ferry boats and had lost about forty keys on a key ring which belonged to the skipper. Peter had been swinging the keys around when they suddenly flew off out of his hand and into the depths of the river Mersey never to be seen again. It took the skipper about two and a half years to replace all the locks and keys to everything.

The cabin door was accessed from a good sized stern deck which once opened led down two steps into a cosy well laid out cabin with combined eating and sleeping accommodation.. Comfortably, it could sleep four adults and uncomfortably seven or eight. Storage room for anything but the bare necessities was quite limited but it was surprising what could be crammed into storage spaces under seating. I thought we had a second wardrobe till I discovered it was the closet for the porta potti which was desperately in need of a good clean up. Once I managed to find out how it all worked and came apart, I gave it just that with an added final generous measure of loo bloo.

Well, it took a few days of 'grime busting' and plenty of soap, water, scrubbing and cleaning to get **'Im-a-wright-one'** looking like **'Im-a-bright-one'**. She looked a different boat, white and blue, shiny, smart and tiddley, all set to go, all 25ft x 10ft beam of her. Finally, a motley crew of landlubbers boarded her, none of us at all familiar with boats and waterways apart from Peter who had lived and worked on and with boats most of his adult life, so we were confident we would be able to leave that side of things all to him and that we would just be the galley slaves and dogs bodies down below. I'd never seen a lock operated, or if I had, had never paid much attention to the sequence of events that operated the relevant paddles and gates to enable boats to work their way either up or down the lock systems. Peter seemed to have the cushy job up on deck, sitting behind the wheel, enjoying the scenery, while the rest of us slaved away preparing and cooking meals, washing up, cleaning, making and unmaking beds with frequent and badly timed interruptions as we approached locks and had to drop everything to dash up on deck, and clumsily clamber on and off the boat, jumping ashore with windlasses and ropes at the ready. The way we shaped up would have had Nelson turn in his grave. On one attempt to throw a line ashore to one of our crew, I cast the rope in the air and knocked his glasses off with it. Well it could have been worse! It could have been his head!

"You are not supposed to lasso them!" yelled Peter. "It's not the Wild West!" I couldn't keep a straight face. It was a classic "Carry on up the Canal" scenario.

Secretly, I thought we sure were all up the bloody creek. The weather was appalling. It was Easter in Antarctica stuff, but with torrential rain instead of snow. Our youngest crew member was full of a stinking cold, forever coughing and sneezing and leaving heavily used nose blowing tissue everywhere, while other crew members chain smoked and coughed and we all inhaled and exhaled the fuggy miasma together as we sat round the mess deck table playing cards, gambling for small change, and drinking copious amounts of whiskey and water, purely for medicinal purposes of course. If we'd have been in a Las Vegas casino, our enjoyment would not have been greater than it was at these card playing sessions, even when we all eventually succumbed to our young friend's germ warfare. While outside the rain and wind constantly battered and buffeted the boat, inside we felt snug and cosy in our nautical smog.

Peter and I often slept out on the deck under the awning, in our sleeping bags, on an airbed and one such night I awoke early, as the first hint of dawn appeared on the horizon, and noticed the odd raindrop plopping down every now and then. The rain must have found a way through the PVC cover somewhere. It was only a few spots here and there, nothing to panic about and I was too warm and comfortable to move and soon went back to sleep. Dawn soon officially gave way to daybreak and I woke again and mentioned to Peter that a little rain had been dripping in through the night but he was too comatose to comprehend such mundane information so early in the morning. I sat up and my eyes, still half asleep, began to focus on some little pink and white wiggly things, on the bed and BLIMEY, in the bed ON US! And worse still. No I wasn't dreaming.

"We've been invaded by maggots," I yelled at Peter as I frantically shook him awake.

What I had thought to be rain dripping in during the night, had in fact been maggots. Peter and one of the lads had been fishing during the day and forgotten to put the lid back on the maggot container and they had all crawled out and been dropping down onto us all night. They were everywhere, even in our hair. We had no choice but to set about recovering what we hoped was every last one which wasn't an easy or pleasant task. I never dreamed in my worst nightmare that I would be sharing a bed with dozens of assorted maggots. The rest of the crew banned us from entering the cabin until we were maggot free, but later that day we paid a visit to the local swimming pool for a shower and in the shower tray around my feet when I had finished were two more maggots. I was just glad they weren't spiders as I was definitely of an arachnophobic nature.

By the end of our canal holiday I think we were all fit (to drop) and had all had a good time and quite an experience. In the weeks that followed, Peter and I often escaped off up the cut on our own and enjoyed meandering along peaceful stretches of canal out in the countryside. The light at the end of the tunnel had literally come true for us. So much so that we nearly knocked the row of traffic lights suspended over the entrance of Foulridge tunnel, off. Life was good again but we found ourselves wanting to spend more and more time afloat and to travel further a field. We realized however, that in a 10ft beam boat we could only travel stretches of canal and locks wide enough to accommodate it, and which would severely limit the scope of travel available to us. Also, 'Im-a-wright-one' guzzled petrol and was far too expensive to use for travelling far in and she was not suitable for winter weather. So, as travelling and serious plans to become water gypsies gradually consumed us, we kept our eyes open for a more suitable boat, one which would accommodate us in a more civilized manner and in which we would be able to navigate all of the waterways. Before long we saw, liked and bought a 42ft narrow boat up for sale in Skipton

This boat had a tiller instead of a wheel and was completely different in every way to the cabin cruiser, but it was exciting to think we were now going to be able to travel and explore the waterways, consisting of over some 2,000 navigable miles of canals and rivers. Firstly we decided to get some alterations done inside and took the opportunity of making our first journey to Wigan in our new boat along with another couple in their boat. This made life easier for us on our maiden voyage than travelling on our own, sharing the locks and swing bridges, some of which were considerably heavy going. All was smooth sailing apart from having a few stones thrown at us near Burnley. We also had some problems with black smoke, making the boat very smelly and sluggish. Our travelling companions on "Geordie Girl" were astern of us as we went through Foulridge tunnel, with our for'd lamp light flooding the tunnel ahead and our diesel smoke blackening all astern with much coughing from our friends behind.

Peter: *"good stuff this diesel eh Geordie? "Luvly day aint it?"*
Geordie:- *"Cough! Cough! Bloody 'ell Peter 'ave you blown a gasket or is Maggie making toast agen?"*

From then on we decided we had better go astern of Geordie Girl as the faces of their crew were beginning to look like those of African natives.

Our biggest challenge now was going to be descending Wigan flight of 23 locks. The only consolation, apart from there being four of us to tackle them, was that we would be going down the locks which would be a lot easier than going up them.

It took us a couple of hours with the help of two very co-operative and helpful lock keepers. I got as keen as mustard to dash ahead and prepare the locks as we approached them. But did so without realising the extent of strain I was putting on my back which had never been A1 since having a prolapsed disc some years previous. It all flared up again and became progressively worse as I continued leaping around locks and quays like wonder woman. So it was just as well that we moored up there at a boatyard to have the alterations done to the boat and allow me some time to rest and hope the pressure on the sciatic nerve would ease up.

It took seven weeks for the boat to have the wood stove moved, the cabin lounge divided to make two cabins, one to sleep in and one to live in. Bathroom pump and water pump renewed; deck plates/boards renewed; steel doors fitted fore and aft; plus lots of minor adjustments and repairs. We had also by this time renamed our boat "Rainbow II". While we waited for the work to be done we decided to go to Skipton and make another journey down to Wigan with 'Im-a-wright-one'. The thought of all the locks and swing bridges and the state of my back was worrying and I knew that I was not yet confident enough to handle and steer the boat on my own so that Peter could open and shut the locks. This was a problem until we had offers of help from family and friends. So, there were no mishaps on the action replay trip down to Wigan apart from when the airbed, which was airing out on top of the cabin, suddenly took off in a gust of wind as we went round aptly nick-named "Windy Corner", and landed in the water but was instantly fished out again.

Also, long before we reached Wigan, we received an unsuspected visit from a marauding posse of family members, one of whom desperately needed an overnight babysitter for our year old grand-daughter Danielle. So it was a real case of 'baby onboard' and we didn't have to rock her to sleep as the boat did it for us. From then on all was plain sailing apart from getting all kinds of flotsam and jetsam wrapped round our propeller. It was unbelievable the amount and variety of junk there was. At least if it was floating we could spot it and hopefully avoid it but if it was submerged, it was like going through a minefield. "Crunch"! We had copped it good and proper this time and came to a grinding halt. Peter, armed with a large knife, scrambled astern and over the side, onto the tailboard and attempted to free us from whatever had caught around the propeller. It turned out to be a large sponge sofa or armchair cushion and was a real struggle to remove, like cutting chunks off a huge cheese. Urban stretches of canal, as you can imagine, were much worse to contend with and we'd count numerous shopping trolleys, rusty bikes, oil drums, plastic containers, pallets and everything else that you'd never ever dream of coming across. Black plastic bags beneath the water were a nightmare for catching round the propeller and would slow us down to a sluggish crawl. However, if we gave a good burst astern on the prop, it would often soon free us up again. We had to watch out that our stern mooring rope never accidentally slipped into the water near the prop blades, as ropes caught round propellers were the ultimate nightmare. During autumn when travelling through wooded stretches of canal thick with fallen leaves, boats often became dramatically slowed down.

Once again we were rewarded with fine views across Wigan and the surrounding landscape as we dropped over 200ft down into the town via the 23 locks. And of course during our prolonged stay in the area over the following weeks we had to visit the famous Wigan Pier and complex of museums, including the largest working steam  engine in the world. We took a look at the old work boat Roland, on display in the garden area and Peter leaned over her side to have a closer look and managed to get covered in tar, the second time in six months.

On one of our trips into town, Peter must have looked like a working bargee, ie, scruffy. He went into the bank to get a few counter cheques to tide him over till he received his new cheque book but the counter clerk was reluctant to oblige and eyed him up very suspiciously. After much wrangling Peter managed to draw out some cash and as he turned to depart he stated, sarcastically and loud enough for clerk and queue of irate customers all to hear, "I've just been let out of prison and I'm dying for a drink."

We moored 'Im-a-wright-one' alongside 'Rainbow II' and were able to recharge our batteries for awhile. The specialist had prescribed "complete rest" for my sciatica, so we decided to take up a bit of restful painting plus time with family so for awhile we were like a couple of yo-yo's However, we were keen to get on with boating now we had the chance and as soon as we could we managed to get a few miles out of the rather drab built up areas of Wigan into the more pleasant terrain of the pretty wooded Douglas Valley. The peace and tranquillity was like a breath of fresh air and we moored up opposite a lot of reeds where the antics of some moorhens entertained us until dusk.

Bronte wood burning stove and side panel showing Bronte character and pen and ink.

Peter by this time had become quite a lumberjack and the pair of us were constantly on the look out for pieces of wood in any shape or form for our wood burning stove.

By the end of October we realized that wood burned so much quicker than coal and that it would be an ongoing daily chore to keep enough stocked up for daily use in the winter months. Under the forward deck boards there was a large hold, ideal for keeping logs in. We picked up any fallen branches or logs in or out of the canal and were forever on the lookout for discarded fence-posts and if they had been treated with preservatives they were considered to be A1 prizes for their wonderful inflammable qualities.

We really didn't ever want to have to resort to buying logs if we could help it as there was so much wood abandoned and wasted since people had stopped having open fires in their homes. It was there for the taking if you made the effort to collect and saw it up.

Mostly we collected dead wood, but when desperate we would mix dead with green before it had chance to dry out so flames would invariably turn to miserable grey heatless smoke. We soon learned which types of wood burned well and which didn't, as we learned most other things in our new life on the water, which was the **hard way**.

Desperate one evening for some wood for the fire Peter went off up the canal bank to where he had seen a very low and 'ready to break off' looking bough of a tree. He hung himself on the end of it and forced it and himself backwards, heaving and bending it back, waiting for it to break off the trunk. But it was tougher and more pliable than he had anticipated and at both his and the branches limit of bendability, he lost his footing down the bank and as he slipped, still holding onto the branch, it almost catapulted him across the canal. Not defeated he went on to find enough wood for the evening fire but not before stumbling down the bank on his arse a few times.

I finished painting two name boards for each side of the boat and Peter fixed them on, but we found that so many people stopped for time consuming chats that jobs became endless tasks unless we discreetly disappeared into the boat when we saw anyone coming.

The nights began to get very chilly and once it was dark and we were in the forward cabin for the evening by the fire, we had to wrap up well if there was little wood to burn. It was especially cold inside the boat below the water line, so when sitting we found that our legs from the knees down felt as though they were at the North Pole compared to the rest of our bodies in Northern England. We soon learned to lag our legs well with pairs of 'long Johns' in addition to thermal vests and layers of warm clothes which for me was also the case when I was in bed plus hot water bottle and even at times a woolly hat. Peter used to laugh and say I went to bed with more clothes on than I wore during the day. And with condensation forever present we had no choice but to live in damp but happy conditions.

We often had to get on the move whether we wanted to or not in order to find wood, and on reaching Burscough and taking on water there, we found a timber yard where the chap very kindly gave us a huge amount of off cuts and was even good enough to loan Peter the use of a wheelbarrow for the job. So the home fires were certainly burning very brightly that night along with an equally bright and colourful sunset.

Strange things happen when living on a boat that never do ashore. We ended up that evening with a canoe on our roof. Some scouts had been canoeing up and down and a lad, very aptly in canoe number thirteen, had come unstuck and unable to man his canoe, so the Scout master asked us if we would return it to base on our way back, which we gladly did.

We were rudely awakened in the middle of the night around 3 am by some idiot on the tow path shouting and screaming. We couldn't imagine who on earth would be out at such an hour in torrential rain and gale force wind creating such a hullabaloo. This went on for about an hour before we assumed the police had been called as there were a lot of lights flashing and a voice trying to calm someone down. As curious as we had been to know what the incident had been all about, we were left guessing. It was far too dangerous to venture from the safety of the boat to see what was going on, especially if you happened to be moored out in the middle of nowhere. More often than not these incidents involved a person or two who had had more than enough to drink. Sometimes groups of lads would untie our mooring ropes or pull up the mooring pins as they passed and set us afloat. It was more annoying to lose a mooring peg than to be set adrift, but often the mooring peg would still be hanging on the end of the rope and thankfully retrievable. Youths often jumped or stood on the mooring ropes to rock the boat as they passed, especially in the areas where the canal towpath was en route to and from the local pub. We used to dread firework night in case anyone took it into their heads to put a banger down our stove chimney funnel, but luckily no one ever did and we never heard of any other boaters being victimised in this way. If the wind was blowing in a certain direction we used to get bursts of smoke blowing out of the stove as gusts blew down the flue. Maybe that is how boaters such as us acquired the nickname of "smokey stovers" The cabin walls (bulkheads) used to get very smoke stained and had to be cleaned often.

Gradually, over the weeks I became more confident at handling and steering the boat which enabled us to share the job of opening locks and swing bridges and made life more interesting too. We put up a good show at Parbold when Peter nipped ashore to operate the swing bridge and couldn't open it with the windlass. No wonder, as he was turning it the wrong way and holding up the 'none too happy' motorists waiting to get through. We were in the slow lane going nowhere in particular, at snails pace, so didn't worry and it gave me plenty of time to show off my newly acquired boat skills. Peter said he would have to buy me a new hat for my big head.

Initially the layout of the boat from fore to aft was:- fore deck leading down two steps into the front cabin, measuring some 10ft x 7ft wide, through to the middle sleeping quarters of about the same size, with double bed. Alongside the bed ran a 9ft long narrow passage with WC (porta potti and hip bath situated in a small cubicle just past the bed). The latter part was partitioned off with a door which we later removed and replaced with a curtain to give a bit more elbow room when squashed straight jacket like on the loo between hip bath and passage bulkhead. Lastly, at the stern end' the galley measuring about 6ft x 7ft wide with a 4 ring calor gas cooker, fridge, sink/drainer, couple of small worktops and cupboards. On nice days it was pleasant preparing meals in there with the door open on to the stern, but in winter it was draughty and difficult to see very clearly due to poor lighting. Not surprisingly I did on occasion find one or two unplanned ingredients in our meals and didn't enjoy once discovering that the mouthful of food I was chewing up included a spider with rough grass-like textured legs. After that I carefully examined my meals and fished out any obvious intruders. Peter used to laugh and say I needed to get some meat down me somehow as I ate very little of it.

We usually had a good breakfast, then a main meal in the evening and although we did little cooking on top of the woodstove it came in handy to keep things hot on. But more often than not I used it to boil up washing on and had a very large metal two handled panikin which I kept especially for the job. I'd wash small amounts daily then hang them out on a rotary washing line which Peter had ingeniously fixed up on top of the gas locker space for'd. When fully rigged with washing it looked like a real fancy set of foresails blowing in the wind, much to the disdain of the occasional immaculate, wine drinking floating gin palace boats passing by.

It wasn't so clever though when the wind was blowing towards it from the direction of the chimney funnel which only stood about 4ft away from it.

I'd hang any larger items such as bedding, over the hedges or on a nearby handy fence. I couldn't understand the snobby mentality of people who looked down their noses at clean washing hanging outside to dry, be it on a line, rotary or otherwise from posts or trees, fences or hedges, blowing nicely in the breeze and acquiring a wonderful fresh air smell that nothing bought in a bottle could begin to equal. The only setback when throwing items of washing over hedges was that some items were more prone to catching and snagging on branches, particularly those of blackthorn or hawthorn bushes, resulting in various articles at times taking on a rather moth eaten appearance.

If washing didn't get dry outside I had to bring it inside and hang it all around the front cabin from small sections of line strung up from hooks overhead. As the cabin was only just over 6ft high, you can imagine this washing completely took the place over. However, I sussed out suitable angles and ways of hanging it all so that we didn't end up continually getting it wound all round ourselves every time we made a move and I had lots of useful hooks strategically placed everywhere from which I used to hang painted items of 'canalia' to dry. Peter was more prone to getting clattered around the head from these overhead hazards than I. Space was something we had very little of to spare.

We ran everything off calor gas or the batteries for things like lights, pump and the small black and white TV. I had no iron, hair drier, electric kettle etc, or running water (without first going to a water point and filling up our water tank). No flush toilet (it was my designated job to empty and clean out the porta potti by taking it to the nearest sanitary disposal station). These were sometimes few and far between so we didn't take these things for granted as we would have done in a house. Having a bath was a luxury and we used to take turns to squash ourselves into the small hip bath once a week and soak. Compared to what some boats had, we were well off and blissfully happy with our lot.

During our travels on the Leeds and Liverpool canal, it amazed me to learn that this manmade trans-Pennine waterway was nigh on 130 miles long and, with it's wide beam locks, could accommodate boats up to 62ft long and 14ft wide. It had taken forty-six years to build being completed in 1816 with the final stretch between Blackburn and Wigan and could claim many great engineering achievements such as the five rise staircase at Bingley. After we had made two or three more trips back and forth along much of it we could well believe that it had 91 locks and 53 bridges to its credit. We sometimes counted them in our sleep. Certain numbers of these locks and swing bridges, mostly those in urban areas such as Blackburn and Wigan had their paddles (sluices) fitted with anti vandal locks and required a special key to unlock them, which made it all the more difficult and time consuming to open and close them. But it was better than having the risk of paddles being left open and causing mayhem.

By the end of October, with the clocks going back we missed the extra hour of daylight in the afternoon. Except Peter that is, as he had put his watch ON an hour instead of back, so he was two hours in front of the rest of us. Time didn't matter much, and we mostly had no time for it. We started playing games of crib in the evenings and occasionally paid a visit to any handy nearby pubs for a bit of company and a change from the boat. One evening we were having a quiet cosy drink, playing a game of dominoes and didn't realize how comfortable we were getting or how much we had managed to drink until the spots on our dominoes suddenly appeared to have more spots on them than all of Disney's 101 Dalmatians put together.

Late Autumn was so peaceful in the wooded valley. We appreciated living so close to nature as against the noisy existence of terraced Coronation street type dwellings with the endless noise of traffic, banging of car and house doors, barking dogs, shouting people, DIY fanatics wielding noisy drills and hammers at unsociable hours etc. We sat out on the bow or stern decks watching the wildlife all around us and discovered that winter months were the best for spotting the beautiful metallic blue flash of kingfishers as they darted along close to the water. We were mesmerized by the antics of the ever present ducks, moorhens, coots, herons, swans, geese and all the songbirds, plus at this time of year dozens of fat oven ready sized pheasants, strutting their stuff, everywhere. Peter viewed them as "meals on wheels" and if one unfortunate 'destined for dinner' bird happened to come his way he would have it and save himself a trip to the butchers. We seemed to be in a 'pheasant plucker's paradise' and early one morning I woke Peter to tell him "There's a big one on the towpath right by the boat." He was up and dressed quick as a flash but not before the 'pheaso' had disappeared into the hedge. However, not one to be defeated, Peter, the ever intrepid pheaso stalker re-moored the boat further along the bank where a number of the mobile dinners had been sighted previously. Then slowly and very surreptitiously he crept along the hedge and up the bank by a big tree to have a look when as he did so two pheasants shattered the silence as they took off in a sudden and explosive wing clapping flight right in front of him, causing Peter to almost die of fright and he returned to the boat with his feathers more than ruffled.

Not to be deterred, occasionally I would find Peter missing and he'd be squatting uncomfortably up the bank somewhere, hiding in the foliage, either at dusk or dawn, waiting to take a pot shot at some unfortunate pheaso. Not exactly the Big Game Hunter, and more often than not' after frustratingly failed attempts we would end up with buying a rabbit from the local butcher and having rabbit stew or rabbit pie which I thought was much nicer anyway.

Well into October and the Crib Stakes began to get very competitive and intense, with nil games to the Big Game Hunter and 3 to "Hippo bum", who shall remain anonymous. By the end of the allotted number of games, I was champ with four games to nil, seven legs to one.

"Maggie the Crib Queen"

    Peter spent many a quiet hour fishing and daydreaming out on the stern deck and I was never happier than when wielding a paint brush in my hand, either painting canalia or the boat. At this particular time, I was painting a diamond pattern on the two steel front cabin doors in red and yellow and when they were finished I painted a cratch board to fit across the bow of the boat, secured in place on top of the gas locker. Peter kept busy by making and fitting inner door panels and came across some good pieces of new plywood in a skip. Most boaters were good "skip routers" and recyclers of useful so called rubbish. We had a lot to choose from in an era of the throw away society and never ceased to be amazed at the awful waste and almost criminal abandonment of good useful stuff, thrown away. Boaters seemed to have an appreciation and resourcefulness for making good use of others cast offs and often left unwanted but useful items neatly in front of the canal sited skips, hoping another boater would be able to put them to some use. It made sense and if a boater knew another boater was on the lookout for a certain article he would soon inform him of its whereabouts if he happened to come across it on his travels. Books were always a welcome find, often left by boaters at the waste disposal points along the canal for others to pick up and read. As it wasn't possible to join a library, with the odd exception if moored a long time somewhere, when constantly travelling, it was like finding a bit of treasure. If I had the chance, now and then when near a village or town I would find some good books in charity shops and be eager to get back to the boat with them and give to Peter. You would have thought that Christmas had come early, he'd be so pleased with them and with me for getting them for him. Happiness on long dark winter evenings was to get warm and cosy together and immersed in good books.

    Boaters were not so generous when it came to 'wood supplies' Wood meant warmth in winter and 'smokey stovers' wilfully competed for it and mostly kept quiet about any finds they came across, until it was safely all stowed on their boats. Unless there was plenty for all, then word soon got around on the grapevine. When the waterways or council workers were clearing areas and thinning certain stretches along the canal, we had a bean feast. It was a matter of pot luck where you were at the time work was being carried out. When wood was being logged and cleared, handy to the canal, I sometimes approached the foreman and asked if we could have some and this was a good and rewarding policy in many cases. Once we came across a farmer and his workers removing all of his old oak fence posts and broken fences around an area of his sheep field and asked him if we could have some. He was very obliging and only too pleased to let us have as much as we could load onto the boat without capsizing it and even got a couple of his workers to assist us. There were other times when there was no one to ask, but equally no apparently obvious requirement or use for the wood that we had come across, so we would gather it up and put to good use. Our thoughts were consumed with 'wood'. We rarely ever passed even a log-sized piece, me especially who Peter called the "wood gnome". Wood stored on top of the boat soon dried out, green or not and we put green logs on top of and around the wood stove to dry. When nothing at all managed to get the fire burning well we'd resort to burning an old boot or shoe to liven it up or shove a rag soaked in diesel oil in. A good blaze made all the difference on a cold night and once the temperature in the boat rose, we'd find ourselves stripping off our layers of clothing and even moaning and swooning about the heat and have to resort to opening the doors to cool down. At times this heat must have equalled that of a tropical dessert, up in the 90s. The wood stacked around the stove flue sometimes became so hot that I used to wonder how on earth it failed not to burst into flames. Flames a foot or more high sometimes shot out of the chimney into the night sky and it didn't do to burn more than a few creosoted logs at any one time. The fire rarely stayed in over night and I cleaned out the wood ash in the mornings and re-lit it. We always made sure we had a good supply of kindling wood chopped or a collection of small twigs, handy.

By mid November we were back in Wigan and desperate to get some more books as we had by this time almost acquired a 'resident status' and been able to join the library there. Peter asked me to get him a copy of 'Les Miserables' and or Omar Khayyam but I couldn't find any so he had to make do with the Diaries of Adrian Mole, instead. He enjoyed reading it in bed until 3pm the next day, feigning flu-like symptoms as an excuse and as the sole active crew member I was kept more than busy cleaning, including the brass, making a stew and fetching bread and milk from the local shop. On my way back I was caught unawares by a Mancunian cloudburst and arrived back at the boat looking like a drowned water rat.

While we were moored near the Pier, we noticed a couple of young teenagers suspiciously eyeing up Peter's fishing rod on the roof, and moved it out of sight. The grey days now mostly consisted of rain and put life almost 'on hold'. Maggie Thatcher resigned from the Government while we continued to play crib and read.

For a change one evening we played Ludo, comfortably, warm in bed, but Peter was cheating (I am allowed to say that as I am writing this book). So, I decided to cancel the game and have a replay at a later date and on a flat surface rather than in bed where the tiddley winks kept slipping off or being deliberately knocked off the board, kind of accidentally on purpose, by a certain ancient mariner. Peter's excuse was poor manoeuvrability due to the onset of a painful frozen shoulder that prevented him from being able to manipulate the tiddley winks properly.

"Alright Enid Blyton" I said. "Goodnight".

Chapter Two

You Can't Sink a Rainbow

By the end of November Peter thought I should get some serious medical advice for my worsening back problem, but we were both reluctant to give in to the idea of having to leave the boat and go ashore again, so we masked over our ailments with various drugs and the boat began to look like a chemists shop.

Infrequently, when out of necessity we needed to move the boat, I'd have to negotiate a lock or two, wind up the stiff paddles and heave open the very big and heavy gates. But when I finally became so bent up and deformed with sciatica and back pain, I knew there was no alternative and that I'd have to get some treatment if we were to ever have any chance of continuing our life on the canal.

Feeling rather dejected we moored Rainbow II at the bottom of Wigan flight near the boatyard and Captain Pugwash, on a small boat there, assured us he'd keep an eye on her. It seemed that no one on the canal ever had a real name of their own. They either had nicknames or were simply known by the name of their boat. Someone for instance might ask you if you had seen "glass-o-wine-Ginger" on 'Boozing and Cruising' or "Soggy John" on "Rising Damp", but rarely the real name of the person.

So, with little choice we became, we hoped, temporarily landlubbers again. Not that at this particular time I cared whether I was on land, water or in an airborne rocket heading for the moon. I spent three days trying to get into pain free comfortable positions, even to the point of almost standing on my head or curled up on all fours on the floor. My daughter must have thought I'd gone strange in the head when she came in one day and discovered me.

"Are you doing Yoga or praying to Mecca?" she asked, giving me an old fashioned look.

I couldn't even laugh or cry even if I had wanted to, it was all too painful. I retreated to bed, and later the doctor called and sent me off to hospital where I spent two weeks confined to a bed, on traction, a sort of 20th century form of medieval torture similar to being put on the 'rack'. I was kept flat on my back with weights attached to my legs to gradually stretch and ease the pressure off the nerves causing the pain. For a while it was even worse till gradually over the days it eased a bit and with daily anti blood clotting injections and valium tablets to relax the back muscles, plus pain killers every four hours things began to improve. Sleep, when it came was such a welcome release from it all. Eating and drinking was difficult, but at times like this you aren't very hungry. I would drink via a bent straw into a cup or glass of liquid which was placed on the bed alongside my head. Likewise, meals were placed the same and I was given a fork and spoon with which to try to manipulate some food as best as I could into my mouth and eat. Much of the time it was very, hit and miss. Sometimes I was given thin soup in a baby type feeder cup, which was a little easier.

Peter came to visit me, all bright and breezy and was always the highlight of my day, but I could sense he was at a loss, even though the family were doing all that they could to help him, which was a consolation to me. He put me before anything and everything (with maybe the exception of fishing!), and was so kind and patient and wanted so little for himself. I thought it was a shame that he was having to go through all this again as he had done previously with his wife who had years of spinal problems and treatment for it.

Finally, after two weeks, bedridden on my back, I was at last allowed to get up. When the nurse said she would help me up the flight of stairs and accompany me to the bathroom, I was a bit taken back and thought she was being a bit soft and over careful with me, until I realized just how weak my legs had become after such a short time confined to bed.

It was miraculous, no pain whatsoever, although the specialist had worried me when he had said that there was no guarantee that things could not go 'pear shape' again and that eventually I might need surgery. Time would tell. In the meantime it was nice to spend Christmas happily with Peter and the family, celebrate a few birthdays including Peter's 65th and go to the theatre to see Ken Dodd.. During this time we assumed all was well with Rainbow II under the watchful eye of Captain Pugwash and the nearby boatyard. We were naïve to the fact that leaving a boat moored up wasn't quite like leaving a house. There were numerous things that could go wrong if a boat wasn't regularly checked out for any length of time.

At last, it was time to end our sojourn on terra firma and make out way back to the boat. Our old engineering friend Leo came with us to check and iron out any mechanical hiccoughs that might have presented themselves, or need a little attention to get us shipshape again.

As we somewhat excitedly approached Wigan and our mooring we were impatient to catch our first glimpse of Rainbow II and as we turned off the bridge road to the canal approach there she was, not our lovely proud floating Rainbow II but a dismal, horribly forlorn capsized Rainbow II. We just stared in numbed statuesque shock at the scene before us. Subsequently, we learned that the Waterways had dropped the water level in the bottom pound where we were moored and Rainbow II had dropped down with the water, her mooring ropes, secured to rings set in concrete, had become too stretched to slacken off and hold her level, so she had accordingly, tipped to an angle as she hung tightly on the ropes one side, and taken on water through her drainage holes which were now at water level. Had her ropes been slackened off it would never have happened. Fortunately, it could have been so much worse, had the water at the edge of the pound been deeper, she would have submerged more, or even completely.

We were devastated, she was inaccessible and at a dangerous and unpredictable angle for boarding safely, plus being awash with water which on the offshore side was 3 – 4ft deep inside her. Our hearts sank with her, down to the depths but our despondency turned to desperation, knowing that the daylight hours were very rationed and we needed to turn all our thoughts and energy into positive action as soon as possible if we were to salvage her. We were angry that no-one had contacted us, especially the nearby boatyard where we had so recently spent hundreds of pounds and where 'Im-a-wright-one' was still moored. Rainbow II was in full view of the unmade approach road to and from the boatyard. What made things even worse, when Peter contacted them, was their offer to "take on the salvage work with your Insurance Company for you." That was like a red rag to a bull to Peter whose answer was to storm into the boatyard, angrily untie 'Im-a-wright-one' and with no messing about, haul her out of her mooring and tie her up astern of Rainbow II. Fortunately before anyone got hurt, there was no time to delay further on negative unproductive actions and the daylight hours were too precious to waste. Our first urgent priority was to get hold of a pump. We managed to hire one and picked it up from a place not too far away. Pumping started in earnest with what looked like, to me, a right old antique specimen of a pump which laboriously and noisily slurped away, sucking the water out of the boat at a painfully slow rate. But our spirits rose once we realized we were most definitely going to re-float Rainbow II even if so much inside her had been ruined, including much of the tongue and groove that covered all the bulkheads. It had swollen and buckled in places, out of the grooves.

As the water slowly retreated I ventured down onto the front deck and inside the front cabin, much to protest from Peter who said movement might alter her position and tip her further into the water. I just shut my ears to the protests and armed with a screwdriver, intent on my mission to salvage just one very precious item – a large framed photograph 24inches x 18 inches, of my six children given to me by them on my last birthday. Thank goodness it had been fixed high enough on the bulkhead to escape the water. I paddled through the waterlogged cabin, unscrewed the picture and happily clambered out again, clutching my picture and family to me.

We didn't manage to salvage all the gear stored under the bed or seat lockers and it was a gruelling task each day taking sopping wet stuff out, particularly the new foam seating, bedding, pillows and sleeping bags. Loads of expensive natural history and reference books were ruined along with my portable typewriter and we hoped the Insurance Company would treat our claim generously.

On returning to the boat one day we found that someone had pinned a large piece of paper over our Rainbow II name board with the words "Mary Rose" appropriately written on it. Humour always seemed to find a way to amuse, however bad things were. But, you can't sink a Rainbow!

It wasn't the best time of the year to sink a boat – no sun or dry weather to help us get dried out but eventually we managed to get the fire going again to speed up the drying out process a bit. But where the water inside the boat had come up to we could see the difference and the mould kept coming back in the cupboards and on shelves. It was comfortable to be inside again, but we still had not got the foam dried out for the seats and the mattress was still not completely dried out. We had to spend as much time as we could aboard with a good fire going and work on repairs and endless cleaning. Everything became covered in thick black oily soot and as soon as I cleaned it all, it was back again and I had to start all over again. The wood stove was leaking from its joints so every time it was lit the air was filled with a dirty fug from it. After yet another cleaning session and 4 or 5 bowls full of black water I realized I was not winning the battle and announced a ban on the lighting of the stove until the leaking parts had been properly sealed up.

With Rainbow II once more afloat and safely moored up under the genuine and watchful eye of one of the lock keepers, we made the decision to take 'Im-a-wright-one' to a boatyard near Hapton and put her up for sale. So along with our knowledgeable and ever available engineer and his son we set off again from Wigan, up the now familiar flight of twentythree locks. At a speed of at most 4 mph, the thought of our journey of about 33 miles and all the locks was equivalent to that of making a trip 'over the sticks' on a blindfold donkey up the Khyber Pass.

It was trying at times, sharing a small boat with three men faffing about under my feet, feeding and brewing up for them non stop, but on the whole we were an amiable crew most of the time and both Peter and I were indebted to them for all the help given to us to make this trip possible.

The first shock Peter and I experienced was, that, early mornings for our engineer and son started at 5.30 am regardless. To Peter and I, this unsociable hour was more like the middle of the night and on a boat any sounds, or movements made were unavoidably exaggerated and shared by everyone whether they wanted to or not. So it was a case of "We're awake, everyone's awake, come on Maggie get the tea made." Bog eyed brews and burned toast all round ensued. Toast that was too burned to eat was whizzed 'Frisbee' fashion out of the doors for the ducks who, really did need to do as their name suggested and 'duck' or risk being decapitated by brittle burnt to a crisp slate-like toast.

Our engineer had his work cut out for him, including many a long spell spent hanging horizontally across the tailboard platform, replacing broken sheer-pins and removing rubbish caught up on the prop, which included a whole supermarket shopping trolley. An essential part of his tool bag was definitely a hacksaw and good pair of wire cutters. He replaced so many broken sheer pins that we had none left in the end, so he improvised by using my hairgrips.

On our travels we stopped short of Blackburn one evening for a rest and the men went off to find some liquid refreshment, leaving me in peace to write some letters. I was glad when they came back as there had been lots of strange and unfamiliar noises, including eerie tappings on the hull, which my common sense tried to tell me was only the familiar sound made by ducks tapping on it with their beaks. 'Im-a-wright-one' was nowhere near as safe and secure from any would be intruders as Rainbow II was and all common sense completely deserted me. My imagination took off and in the space of half an hour, peeping Toms, murderers, ghosts and ghouls, aquatic monsters and thieves had, in my mind, intruded upon me. I was so relieved when the men clambered back aboard but did not for a minute own up to having been anything but quite calm and relaxed and quite surprised they were back so soon. After three days we arrived at the boatyard where we were to say a sad farewell to 'Im-a-wright-one' and lots of happy memories. Parting with a boat was truly very painful.

Now we were able to just concentrate on one boat and hopefully start planning to explore more of the canal system. But we still had lots of work to do on Rainbow II after the sinking episode. Even when we assumed that things were replaced and fixed, invariably they weren't and further successive attempts were required to put them right. The first time back aboard that I decided to take a bath, as fast as I filled it up, the water all ran out from somewhere under the bed. We seemed to be forever awash rather than afloat. The pump had to be stripped down and fixed.

We decided that we desperately needed a break from Wigan and set off down the Leigh branch of the canal, which connects with the Bridgwater canal. The scenery was all new to us and we passed a lot of typically no-mans-land terrain, bleak, flat, derelict and largely flooded due to mining subsidence along with some still working mines. But once past Leigh the surroundings became more scenic and wooded. The canal also turned a distinctive 'ochre' orange colour, near Astley Green, due to iron ore mining. It was like boating in tomato soup minus the croutons. Coming into Worsley was like entering a different world, with its many historical and listed buildings, many of which had a tangible air of antiquity attached to them. The old canal basin still remained with its entrance to the forty-six miles of underground tunnels where coal was extracted and brought out in special tub boats, each able to carry up to 12 tons.

This was certainly a popular place, as we soon discovered when we tried to find a mooring space among all the other boats. Peter decided to squeeze us in behind a large sparklingly '*posh*' fibre glass cabin cruiser and came within a hair raising cat's whisker or two of running into it when our engine decided to just cut out at a crucial point in the manoeuvre. Unlike vehicles on wheels which respond instantly to their driver's commands, boats are not so obliging, have a mind of their own and **do not.** They are also much influenced by things such as wind, currents and sheer momentum which forces a boat of some considerable tonnage to carry on moving long after her engines have been stopped. Having a slight bump with another narrow boat was usually nothing much to worry about but fibreglass boats were craft to be avoided at all costs as they were as vulnerable as floating meringues. The following day, after taking the boat a short distance to a boatyard for fuel and calor gas, we returned to the same mooring, only this time Peter decided to squeeze in front of the cruiser. No problems as we slowly glided in and went astern to stop and position us nicely in the mooring space. I wondered why Peter had suddenly turned a nasty ashen grey colour, then, I realized that our engine had cut out AGAIN and was not responding to his instructions. It was time to panic and do impressions of a demented windmill in a force 10 gale with arms and legs flying here and there, and a numb brain trying to link in with a positive plan of action. At the last minute all I could endeavour to do to soften the inevitable blow to the cabin cruiser was to shove out with my feet on her as we collided. I fully expected her to crunch up under the blow, like a cream cracker in the jaws of a whale, but the impact sounded worse than the outcome and miraculously there wasn't a mark or any damage done, partly due to the fact that the cruiser was loosely tied up on her ropes and able to move about freely. Peter leaped ashore and smartly grabbed hold of one of our small rope fenders, which was hanging from the grab rail. The fender slipped off the end of the rail as he heaved us in on it and he almost did an Olympian back somersault as a result. At this rate our chances of travelling far before first ending up in court or hospital didn't look too promising.

Thankfully, the rest of the day was mercifully uneventful and spent painting various parts of the boat and generally sprucing her up. A large species of black goose decided to come aboard and investigate us and scrounge for bread at the same time. It was no wonder there was often not enough bread left for us. One goose, swan, or duck lucky enough to get fed, would invariably be joined by a few hundred or more of its kind, all squawking, splashing and very disorderly trying to establish a pecking order. Reinforcements of bread would be brought up from the galley to make sure every last duck, or even a sparrow, had received a crumb or two.

"Be nice with orange sauce" laughed Peter.

Peter had made 80 pints of homebrew ale which he had transferred from ferment bins into two beer barrels and was eagerly anticipating their readiness. He lovingly stowed them up front on the foredeck locker. It made sense, with the ever-increasing price of beer in pubs, and for the price of about 15p he'd be able to pull himself a nice relaxing pint at the end of the day. **And,** being partial to a nice glass of ale I just might join him.

At this stage in time, we now had to have a serious discussion and decide what we were going to do with our two moggies, who were temporarily being looked after by the family. We really only had one acceptable option and that was to turn them into 'ships cats' So, we went out and bought harnesses and leads and Peter put up a couple of nice 'viewing' cat shelves by the windows and fixed some wire mesh over the doorways so they would be able to look out but not get out until they were settled down. All prepared for the moggies, we set off to fetch them and also to spend a couple of days sorting out some last minute jobs ashore.

On our return Peter was eagerly anticipating two brewed and ready barrels of beer waiting and ready for him to get started on. As we approached the boat he thought I was joking when I said "Its gone Peter – the beer's gone!" I thought I must have been seeing things. Perhaps he had moved it before we'd left. Peter's worst nightmare! It was true, all 80 pints, barrels and all, gone, stolen. This was just one of the many lessons we learned the hard way. This one was to lock everything up. One of the many passers by we often chatted to was of the opinion that 'students' had more than likely been the culprits. We hoped whoever it had been had suffered terrible hangovers and bowel problems as a consequence, along with other unpleasant symptoms.

'Two little beer barrels sitting on the barge
One for Peter and one for Marge
Along comes a thief to steal them right away
Now Marge and Peter are sober.
Night and day.

However, with the cats to think of, we had no time to dwell on nicked beer and Peter soon had a fresh lot brewing. It was an anxious time, making sure the cats were safely in and doors shut. Old 'Blobs' the ginger and white feline trainee able seaman was well into his teens. He took remarkably well to the strange new settings of the boat and didn't seem to be bothered much where he was as long as he had food on his plate and a nice warm place to sleep.

Younger, black 'Jesse' was much more nervous and spent most of his time in the early days of his boat life, hiding under the bed, especially when the engine started up. As we looked under the bed all we would see staring back at us from out of the darkness were a large pair of green eyes.

Blobs was first to adapt to the role of Canal cat and also to be allowed to venture off on short runs ashore off his lead; but not so for some time for alley cat Jesse. We just did not know what to expect or dare risk him going off and getting lost and if we were to let him free too soon there was always the additional fear that he might fall into the canal and drown. The leads attached to their harnesses were far from ideal and were forever catching round obstacles and pulling them up short in a nasty and ungainly tangle, so they had to be closely supervised at all times when out on them. We now know that as long as we had kept them in initially for a number of days until the boat and accompanying smells were familiar to them that we could have let them out free and they would have returned to the boat all right. Yet just one more lesson that only time and experience was to teach us.

There was nothing to stop us now we were a full crew of four. It was the end of April, a perfect time to GO. We filled up with water and set off down towards Barton Swing Aqueduct which is classed as one of the Seven Wonders of the British waterways. It was built in the 1890s and comprises a 243ft long section weighing 800 tons that swings across the Manchester Ship Canal. We made our way through the large industrial area of Trafford Park to Waters Meeting junction and were glad we were not destined to go up the main line to Manchester which we had heard such spine chilling tales about, of grim and gloomy oppressive factory buildings, festooned in a mangle of hissing steam pipes, disused docks, high claustrophobic walls with all manner of unattractive unintelligible writing, to those that is, not versed in the knowledge of deciphering graffiti. Rubbish strewn stretches akin to Council tips both in and out of the canal. Worse, was the ever-present threat to boaters from yobs deliberately preying on them from bridges and the towpath. We received warnings of "whatever you do, for love or money, don't moor up or stop anywhere until you get to Hulme lock". We wondered why anyone other than out of sheer necessity or madness would ever want to go up the main line. It sounded like a trip into Dante's Inferno, and for us it was far nicer to head towards Preston Brook and the refreshingly pleasant Cheshire countryside.

We stopped at Lymm, an idyllic little town with pleasant moorings. Blobs and Jesse came out to have a look around and Jesse was very interested in the ducks. At the end of one garden that came right down to the water's edge, someone had made a little 'dog kennel' sized duck shelter complete with gangway down into the water. Two ducks were keenly eyeing it up but inside, all cosy like and staring out, was a real mean looking cat, waiting and hoping for a duck dinner to waddle within paw/claw reach.

We settled down for a relatively early night, in what should have been all consuming tranquillity and peaceful quiet of the evening, but at 9 pm the church bells were clanging out like crazy in an ear splitting frenzy, which seemed strange, especially on a Thursday, in what otherwise appeared to be a sleepy little haven. Perhaps it was novice bell ringers practice evening. Quasimodo would have turned in his grave and I don't think a living soul within a radius of twenty miles could possibly have had a problem with earwax.

As we had arranged to meet some friends in Preston Brook at the weekend we moored short of the tunnel which was like being moored on the M6 with boats passing every few minutes, coming and going through the tunnel, many going too fast and giving us a good old rock around the clock as they did so. Monday, it was our turn and coming out of the long and crooked tunnel, which was not wide enough for two boats to pass each other, we reached Dutton stop lock and were now on the Trent and Mersey canal. All was beautiful, quiet countryside and woods, such a contrast to all we had left the other side of the tunnel. I likened it to something out of Alice in Wonderland.

At the first chance possible we wandered blissfully along this part of the canal, which in part is high up and overlooking the River Weaver with some very spectacular views across the valley. Especially enjoyable and scenic stretches of canal were always firmly imprinted on our minds and fondly remembered, and this was always one of them.

In less than two weeks Blobs had acquired his sea legs sufficiently to be allowed off his lead and was promoted to 'Leading seaman'. Jesse was less nervous and enjoyed himself out on the bank when we moored on quiet country stretches. I spent some time painting rainbows, on the gas locker cover, the boat pole and the stern seats. We could have happily stayed here for months, but that would not have been travelling the canals as planned. We pushed on heading towards Middlewich and along our way saw a farm worker muck spreading in a field adjacent to the canal. He seemed to suddenly and deliberately rev up and head towards the canal and us, spreading muck thick and fast so that the foul smell fell on us like a blanket. Peter said that the chap was laughing his head off, but we weren't as the smell was like rotten eggs. At least, none of the foul stuff landed on the boat which was one consolation.

At Middlewich we stocked up with supplies and continued on our way. The big lock there had a very stiff gate which didn't do Peter's sore back any favours. We continued slowly on our way, through nine more locks to Sandbach, arriving just as it grew dark. It had been a tiring but rewarding day with new sights and experiences, some nicer than others with the additional bonus of sightings of herons, long tailed tits, kingfishers, Canada geese with a nest, a pair of grebe and a colourful bullfinch. Peter was happy to settle down and read a condensed Readers Digest which I had picked up for him in a charity shop.

The following day was nice and sunny so while I busied myself collecting kindling wood, cleaning the brasses and windows, emptying the porta potti and doing some shopping, Peter fixed the headlamp onto a bracket on the roof so that it was a permanent fixture. He then, very tactfully tried to scrounge a few maggots from the fisherman on the bank. But with no luck, so I dug him a few worms later when I returned from town. There wasn't a very good rapport between fishermen and boaters on the whole and we found that a lot of fishermen tended to be very po-faced. Peter certainly was not in this category. Although he was 100% a fisherman, he was never ever even slightly chamber-pot faced, and had a job to understand those who were. There seemed to be no pleasing some fishermen, whether you slowed right down and kept to the middle of the canal, or carefully altered course, or stopped completely midstream when they caught a fish. The irony of it all was that the canals were initially constructed for boats and had they not been, they would never have been there to fish anyway. We looked upon it as a great facility for all to enjoy and to respect everyone's pursuits as much as possible, though there were always some whose lack of consideration upset the balance and caused trouble.'

Our aches and pains were eased away as the May sun came out and warmed our bodies and we set off the next day up the ten pairs of locks to Hassall Green. We had a short rest before continuing up four more to Rode Heath and moored up for the night bathed in the pinks and reds of a perfect sunset.

Peter was always making me laugh, typically, when on the following morning, he got up and still half asleep put his boxer shorts on upside down, trying to get into one leg of them. He almost succeeded as they were a well worn and stretched, wide legged, two sizes too big for him pair and as I cracked up laughing he said

"Hey Mag, I've got my underpants on upside down and my voice has gone all high".

I wasn't at all surprised.

His back seemed a lot better but then he developed 'gout like' symptoms in his toe, which soon disappeared when I threatened to cut his beer consumption.

We spent a lazy day and wandered along a stream into a wood full of comfrey plants, so I gathered a good bunch to add to our bathwater, as it was said to help ease aches and pains if used in this way. Peter did a bit of fishing and Jesse fell into the canal when he jumped off the boat on his short lead. In a flash, both Peter and I dashed to pull him out. I wrapped him in a towel and he was soon dry and washing himself. From then we decided it was more hazardous for Jesse being on a lead than off it, but we couldn't help feeling apprehensive about him, that he might wander off and get lost or get himself into some dangerous predicament. After all they never had much chance to get used to one territory, which they would normally do living in a house. But we were underestimating the ability of cats to know and find their way around while travelling on canal boats and Jesse soon proved this to us, along with his mousing skills and we'd watch him make his way along the towpath, his ears tuned in to numerous sounds around him, which our ears were not capable of picking up. He'd stop, listen and raise himself up on his haunches, meercat fashion and expertly time the moment to pounce on his unsuspecting victim, usually a mouse or shrew and retrieve it in his jaws. Mice were a natural food and no doubt were much more nutritious than tinned cat food. It certainly must have done their teeth a lot more good and been healthier than sloppy soft stuff from a tin. Every part of the mouse was usually eaten with the exception of the gall bladder which was always expertly dissected, as good as or better than any surgeon's knife could have done, and left intact, most often somewhere on the decks inside the boat for us to find and dispose of. No doubt they were probably very bitter, but we didn't know for sure why they never ate them and how they instinctively knew not to. We also discovered that cats (all of those we had) never ate a shrew, or, on the rare occasions they caught one, a mole.

Up relatively early and heading for Kidsgrove with twelve locks knicknamed 'Heartbreak Hill' to navigate, most of which were through lovely countryside, we were in no rush and reached Harecastle tunnel about 3pm. The tunnel is one and three quarters of a mile long and took us forty minutes to get through. It was quite a creepy feeling in the middle, almost claustrophobic at times, narrow and dark, the low constantly dripping roof silhouetted in the beam of our headlight. It was hard to imagine how in the days of the horse drawn barges, the boats would have to be literally 'legged' through the tunnels by the 'leggers' lying on their backs and pushing their feet along the tunnel roof or walls. There were often fatalities, men falling off into the water and being drowned or crushed between the boat and the tunnel. The first Harecastle tunnel was built in 1777 and took eleven years to build. Since then there had been three tunnels made but only one now remained in use.

Once through the tunnel we decided to push on through Stoke-on-Trent and five big locks. A pleasant young man, who was trying to sell his water colour canal scenes, helped us through some of the heavy steel gated locks. Going through the Stoke area was a bit grotty until coming into the picturesque countryside of Barlaston where we tied up at 9pm and relished our late dinner of stew and dumplings. We were quite pleased with our day's achievement, even though we had only covered about fifteen miles in all, and slogged through eighteen time consuming and energy sapping locks and the tunnel, all at a leisurely and enjoyable pace.

We were often delayed setting off on our journeys when one of the cats decided they wanted to stay ashore. Blobs decided to go walkabout and disappeared the following day. We panicked and searched everywhere for him and thought the worst, then he suddenly appeared all nonchalant, nose and tail in air and casually jumped onboard. Peter wasn't so lucky jumping ashore after coming down our 1st lock of the day and landed in thick deep mud up to his knees, quickly scrambled astern and stripped off his jeans up on deck just as a young woman appeared on the towpath near us and Peter almost fell down the stern hatch clad only in shirt and underpants, in his rush to get into the privacy of the cabin and get some more trousers on.

We moored up later in Stone and I left Peter while I went in search of a chiropodist, hopeful that I would be able to find one and get some treatment to relieve a painful corn which I had been trying unsuccessfully to treat myself for months.

Oatcakes as only the natives of Stoke know how to make, for breakfast, with bacon, eggs, beans and Cumberland sausage for Peter, egg and beans for me. Then, we had yet another trip ashore for groceries. Peter carried some bags back to the boat for me while I nipped to some other shops and as he stepped back onto the stern of the boat he got a whiff of smoke, so ran to the for'd gas locker and smartly turned the gas off before running back astern and opening the stern doors. Smoke was pouring out from behind the fridge. Peter yanked it out and found the pipe at the back of it on fire. On closer examination after he had sorted it out and made it safe, he found to his disbelief that the previous owner had installed the fridge using a piece of garden hose for a gas pipe, which, being uncomfortably close to the pilot light had eventually caught fire. We couldn't believe our luck, how near to a disaster we'd been. Jesse and Blobs had a narrow escape too, as there was only one way into the boat on returning to it, and that was through the stern doors, the forward doors being bolted from the inside.

"What do we need a fridge for anyway" questioned Peter after 'Dusty' another boater we had befriended at Stone, safely sealed it off for us.

"Not a lot really" I replied, "Especially in this country with its mostly cold all year round temperatures and even colder on a boat below the water line".

Both Peter and I had grown up in the days when no one had fridges, so the thought of being without one was of no consequence. Besides, the boat fridge was very small and with just a tiny freezer box, neither here nor there. We both agreed that a cupboard would be more useful, so the fridge went in the skip and we felt a lot safer. The extra storage space it freed up was also a bonus.

In the summer it was nice cooking in the galley which was aft, but it did have it's disadvantages being by the stern doors, which had to be open so often with one or the other of us clambering in and out on deck all the time, plus the cats coming and going. When it was cold and the doors managed to be shut for awhile there were gaps around and between them so it was very draughty. Peter fitted wood panels over the steel doors which eliminated some of the draughts, but when the doors were open it was a case of carry on regardless.

Considering that it was now the middle of May, we were having a very cold windy spell of weather which didn't make us feel like going anywhere.

Peter pottered about doing a few jobs such as moving a barrel of home brew onto the portable gas fire, putting a chain around it and securing it to two hooks attached to the bulkhead, not as a precaution against theft but to prevent it sliding off onto the floor if the boat moved.

Eventually we decided regardless of rain and wind to move on and head for Great Haywood and see how far we could get. We were completely exposed to the weather up on both decks, so whoever was steering the boat needed to be well wrapped up and in waterproofs, with lots of hot tea, coffee and butties supplied at regular intervals. We noticed the bridges were very low on this part of the canal and we always slowed down as we approached blind ones, but one day met another boat coming the other way that didn't. Peter quickly moved over to avert a collision but the woman steering the other boat panicked and just rammed into our bow. On a quick inspection from leaning over the bow, while still on the move, we didn't appear to have any damage but once we were moored up and had a closer look we discovered a dent in our port bow, but nothing too serious. We tied up at a very wide, almost lake-like part of the canal called Tixall Wide, where there were numerous Canada geese including one pair with five young ones, two pairs of nesting grebes and coots. Stew, which seemed to be our staple diet, always went down well at the end of the day and one large pan full would provide us with two days dinners.

Our travels from Rugeley to Fradley junction took us 8 hours through some beautiful 'miles from anywhere' countryside and woodland right down to the canal banks, full of bluebells and red campion. Large cushion-like tufts of delicate white stitchwort flowers edged the canal banks. We used to call them bachelors' buttons or milkmaids when we were children. Alternating with them grew clumps of 'Large bitter cress' and intermittent splashes of pink 'May flowers' also known as 'cuckoo flowers' or 'lady's smock'. All this woven together into a floral tapestry with the finishing touches of lace like umbels of 'Queen Anne's Lace' more commonly known as 'cow parsley' or 'keck'. Spring at its very best, with the first hint of the hawthorn 'May' blossom mingling with the overall smell of every other blooming herb, filled and overflowed our senses with appreciation of such a magical 'potpourri'.

We attempted to moor up in this spectacular area past Handsacre but the banks were bad and we kept going aground so had to carry on to Fradley junction where we took on water and carried on onto the Coventry canal. This canal seemed quite deserted and unused in comparison to the Trent and Mersey, apart from a lot of boats moored up privately at the bottom of gardens. We finally tied up at a pretty village called Hopwas which was true to it's name, as there were hops growing everywhere. More bowls of soup at the end of yet another perfect though still cold day.

Waking to find a warmer day we decided to stay put and make the most of such a quiet spot with wooded hills one side and the river and open fields of grazing cows, corn and yellow oilseed rape on the other. It wasn't such a pleasant place for the cats, however, as the towpath seemed to be the main dog walking route and we were constantly on the lookout if one of the cats ventured ashore. We were happier when they didn't. Blobs wandered along the roof and onto the stern deck and sat dozing in the sun. I was sitting up for'd when a woman walked past followed by a Doberman dog off the lead, which caused me some concern. I was glad that they had come from the direction of our stern and were not heading that way. I looked up and acknowledged the woman and her dog and half heartedly said, "I hope he's cat friendly, my cat is ashore?". I felt sure that the dog himself must be just a big old pussycat otherwise he would have been restrained on a lead. I was quite shocked when the woman replied in a hoity toity voice, "Oh he would have had it if he had seen it". I was rendered speechless. Later on I was chatting to a man with a dog and he said the woman was a pain in the neck with her dog and should have it on a lead as it went for everything it saw. We were more observant and cautious of dog owners after this eye opening attitude and were especially on the alert for greyhounds off the lead after an owner with one such dog, informed us that it had killed a few cats. Most owners were respectful but there were always the few who had no regard for others pets. Many a time Jesse was chased up a tree, often to the amusement of the dog owner. We were glad of the trees at these times, but although Jesse could soon shoot up a tree to safety, he had no head for heights and no idea how to get back down a tree once up it. So we would have to wait sometimes hours before he'd manage to get down. He would sit up the tree meowing as we tried everything in the book to coax him down. Just one big scaredy cat! Usually, some hours after dark he would finally manage to get down, probably forced down by hunger pangs.

During the times when the cats had to be confined inside the boat, for their own safety mostly, the litter trays had to be used, and 'nasties', in such confined quarters, quickly disposed of. Gas masks would have made life more bearable at these times. We always shut them inside the boat when we were travelling as we were sure one or the other or both would be tempted to jump ashore as they pleased for a bit of shore leave and that would have been so easy for them to do at the walking speeds we travelled at.

Chapter Three

A New Crew Member

Before moving on towards Atherstone, we spent what seemed like a lifetime searching for Peter's hearing aid, high and low, emptied rubbish bin and bags, all to no avail and we just had to hope it would turn up later.

We stopped short of Atherston's eleven locks, overlooking a field with two horses and a foal, sheep the other side of the canal and three or four other boats moored up nearby. There was a little black and white stray cat on the towpath near us. We recognized it as being the one a boater had told us about earlier on in the day, at the last locks. He had said it had spent the night with them on their boat and was in the habit of going on and off anyone's boat. It was only a young cat, cute, little black and white thing which probably had been lost accidentally, or, deliberately cast adrift from a boat. Not long after we had moored up, the little cat found Peter's lap and settled down purring away. I gave it the milk and meat that our cats had left. It growled and hissed and spat non stop at Jesse and Blobs and wandered freely in and out of the boat as it seemed to do daily upon any boat that stopped on this stretch. At 11.30pm it was under the bed somewhere and stayed there all night. Blobs gave it an occasional nasty hiss. We fed him the next morning along with ours and he stayed around on and off till Jesse chased him off the boat and he then disappeared out of the blue. Peter went up and down the canal towpath looking for him but we came to the conclusion that he was, by now, probably miles up the locks and canal on some other boat and that with a cat like that it would be very difficult to keep him pinned down to one boat. However, he was a lovable little thing and we hoped that he would be alright wherever he was and couldn't help feeling a bit worried about him.

Moving on, not far, just up a couple more locks, and who should come jumping aboard, none other than our little four legged stray. It seemed he had taken quite a fancy to us too, regardless of unfriendly vibes from Jesse and Blobs. He stayed with us as we gradually made out way up the rest of the locks into Alveston where we stopped for the usual grocery run ashore, also to buy a cat collar and name tab for our new crew member A.B

Ibley Dibley. Peter and I had the grumps with each other on this particular morning, so it was our turn to be hissing and snarling at each other. Not for long though. Peter accidentally knocked his glass of ale off the boat into the water where it miraculously managed to land upright and float with contents intact. That broke the ice and we laughed as we slowly reversed to recover it.

Then at Hawkesbury junction we nearly split our sides laughing when we watched a chap standing on the bow of his boat, windlass in hand, poised to jump, while his wife on the stern concentrated on steering the boat slowly across the wide lock pound towards the lock gates. Suddenly the bloke leaped off like a kangaroo, about 15ft from the bank which had been his hoped for destination, and landed unceremoniously in the water, disappearing into its murky depths.

Moments later he shot to the surface like a shark chased seal and amazingly still clutching the windlass in his hand. What a hero! His wife shouted excitedly down to the occupants of their boat to "Quick get the camera, dad's in the water!" We had fully expected her to be shouting for help. Maybe she wanted to capture the episode for sending in to "You've Been

Framed". I wished I had had my camera handy too, as once we realized the chap was not in any danger of drowning and was soon recovered from the water, we just kept laughing our socks off every time we thought of it. Surely the chap had realized that no one on the planet apart from some Olympic wonder could have jumped such a distance. Perhaps he misjudged the speed the boat was moving and anticipated that by the time he had jumped and landed, he would be home and dry. No chance!

After two days there was still no sign of Peter's hearing aid, so it was a good excuse to 'shout at the Captain'. Poor Ibley Dibley jumped up onto the wood stove which was red hot, yelled and shot off. Jesse did the very same thing the previous week, so I put a kettle full of water on top of it to stop them jumping up again. We put some Vaseline on their paws, but there were no visible signs of any blisters or damage.

On our way heading towards Braunston we stopped for a bite to eat and to give the cats an airing. Ibley Dibley ran straight up a tree like a squirrel and we thought "Oh no!", thinking he would be another Jesse and not be able to get back down but before we knew it he was back down in a flash, didn't even bother to turn round, just came down as he had gone up, spread out bat like, head up, tail down, four legs spread round the tree, no messing. We hoped Jesse was taking notice. Blobs, oblivious to all went on his usual "I'm off home" walk about, off up the towpath, head and shoulders down. Jesse was only interested in disappearing into the woods and all over the place mousing.

"We're getting more like a floating cattery every day" said Peter.

We passed through Rugby, only stopping for a paper. The canal route was very pleasant and avoided any urbanity. Long stretches of very straight canal with high banks each side, thick with hawthorn, so our views of the surrounding countryside were mostly blotted out. The towpath was almost non existent in places and the banks impossible to moor up on so we just kept going. Ambling along and approaching one of the few bends, a boat came hurtling round it like a bat out of hell, and the young woman steering it just threw her hands up to her face in a panic, leaving the boat heading straight for us. Thankfully her husband had the presence of mind to quickly alter course in time to avoid us. We became very wary of holiday boats.

Finally we found a place to moor up and Peter began tying up the boat when he stopped in his tracks and nearly fell backwards as a most foul smell hit him. It was one of those awful smells that you couldn't live with and although we didn't have a clue what it was and where it was coming from we had no choice but to shove off again and hope we could find a pong free mooring for the night. It was 9pm before we did.

Just outside of Braunston, the weather turned nice and we heard the call of the cuckoo, now all the way back from wintering in Africa. We caught up on some jobs around the boat, more painting and cleaning and Peter fixed a large brass bell that he had been given to him one birthday, up on the stern and gave it a good ringing as he shouted "Ice cream, roll up". I got stuck into a pile of washing, doing smaller stuff in the sink and larger stuff in the hip bath, kneeling over it and rubbing and scrubbing as best I could. I used a small hard brush on stubborn marks and dirt, as canal life provided us with really dirty gear. It was real washing, not like the clean looking stuff people just pile daily into their washing machines these days. They wouldn't have been so keen to wash so much clean stuff if they had had to do it the hard way before washing machines came in. Thinking back to when I was married, I didn't have a washing machine until my third baby came along. Here on the boat, I mostly washed a few bits each day to keep on top of it and hung it out until it stopped dripping, then brought it in and hung it on the hooks and short lines all around the boat. It soon dried in the fore cabin where the wood stove was.

One day while enjoying playing one of our very tense and crucial final legs of cutthroat crib, consisting of about ten games, each of three legs to a game, over a certain number of days, all very matter of life or death stuff, a boat went tearing past, sending the crib board and cards all over the place, so the final was postponed. Boats had been passing all day and many of them not slowing down sufficiently, as was the general rule when passing moored boats. Our bow mooring peg had been gradually working loose as we were rocked backwards and forwards by these speed merchants, till it gradually worked loose and slipped the mooring rope, setting our bow free to swing out from the bank. Peter went out to re-moor it and gave the last offending boat a shake of his fist as he did so. I remember at one mooring we had with many other boats, one irate boater on the receiving end of being constantly shaken around by boats going past too fast, ran out and yelled at a holiday boater "You're going the wrong way, Silverstone is that way".

Arriving in Braunston there were more boats than we had ever seen all together, all gathered ready for the big boat rally at the weekend. With everywhere so busy, we decided to keep the cats confined to the boat.

The litter trays were in full swing with Jesse first in on arrival, Blobs at supper time and Ibley Dibley at 1.30am. It was a real 'one two three o'clock Pooh!' Just dropping off to sleep all warm and comfortable, the last thing we felt like doing was getting up to clean out a litter tray. No fault of the cats, as they had no option, not being able to get out. Next morning we decided to risk letting them out, under our supervision. Curiosity killed the cat, it is said. Well, both Jesse and Ibley Dibley went straight onto the stern of the boat in front of us. Little did they know that up on the bow sat a large golden Labrador. Blobs went off as usual in his oblivious style of 'couldn't care less' walkabout, but had the sense to quickly turn in his tracks when he saw the dog. We always felt happy if there was a nice thick hedge along the towpath with cat sized gaps in case the cats needed a quick escape from man or beast.

At times I began to wonder if we were suffering from a dose of 'Cat Paranoia', or were just soft in the head, or maybe both! We were always on edge with them in built up areas and many things had to be taken into consideration before we could moor up. Was there a road or railway line too close? Was the canal bank cat friendly so that if they fell in they would be able to climb out again? Mostly banks were earth/grass or concrete which was fine but we always avoided the steel corrugated type edged canal sections fearing that if one fell in they would not be able to get a grip on it and climb out. Their safety was always one of our main priorities but we didn't always get it right as time would tell.

Another problem was that they all liked to walk around the outside of the boat on the narrow gunwale which was only about three inches wide and divided the hull from the upper structure. This was alright except when one cat was approaching along the waterside gunwale from one end and one was approaching from the other end, the inevitable outcome was a head to head confrontation, with no way for either cat to turn around, or jump up onto the roof. It was a stalemate situation with just a very slim chance one might be able to back down and retreat if he had only a short distance to go, but mostly it meant a big splash for one or the other and a desperate bid to swim the length of the boat and scramble up the bank, or be fished out by one of us if we were aware they had gone overboard. We were geared up to the sound of these "cat in the cut catastrophes" and on our feet to the rescue in super quick time. They could swim, but they did not like doing so one bit and their little eyes were full of terror when they had to. Once they were safely onboard they did look so funny and more out of relief that they were safe we always had a laugh at the sight of them, all thin and scrawny with sopping wet flat fur.

Peter came up with an idea of blocking off the water side gunwale but we couldn't think of a temporary way to do it, so all we could do was put a board wedged each end to block it off and this seemed to work. We also devised a "fall in the water safety plank" which consisted of a 4 or 5ft long plank of wood suspended on ropes from the grab rail and hanging so that it sat amidships in the water alongside the boat, waterside, so that if a cat fell in it would provide a platform for them to get on. I don't think it was ever used for this purpose but many a duck found it very accommodating and one even brought its whole family of about 11 ducklings to enjoy a siesta on. If the canal was a bit choppy in a wind it used to clonk and clang against the side of the boat a bit but we got used to many of these strange noises which more or less just went with boating.

The worst noise was from the engine, which had to be run daily to keep the batteries charged. No problem when travelling, but moored up for any length of time, our hearts would sink if the engine didn't fire due to flat batteries, but then again it was all part of boat life. We had a little black and white TV and rationed viewing times for special programmes, not so much in the summer when we were mostly outside, but during the winter months when it gave us some entertainment. Then when the world cup football matches were being played, Peter was like a cat on a hot tin roof, planning life around footy and desperately wanting a colour TV and a mooring where we could definitely be sure of getting a good picture without having to go out on the foredeck in all weathers and wave the TV aerial around manually, to find the best place to prop it up in order to get a picture. Anyone passing must have thought we'd lost our marbles. Sometimes I'd end up standing out on the deck, in the rain, clamber up onto the side seat to gain some height, then slowly and meaningfully wave the aerial about while Peter gave directions from the comfort of the cabin, such as "no good, – no good, – bit better, – hold it there, – bit to the left, – no too far, – you had it then, – now you have lost it, – no good, – YES STOP THAT'S IT!!. Well it might have been IT, for him, but for me it was far from IT, as I hung precariously over the side of the boat hanging on to the rail with one hand and the aerial at an angle of 90 degrees in the other. I just had to move and resume a more secure position and risk the wrath of the Captain.

"NO, NO GOOD NOW, YOU'VE LOST IT" Then Peter would have a go and I'd have my turn of shouting instructions as to where to put the aerial, and yes often I did feel like telling him just where to put it. But as with most things, we saw the funny side and took it all in good humour. We did buy a small colour TV which could be run on 12v or 240v, but it had a voracious appetite for battery juice compared to the black and white one, so we really did have to ration it and run the engine more to keep the batteries topped up. We invested in two more big batteries to help alleviate matters so then had a total of 4 linked up and this made a big difference.

Nothing made much of a difference when some months later when Peter plugged the TV lead into the wrong socket and blew it up. He got lucky as it was still under guarantee and replaced

"I think the weather forecast is bad Pete"

"No its just a Newsflash Mag!"

It made a change for us to be in the thick of a boat rally and we enjoyed admiring the many boats and their various decorated canal ware and many individual traditional styles, especially the beautifully painted milk churns and Buckby cans. We enjoyed the special firework display and a good old singsong in the beer tent later where a folk group were playing.

During the night someone deliberately cut through one of our mooring ropes in two places, but luckily a knot and part of the rope kept us secure till we discovered it in the morning.

Peter, being a seaman, was an expert with ropes and soon got down to making a very neat job of splicing the rope together again. He could have earned us a few bob making rope fenders, but said he'd done so much of it in the past, that he'd lost interest in it now. Instead, he began to whittle away at making walking sticks, when he wasn't working around the boat, or fishing, finding wood and sawing it up, or watching soccer, snooker or cricket. Life was very happy and rewarding at the end of each day. We both loved reading and our midship cabin double bed was a luxury after the cramped quarters elsewhere in the boat. Three cats insisted on sharing it with us and would plonk themselves right slap bang on top of us, trying to usurp book space to their advantage so that we gave all our attention to them. We were too soft not to give in to them, even when they positioned themselves so that our limbs went numb due to cat pressure on blood supplies. Ibley Dibley always wanted us up early in the morning and used to perform bat like performances leaping from the two shelves we had, onto the bed and if that didn't work, which mostly it didn't, he'd jump down onto the deck at the side of the bed and furiously scratch and rake his claws up and down the lower sliding bed locker panels. This made an alarmingly noisy racket and as soon as we chased him off he was back and at it again and scampering around enjoying every minute of the game. It worked too, with one of us getting up to feed the cats and make a brew.

We continued to enjoy another day of the boat show, watching Morris dancers and looking around at the many new boats on display, in various stages of construction.

Jesse suddenly started to turn on Ibley Dibley and kept going for him all day. He must have been having a 'bad fur day'.

Reluctant to leave the happy atmosphere of the boat rally we hung on for another day and made the most of the nice weather, with Peter painting around the stern of the boat and me doing some washing and hanging it out on the hedges to dry. All three cats disappeared and caused us some alarm when none reappeared after some hours and later had us searching far afield, up and down the towpath hedges, endlessly calling them and banging a fork on a saucer in hopes they might think it was feeding time and condescend to come back. But cats, we soon learned' were a law unto themselves and only do what they want to do, when they want to. Jesse eventually came leaping aboard with a mouse dangling from his jaws, so we knew what had been occupying him ashore. Ibley Dibley wandered casually aboard quite unperturbed and sat watching Jesse scoff the mouse, but Blobs was nowhere to be found and as the time went on we started to get quite worried about him. We were hoping to set off that evening towards Napton but it all depended on if and when Blobs was found. So we had dinner and still no Blobs and had to spend more time endlessly wandering about like lost souls, looking for him. I don't know why but I knelt down midships in the narrow gangway alongside the bed and peered underneath, moved various articles so as to see further under and around the bed. It was dark but as my eyes acclimatized and fixed on a shallow sided cardboard box, two luminous eyes stared back at me. I reached in and pulled the box out with Blobs in it but he didn't budge, just yawned and stretched and stayed put. It was far too late now to move, so we spent another night in Braunston.

English weather was so unpredictable! It was no wonder that the British talked about it endlessly. Suddenly it turned more like October than almost June and was very cold. There was a notice from British Waterways (BWB) ahead of the seven locks at Braunston to the effect of requesting boaters to wait and pair up with another boat before using them, in order to save water. We paired up with a man on his own with a longer boat than ours.

These were the first double locks again since the last one at Poolstock on the Leigh branch of the Leeds and Liverpool. It had been all single narrow locks from there, so it was a little strange being back to double ones. As we finished the last lock, we were now only a few hundred yards from Braunston tunnel which was opened in 1796 and is just over a mile long, and wide enough for two narrow boats to pass each other in, as we soon found out when about nine boats did just that before we came out the other end. While in the tunnel we couldn't see the light at the other end for a long time. This was due to there being a bend in the middle of it and we felt as though we were going into a black bottomless pit until the little spark of light glinted reassuringly way ahead of us.

Once away from the hustle and bustle of Braunston, we were able to get back to some peace and quiet and recharge batteries, including ours. Peter soon got down to catching a few fish and the cats, not to be outdone caught mice. Peter then thought that pigeon pie would be nice for dinner and sat astern with the air rifle at the ready in case one appeared. I didn't like the idea much but wasn't too worried as the chances seemed about a billion to one, not of a wood pigeon appearing but of Peter getting it if it did. We kept hearing pheasants clucking and they seemed a more likely option for the pot. We watched a kingfisher flash along the bank and saw two jays, then amazingly a rook suddenly swooped down over the canal and took a fish from the water, which we had never seen done before.

At night we left the stern doors open, so the cats could go out when they wanted to and spend some quality nocturnal moggy time ashore. They had all settled down well and adapted so easily to life aboard. We really were all shipmates and as the weeks and months went by, our understanding and knowledge of cats grew and we learned so much about them which endeared them to us even more. Perhaps we did mollycoddle them a bit. Peter was worse than me, he would get in and out of bed at the slightest meow to see what they wanted, let them out, let them in, draw the curtain above the cat shelf so they could sit and look out. They were so amusing to watch too and provided us with much entertainment.

By the end of May we were still consuming bowls of stew and dumplings and waiting for some warm summer sunshine to show up.

Often, canals and railway lines ran in close proximity to one another and a very quiet and remote mooring could suddenly be shaken violently by a length of noisy passenger train carriages thundering across what a few minutes ago had been a scene of rural tranquillity. One day, completely on our own, not a living soul or dwelling in sight, in any direction, such a train sped into view across the field and suddenly came to a grinding halt almost opposite us. We could see people staring at us from the many windows as we stared back at them and as the minutes ticked on and the train showed no signs of continuing its journey we began to feel uncomfortably over watched. I wondered if some of the passengers watching us wished they could have changed places with us and felt sure they did. The train was stuck there for a good two hours then finally about 10pm a large engine arrived and towed it away.

My brother Gerald and his friend Freda had arranged to cycle out and meet us at Blisworth so we had to stick to a timetable and travel on to make sure we were there when they arrived. This accomplished, we all set off the following day to navigate through Blisworth tunnel which was the second longest navigable tunnel in the country after the Huddersfield Narrow canal at 3,056 yards (2794m). It was also very big, high and wide inside in comparison to others such as Foulridge and Harecastle and it didn't seem to take us long to get through. In the late 1970's its lining had deteriorated so much that the tunnel was closed for four years and millions of pounds were spent re-lining the bore. We found Stoke Bruerne, the other side of the tunnel, a very nice example of a canal village, though perhaps over exploited for tourism, but still a nice place to spend some quality time, with perhaps a visit to the canal side museum to learn something of the history of the canals.

We shared the next set of seven hefty locks with another boat and really enjoyed the scenery between Stoke Bruerne and Yardley Gobion and two or three particular spots which' over the years' became, firm mooring favourites. One of them was opposite a derelict and burned down farmhouse called Isworth and the other up by the weir at Grafton Regis. The latter, in time, we came to look fondly upon as home.

Freda, Gerald and Peter went to investigate the remote farm ruin across the canal and we wondered about its history and what had caused the fire. Some of the rooms were still intact but carefully climbing up damaged stairs out of curiosity was probably not a sensible thing to be doing, but such is human nature. We came across a piano, or what was left of it and I felt a bit sad seeing it there with not a tune left in it anymore. However, we had to find wood for the fire and there was quite a bit laying around the farm which many willing hands soon had logged, while I, – wait for it – made the stew and dumplings. Ibley Dibley enjoyed cooked perch.

Flaming June was right, bloody awful and raining cats and dogs. Nevertheless we all went for a walk and came across a bees nest in the ground which had been dug into, maybe by a badger. After more wooding and logging we settled down to chatting together, playing crib and Freda knitting in the cosy fore cabin.

Freda and I were not at all amused when Peter and Gerald spotted three nice plump Aylesbury ducks on the canal the following day and suggested one would be very nice in the oven. We took umbrage and walked off in a huff. They scuttled any attempts to provide a duck dinner and all three ducks were intact swimming around when Freda and I returned. On our walk, we had met an elderly farmer who chatted to us and asked me if I was collecting grasses, as I had picked a few and had them in my hand to take back to identify later. He asked if we would like to look in his meadow which he would soon be using for hay making, so we followed him into the field and found a lovely variety of grasses including sweet vernal grass, Yorkshire fog, rye grass, crested dogs tail, meadow barley, wild oat, cocksfoot and meadow foxtail, also lots of the eye catching yellow rattle, ragged robin and a small patch of bright yellow marsh marigold. He was interested in encouraging a variety of flora into the meadow and wouldn't use any harmful sprays on his fields. He also had a field full of broad beans all in flower and the perfume from that field was wonderful. As we left the field by his farmhouse gate, he pointed to a Judas tree in his garden which was in full bloom and just a mass of amazing magenta coloured blossom. We felt happy to have met a man with such commendable environmental values.

Coming into Cosgrove, passing first, beneath a rather unique stone bridge, somewhat out of place on the canal, all decorated in Gothic style, we found a nice almost backwater village nestling around the canal, the kind of place you want to stop and explore, but we saved that for another time and carried on across the Ouse aqueduct and on through about ten lock free miles of Milton Keynes to Fenny Stratford, and on to Soulbury three locks.

Having moored some distance on from the locks, I awoke the next morning to melodic birdsong and watched a little blue-tit flying back and forwards with food in it's beak for its young. It kept visiting a section of fence along the towpath and suddenly alarm bells began to ring, as Jesse was nearby sitting looking up at the fence. We could hear chirping of the young birds coming from somewhere near too, so we chased Jesse in and went to investigate. We were amazed to find the nest was right down inside the fence post itself with a lot of hungry little chirping beaks. We decided

Cinnabar moth and caterpillars feeding on Ragwort

Crested Dogtail

Corncockle

Meadow foxtail

Herb Robert

Rye Grass

we would move on as soon as possible and leave mum and chicks in peace, but not before a near fatality occurred. We caught sight of Ibley Dibley balancing precariously right on top of the fence post and scooping his paw down inside it, trying to reach the chicks. We soon put paid to his little game and all moggy shore leave was stopped until we found an alternative mooring. But it wasn't easy in the Spring to avoid every vulnerable and potential cat victim. Jesse and Ibley Dibley became lethal hunters and baby rabbits became a favourite, if and when they could get them. Mice, formed the greater part of their diet, and' I am glad to say, they did not often catch or seem to particularly hunt songbirds. Spring time was perhaps the exception with so many vulnerable fledglings around. Old Blobs was unusual as he appeared to be completely devoid of any hunting instincts and apart from one rare occasion I never ever saw him chase or catch anything all his life. Maybe he just liked his meat out of a tin.

Most of the prey they caught they bought back to their lair, the boat, so that was distressing enough especially if victims were still alive. I could often get them off Jesse who was a very gentle natured cat. I'd known him to just gently drop a little rabbit into my hands when I'd cornered him with one. How could anyone not try to save anything once having seen its beautiful bright eyes full of precious life? Well that is how I felt and if I could save anything which was as far as I could see not injured, I would and release it at a safe distance from the boat. Many times it was impossible to save things though and at least death was usually dealt quickly with a bite to the back of the neck. Then we had to put up with much growling, especially if we were anywhere near the cat with the victim, while they ate it. After all it was a good meal and would have been stupid not to have let them eat things once they were dead. As with mice, the whole rabbit would be scoffed, fur as well, with the gall bladder left and often the little white bobtail, maybe an ear too. I couldn't believe it at first that they could eat fur, bones and everything like that, but they did.

Jesse trying to look like a 'blue-tit'

One day we discovered a lot of water down in the bilge astern and hoped our water tank hadn't sprung a leak. We pumped it out and decided next time we were in town to get some catering dye to put in the water to determine if the tank was leaking. However, more important things such as fishing, took over, that is when we weren't running aground. The canal seemed very shallow around Stoke Hammond and we spent quite a lot of time sitting stuck tight, like a hippopotamus in the mud, unable to get off and away from the bank. Peter tried reversing, hoping to pull us off astern and we had to all stand on the waterside gunwale, rocking up and down and limbo dancing, hoping to get the boat to move. Sometimes this worked but this time nothing would, including levering boat poles under the boat, both from the bank and from the boat pushing onto the bank. But no amount of shoving and swearing would budge her. In the end we hijacked two passing boats who towed us off.

The soil around Pitstone consisted mainly of clay as I soon discovered when searching far afield for Jesse. The clay stuck to my boots like glue and I returned to the boat a good few inches taller than when I had left it. Jesse for some reason kept disappearing and wandering a long way off, way up the edge of a ploughed field towards the road. In the end we brought him back and shut him in for safety. Later on when it was dark he escaped again and Freda and I went to look for him which wasn't such a good idea, trying to find a black cat in the pitch dark. He came back of his own accord, when he was ready.

Peter drew our attention to a gathering of dozens of enormous carp, swimming around the stern. He was throwing bread into the water and they were coming up, opening their big round toothless mouths and slurping the bread with loud lip slapping noises. They were almost taking bread from Peter's fingers. They were 6 – 8 pounders and it was fascinating to watch them. The water was boiling with action, talk about shark infested seas. Suddenly Gerald grabbed some bread and disappeared up for'd with Peter's landing net.

"You'll never get one like that" Peter shouted after him "They are far too quick for that"

Within minutes the cry went up "GOT ONE, GOT ONE", and Peter had to eat his words.

Blimey! That ONE, was more like Moby Dick than a carp, it was humongous and quite a struggle to lift up into the net, bring aboard and swiftly dispatched to carp heaven.

Peter

> Nah! You'll never get one like that Gez! They're far too quick.
> BLOODY 'ELL he's got a WHOPPER!

"It's a delicacy to eat in China" said Gerald as he and Peter carted it off to the galley to prepare for the oven.

"Send it to the Chinese then", I muttered in disgust.

I can't quite remember the recipe they used for the carp dinner but do remember that there was a distinct Hells Kitchen flavour of diesel oil attached to it, when I was forced to "go on just have a taste." But it didn't seem to curb the men's appetite for it.

Peter stumbled up onto the stern deck early next morning, clad only in a pair of bright green stripy underpants and had a leisurely pee into the cut while he was there. The peaceful country scene before him was shattered as a crowded commuter train appeared from nowhere and thundered across the landscape, passengers all getting a good eyeful of Peter caught literally mid stream. Peter froze but continued to pee down his leg when another train thundered past in the opposite direction. He resolved to 'pee bank side' in future.

It wasn't at all practical for us to use the porta potti every time we needed a pee, it would have filled up in one or two days and nights and the distance between sanitary stations to empty it, were miles between each other along with water taps for taking on water. So unless you had a flush toilet with pump out system fitted, you had to have a bucket and chuck-it when you were not within easy reach of a sanitary station. We had no problem with getting back to nature and the night bucket was emptied ashore in the fields or hedges, wherever. I remember (how could I forget), one early morning taking the bucket up on deck, ready to clamber ashore and empty it. We were out in the sticks and normally didn't see a soul for hours, when suddenly out of nowhere a couple with a dog appeared on the towpath, heading towards the boat. Clad in my long winceyette nightie, I quickly turned and dashed back into the boat down the two steps into the cabin. But as I did so the hem of my nightie caught on the metal step plate at the top of the step, pulling me up sharply backwards, forcing me to lose my grip on the bucket which shot upwards and outwards, throwing the contents with some force all over the cabin. I spent the best part of the day stripping the foam cushion seating covers all off, washing them and everything else that had been on the receiving end, floor, mats, wall, soft cushions and rinsed and re-rinsed till all was fresh as new mown hay again. Drying it all however was a different matter and took some days until all was back to normal. We managed to see the funny side of it though and considered it could have been a lot worse, for instance if Peter had been up and sitting in the direct line of fire.

One thing about living on a boat with just the basics, you became very earthy and back to nature, which Peter and I adapted to easily, whereas many others would not have been able to have done so. I spoke to many women who said they could never live like that, going behind hedges to relieve themselves if needs be, or living without all the mod cons they had and their car. More men seemed to be able to adapt to this lifestyle than women, so it must have been more appealing and suited to a man's requirements.

While Gerald and Freda were still with us, Peter gave us an interesting lesson in knot tying, which he was quite expert at. I can't say the same for Freda and I, even though Peter had some very supposedly easy ways of teaching novices like us, plus lots of patience. He demonstrated time and time again and with one particular knot he used helpful terminology for parts of the rope, for example, while he was holding the end of the rope in one hand and a section of it in the other he would say things like, "The rabbit goes round the tree and through the hole". Hey presto he ended up with a marvellous knot, but I don't know where my rabbit ended up, hanging from the tree I think, as I invariable ended up with what Peter would call a "bunch of bananas" (something ruder actually which I will leave to the reader's imagination). I couldn't tie anything in the end as it all became far too hilarious.

Gerald and Freda left us at Marsworth and we decided to find a quiet mooring so that the cats could spend some free time ashore in safety. The nearby Aylesbury arm seemed the ideal place so we headed for the locks which would take us down to it. There were about seven all quite close to each other but once through them it looked as though there were some nice open stretches of rural canal before anymore cropped up. Down we went, one, two, three, four, five, six and with some relief into the seventh from which we could see all that lay ahead of us. Well, it wasn't quite what we expected by any means as all we could see was a vast muddy dewatered stretch of canal before us with just a narrow channel of some few feet of water running down the middle of it. So, we were literally stuck up the creek without a paddle. There was no going forwards or turning round so we took the only option available to us and went backwards through the pounds and locks, one by one. The boat didn't respond the same when going astern, it was more like a drunken pig, all over the place, so we tied a rope to the stern which I held the other end ashore and while Peter reversed I kept the rope tight enough for him to keep the boat going straighter than she would have done without it. I now knew how hard those horses who used to pull the boats, must have worked. They regularly had to haul loads of seventy tons or more. We moored in deep water in a lock pound with some other stranded boats, also unable to turn or move on. One irate boater went off in a huff to see if there were any BWB workers around but there were none to be found. One option was to go to the top lock and open all the paddles on every lock all the way down, flood the dewatered section, then go back up and shut all the paddles. But before doing that it would be necessary to go past the dewatered stretch to the next lock and check the paddles there. We all opted to sit tight and wait for BWB to sort it out, hopefully next day. Kids or inexperienced boaters had probably opened up the paddles further down and failed to close them after use, hence draining all the water.

Sure enough BWB workmen from the yard put matters right the next day and apparently it wasn't the first time this had happened. There are a total of 17 locks on this 4 mile arm which runs through the Vale of Aylesbury and it was worth the trouble as it ran through our favourite kind of uninhabited countryside. In contrast we found Aylesbury terminal basin disappointing, with a number of boats in long term moorings and limited free space restricted to about 100yds for visiting boats. Tall dowdy redundant looking office blocks overlooked the basin and not far away ran a busy road. The atmosphere felt unwelcoming and after visiting the local food store, at around 5.30pm we headed back towards Marsworth, stopping after six locks for the night. Heavy showers and strong winds prevailed, the cats were happy to be free to roam and we were happy to be snug, warm and peacefully holed up with an appetising plateful of stir fry which made a nice change from stew.

The weather continued to be horrendous so we didn't venture far but we really did need to get to a sanitary station and empty the loo. Unfortunately the nearest one was either at Leighton Buzzard some twelve locks and eight miles away or Cowroast seven locks and six miles away. Neither of us was inclined to be "back to nature" enough to want to resort to going out in stormy weather conditions to find a hedge to squat behind either. Boaters caught in this rather emergency situation, had either to become seriously constipated or take their waste into a wood or field and bury to decompose. I left it to Peter to solve the problem and he decided as we had no spade aboard that all he could do was to deposit the waste in a very deep, watery ditch running along the hedge, which he said would soon disperse, especially with all the rain we were having, and would make the hedges a lovely lush green and wouldn't exactly pollute the planet anyway. So at the chosen hour, almost crack of dawn he was ready to do the dirty deed, but unbelievably, what was once a deserted stretch of canal had become alive with dozens of competitive fishermen, so it was hours before Peter could accomplish his mission.

Blobs fell into the canal and scrambled out on his own, and sat in the boat in a puddle of water, licking himself dry. Not to be outdone, Ibley Dibley was eyeing up some ducklings, tiny little balls of yellow fluff swimming about in the water. As they neared the bank he stealthily leaned down over the bank, waited for a duckling to swim within striking distance, then quick as a flash struck out for it. He must have lost his balance as with a big splash he fell in, and we rushed up on deck to see what all the commotion was about as ducks squawked and splashed and Ibley frantically tried to claw his way up the metal sides of the boat. I quickly reached over the side and yanked him out, took him below, wrapped him in a towel and presented him "gift wrapped" to Peter to dry.

Jesse came bounding into the boat and dropped a very alive mouse. I'd just got into bed so I jumped out, shut Jesse in the galley and Peter managed to catch the mouse before it had time to scurry away somewhere inaccessible, and put it out in the hedge bank, where it shot off.

Continuing back to Marsworth, Peter did his good deed for the day and helped an elderly couple through the locks. On completing his saintly mission he slipped and slid arse over head down the bank. Later on when we were moving up the locks he did an action replay and landed flat on his back, legs thrown up in the air, then down and all I could see as he lay flat and winded, was his hat above the long grass. I did, briefly, consider packing him off to the circus.

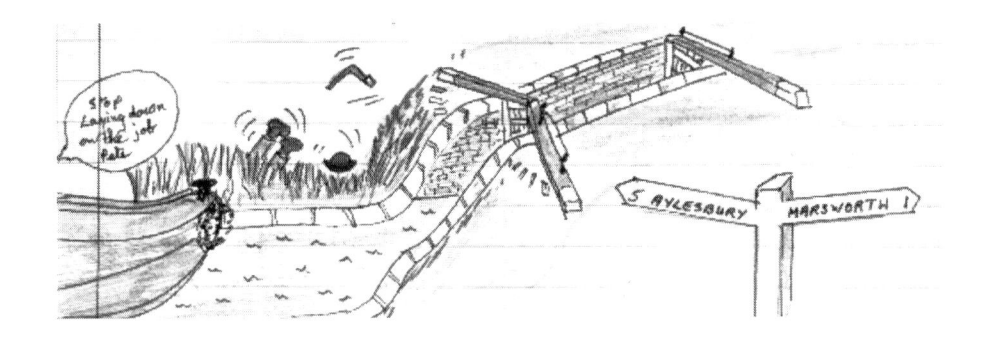

Chapter Four

Cat-astrophes and Corncockles

Back at Marsworth, we had a very nice interlude when a surprise posse of family and friends descended upon us from as far away as 200 miles, bringing wonderful presents and cards for my birthday. I felt very humbled and happy to see everyone and that they had all come especially for me. Only the weather put the dampers on the celebrations and although we tried to sit outside when we thought there might be a lull between showers, we were soon scuttling back to shelter from more downpours. At times the crowded boat resembled a rush hour train carriage with standing room only.

When everyone had departed, the trip boat passed by and a woman shouted to Peter who was up on the stern having a glass of beer.

"Hi, I'll join you on the way back".

I was sitting up on the bow and as the boat passed by, the woman spotted me, her flirtatious smile disappeared and she shouted back to Peter

"Oh your wife is with you, maybe I won't".

We had a good laugh and Peter was quite pleased with himself. I thought that from then on there would be no stopping him and it would be a case of 'mirror mirror on the wall', all day long.

It wasn't all pleasantries though, as there were two dogs on a boat just two along from where we were moored, a collie and a lurcher and the owner came along to warn us that they chased cats and rabbits and would kill any cat they caught. But although it was too nerve wracking to stay much longer, we had an appointment at the vets the next day so could not move on till we had been to take Jesse for his vaccination programme and also Blobs for a check up after his course of antibiotics that he had been on for some congestion in his lungs. Blobs did a whoopsie in his cat box while we were on the bus. Phew! One way of emptying the bus of passengers!

A further trip to the vets, this time with Ibley Dibley, safely secured in Peter's fishing basket. We left him with the vet, to be neutered and picked him up later. The vet surprised us when he told us that Ibley was probably between two and three years old. We'd thought he was just under a year old. He really was the image of Felix (in the cat food adverts) and just as cheeky.

It was with some relief, we moved away from any threat of killer dogs. We had initially intended to only go up four locks at Marsworth where there was a water tap, but when we got there we just could not get in to moor near enough to the tap, try as we might, so had to continue up more locks as far as Bulbourne junction. The weather was terrible and raining cats and dogs. I had caught a flu-like bug, so was dosing myself up on powders and just felt like going to bed. However, it required two of us to navigate the locks. So' clad in thick waterproofs, we hoped it would not take us too long to get to Bulbourne where we could moor up again. Once up at the Junction, somehow we managed to miss the water tap and as there was no way of turning the boat anywhere, we just had to carry on to the first winding hole so we could turn and go back to the tap. Being so exposed to the rain and wind, even though we had waterproofs on was miserable, but there was no alternative so we kept going heading for the winding hole. Our luck just wasn't in this day as when we reached it, there sitting like the magic circle, all around it on the banks were about 5 fishermen, all firmly established with their little green tents pegged in place too. The rules were 'no fishing in winding holes', but rather than create a life or death scene which surely it would have been if we had asked them to move, we plodded on, more miles to Cowroast where Peter, already soaked, managed to get an additional free shower when the water hose slipped off the tap and the water shot all over him. All this just to get water! As to continue onwards would have meant many more locks, we turned round and moored along the Tring summit which was lovely, away from noisy roads and with high wooded banks each side and lush greenery. We were just glad to get down below into the dry cabin, stoke up the stove and get our waterproofs off. I felt like death warmed up and I hoped Peter wouldn't catch the nasty bug too.

Ibley Dibley was making one heck of a din up on the roof early next morning, disturbing our sleep as he thumped and thudded around. Peter took a look to see what he was doing and found him leaping around with a dead mouse, throwing it up in the air and repeatedly pouncing on it.

Thankfully, I felt a lot more human the following day and as the rain had stopped we decided to walk to the hotel near Tring railway station and treat ourselves to a meal. But the somewhat sour-faced barmaid informed us that they had had a busy day (this was at 1.30pm on a Wednesday) and we were too late for a meal, but in an off hand manner added that she could make us a sandwich. We decided to do without and walk on instead to Aldbury and, as we left the hotel, an elderly man pulled up in a Land Rover and asked where we were going. He gave us a lift to Aldbury which was only about a mile away and told us that we might get a meal in the Greyhound. He had heard our conversation at the bar in the hotel and thanks to him we were just in time for a meal at the Greyhound. Aldbury, a pretty village with a duck pond and stocks, was on the doorstep of Ashridge park, the ancestral home of Francis Egerton, the third Duke of Bridgewater who started the canal age. Within the splendid estate stands the 200 foot high column which commemorates him.

There was lots of wood lying around so we made the most of collecting and logging up as much as possible. Peter fitted some hinges to the front cabin locker seats to make it easier to stow gear away. He also added some sugar to his latest batch of home brew and disappeared in a frothy cloud which erupted from the beer barrel like a volcano and went everywhere.

Part of the Ridgeway walk crossed the canal at Tring summit, and it was a very pleasant area to explore. We enjoyed many walks ambling along hedgerows and fields, stopping to admire anything that caught our eye, such as the breathtaking sight of a field full of pastel blue flax flowers and equally lovely finds of individual flowers, which at this time of the year included those of the pretty pink and white field bindweed and the many flowered, dark maroon tipped, pink common fumitory and numerous other arable field loving plants such as charlock, camomile, heartsease and wild turnip. Peter found some of the nicknames amusing such as "Jack-go-to-bed-at-noon" which describes the flower perfectly as it does just that, closes up at midday. Then there was "Jack-run-up-the-hedge" running along the hedge banks, sending out shoots and runners and little lilac coloured flowers as it went. 'Jack' seemed to be a terminology used for many plant nicknames, perhaps just referring to a herb of such. Bowers of fragile pink June dog roses and white field roses, hung delicately from branches that scrambled erratically over neighbouring hedges.

From delights such as these we were soon brought back to earth by things like a blocked bath pipe. Peter had to scramble under the bed with the torch to locate the pipe while I leaned over the bath the other side of the adjoining bulkhead to the bedroom, trying to locate the other end of the pipe under the bath outlet. We succeeded in dislodging the bath outlet pipe and lost the nut that held it all together so then tried various ways of putting it right without the nut, as the only way of retrieving that would have been to remove the tongue and groove bath panelling and get to the space around and under the bath. Even then there was no guarantee we would have found it. We tried plan A, plan B, C etc and three hours later, all plans exhausted, including us we decided to leave it till the next day. Peter sat out and had a beer and got chatting to a chap who often passed by the boat with a lurcher, gave him a beer too and the chap said he would drop us off a rabbit when he next passed by.

Jesse took to staying out most nights enjoying hunting in nocturnal oblivion to man and most beasts that in daytime proved some threat to him. We relished each wonderful lazy summers day with our only neighbours being mostly those of the natural world. We leisurely watched the birds and rabbits and could almost see the foliage growing daily, nettles and undergrowth competitively crowding out everything and becoming so dense in such a short time compared with the relatively bare banks of early Spring. A water rat would suddenly appear and run along the bank and disappear behind a clump of water figwort. Any dead wood that was lying around on the banks soon became completely covered and hidden. Herb Robert with its bright little pink flowers struggled up high and strong above all, branching out strongly on bright reddish stalks and quite defiant above even the tallest nettles.. The cats slept during the day, conserving energy for their nightly pursuits. Two agitated men ran along the towpath one day, shattering the peacefulness of the afternoon with a couple of police in hot pursuit. I had gone off to find a shop, in the direction of Tring so didn't see them, but Peter saw them run past the boat cursing and swearing as they went and was somewhat concerned for my safety and glad when I returned none the worse for wear.

We encountered a solitary lone hermit type boater along this stretch of canal, purposely moored up on the opposite bank for added privacy and isolation from the world.

We rarely saw any signs of life and the boat almost blended into the rusticity of its moorings, with green algae and grime obliterating any original colour it might have had and cobwebs replacing any signs of curtains. The boat was covered in a variety of junk and layers of dirt which appeared to have been unmoved for years. Three old Wellington boots on top of the boat contained a healthy crop of herbs growing from them. Sometimes a brief glimpse of a man would be seen and we wondered what kind of life he had led and what had caused him to become a recluse on the canal. He had a fierce looking German Shepherd dog, which, in time we learned had a bark worse than it's bite.

One day we bumped into the man and managed to exchange a few words and we were quite taken back by his well educated manner, well spoken speech and tidy appearance. He had a military air about him, officer like. In comparison to the state of his boat, we had not expected such a contrast as we'd felt sure that he would be of a similar rough nature.

He told us that he had lived on his boat for twelve years. We noticed he had a severe indentation on one side of his head which must have been from a serious head injury or operation, but all else about him remained a mystery. Personal disasters in life can change so called normal lives into complete opposite ones and none of us can foresee what life has in store for us. I was often reminded of the truth of the saying "There but for the grace of God go I".

Even when we were asleep, our instincts seemed to be more alert and sensitive to dangers than they probably would have been had we been living a more normal existence in a house. A splash at 4.20am woke us with a start and Peter jumped out of bed and ran up on deck, still half asleep but in time to witness a water-rat-like-Jesse come scrambling aboard after yet another fall into the water, the result no doubt of hunting water voles. The cats were becoming quite an aquatic breed of moggies. We were not unduly worried as the banks were low and the canal quite narrow, but we were a little concerned that they might end up on the opposite bank and then be unable to get back to the boat. With most bridges a considerable distance away from our mooring, they would not find them. We had also heard unnerving tales of foxes catching and killing cats and did not know how true this might be.

SWIMMING TRIALS (Splash In Championships)

Jesse	Blobs	Ibley Dibley
2	1	2

Rules
1. No Dog paddling allowed
2. No fishing while in the water
3. No attempts after dark

To our delight we had found signs of badger activity on our journeys but always kept this to ourselves and close trustworthy friends and family. We had heard these wonderful nocturnal creatures grunting at night and seen their sets during the days along overgrown banks of elderberry bushes.

Summer officially came in at long last at the beginning of July, hot enough for us to sunbathe in. Peter devised a wonderful splash pool out on the bank, where there was a nice bath sized hollow. He lined the hollow dip with the double deflated airbed and then connected the hose to the sink tap and filled the dip with water, then clad in our bathing gear we took turns to wallow around in the cool water. Since our bath times had been curtailed due to not being able to repair the pump and pipe, it was even more enjoyable. I felt like a bird having a bath in a puddle.

Gerald turned up out of the blue a few days later and helped Peter to secure the bath pipe to the plughole outlet. It was so difficult to get at and impossible for one person to fix on their own and Peter and I had not succeeded with two of us either. So, with Gerald squashed flat under the bed with arms stretched over his head and hands reaching blindly through the small opening in the tongue and groove bulkhead to the underside of the bath, he felt for and held the relevant part where it was required, directed only by instructions from Peter as he leaned over the bath, to 'left a bit', 'up a bit', 'hold it there', and after about an hour and many failed and frustrated attempts to suspend bolts and nuts in various positions down the plug hole, managed to secure the unit. There has, surely, never been a plumbing job quite like it before and it had to be heard and seen to be believed. On 'job completion' it was far from ideal as we now had a 1½ inch bolt sticking up out of the plug hole.

"Could be very painful that," I pointed out to Peter.

"Yes" he agreed, laughing. "Singing in the bath could become very operatic".

Although we would now be able to fill the bath without the water running out underneath it into the boat, the downside was that until we could get a new pump and the correct bath fittings, the only way to empty the bath water would be by bucket and chuck it. At least we would be able to have a nice hot bath.

Gerald gave me a little bike that he had had in his garage for some time and never used. It needed new brake cables, new back wheel, tyres and a good clean but would come in very handy for me to fetch shopping on.

Rewarded now with endless hot sunny days, our number one priority was to make the most of them. We decided to walk towards Aldbury again, and set off with some sandwiches, lettuce, tomatoes, beetroot, cheese and crackers and one apple to share. Before we reached the Ridgeway path we were heading for, I nearly did a backward somersault when with almost disbelief I spotted a 'corncockle' with about five flower heads on, growing at the edge of a field. I had never found one before and, like cornflowers and corn marigolds they had mostly disappeared from our cornfields due to the use of pesticides. We ambled on up the Ridgeway, through the woods, climbing up onto down land where we had panoramic views across the mostly flat countryside, a patchwork of fields of mostly green hues with the odd yellow patch of oilseed rape and an even more dramatic field of brilliant red, dense with poppies. Horses and cows lazily grazed and everywhere was alive and buzzing with bees laden down with bulging pollen sacs. We marvelled at insects of all shapes and sizes and amazingly bizarre colours. Tiny metallic silver ladybirds and one bright almost luminous lime green bodied spider. The reservoirs of Marsworth in the distance mirrored the azure blue sky and we sat in the sun on the down land among the anthills which were covered in wild thyme, rabbit holes, springy banks of golden yellow rockrose, sweet smelling bedstraw and various grasses. We found and ate quite a few deliciously sweet and tasty wild strawberries, along with our packed lunch and like 'mad dogs and Englishmen', sweated happily in the noonday sun..

Once refreshed and ready to continue our walk we came across more downland plants to enjoy, including 'dropwort' which looked something like 'meadowsweet', the delicate 'fairy flax', 'alexanders' 'hawkbits' and the wild snapdragon toadflax with its creamy yellow orange tipped flowers. For the first time that year we watched speckled wood butterflies flitting erratically here and there and also the marbled white, whose lava feed on grasses such as cocksfoot and timothy. We continued our walk up onto Pitstone Hill looking over towards Ivinghoe, the windmill and the large white scar of Pitstone Cement works which dominated the scene. Scrambling back down and along the bottom of the hill we came across numerous bright magenta pyramid orchids growing alongside what looked like groups of common spotted orchids, but as the area was fenced off we couldn't examine them closely. Little clusters of bell flowers popped up here and there along our way and as our route for a while took us along a quiet road, a different type of species of plants sprung up around us. These were bold and massive clumps of marauding rosebay willow herb spikes and impressive strange and exotic looking lofty stands of mullein with their wonderfully soft downy leaves, nicknamed Adam's flannel. Dense clumps of black horehound and outbreaks of bright purple knapweed, to name but a few were also well established. As we made our way through a field we spotted a huge bull with a head like a bison among cows and young calves. Peter quickly shifted to my right side as we passed them, even though a fence divided us from them. He was taking no chances and tried to look invisible as we passed by. He'd had too many nasty encounters with bulls in the past and didn't fancy any more. On our way back we found a Nikon 35-80mm zoom, macro camera up on a bridge at Tring so walked in to the police station to hand it in and were told that if it wasn't claimed in four weeks time it would be given to us, but we hoped it would be recovered by the owner.

All three cats were asleep in the boat on our return. After a rest, Peter did a bit of fishing and caught a few small fish which Ibley Dibley munched up raw, but Blobs wouldn't touch them until they were cooked to his liking and Jesse much preferred fresh mice, while Peter dreamed of pigeon pie. We discovered that wood pigeons seemed more often than not to perch up in ash trees. I could sense when Peter was up to something dastardly. He disappeared that evening, stalked off up the overgrown bank to lurk among the bushes below an ash tree, nearly treading on Jesse who was curled up fast asleep up there. He later related the tale to me of how he had got a nice fat pigeon in his sights, brought the barrel up, only to catch it under a rose bush branch as he did so and by that time it was too late and pigeon pie was off the menu once again. So to make up for his loss and to cheer him up I made a chicken pie, albeit with tinned chicken, he enjoyed it just the same and always swore that my pastry was the best on the planet.

There was another treat in line for Peter when he got talking to a local fly fisherman who said he would invite him as a guest to a fishing syndicate he belonged to at a nearby reservoir. So, in order to be nearer the venue, we took the boat up the short Wendover Arm as far as the Tringford pumping station. The next day although it was very windy, we went to the reservoir and Peter went out onto one of the strategically placed fishing platforms around the reservoir. There were one or two other chaps fishing and one in a boat. I left Peter settled and in his element and went back to the boat to do a few chores and make him a sandwich or two which I took back to him later in the day, by which time he had caught a nice sized rainbow trout. When we returned, the boat was surrounded by coarse fishermen, so rather than disturb them with moving, we stayed put for the night and were up early the next morning 6.30 to get the boat back to Bulbourne. This involved pulling it back on ropes to the turning point, so with Peter on the ropes ashore and me onboard astern, after a delayed 30 minutes searching ashore for Ibley Dibley, we finally managed to get there. Everything, or much of this new found boat life was so much slower and often much more arduous than conventional life ashore, but we felt more alive and happier for it.

Every day brought something different into our lives including much to laugh at.

One very hot day, Peter decided the canal water looked so inviting that he had to take a dip in it to cool himself down so, clad in his swimming trunks, he lowered himself down over the side of the boat into the water. When he emerged and dried off in the sun, he had a pale grey elephant-like film of clay all over him, so had to get bowls of water from the boat and rinse it all off.

My almost 80 year old mother came to join us for a week's holiday and on the first day with us got chatting to a fisherman, informing him that "Oh he (Peter) catches them for the cats!" I don't think Luton Angling Club would have been pleased to know that.

At Cowroast Peter went into the canal cottage garden and released two sheep that had apparently been put to graze on the garden lawns and both had their heads trapped in a nylon mesh netting around it.

The Good Shepherd

Mum fell off her chair up in the bow as we went through the lock and hurt her arm. I made her a cup of tea and she soon recovered her sea legs. On the Monday, we left her on the boat with strict instructions not to move (put a chalk mark round her) until we got back and went into Tring for some stores. We decided to take her on a trip to Leighton Buzzard and on the way came to a lock where there were side ponds covered in green algae that looked like immaculately mown lawns. Jesse disappeared and I had a horrible feeling that he might have jumped down on the pond thinking it was grass. I called and called him and dashed past the ponds to look but I knew he must have jumped down into one of them and I panicked as I looked furtively down into the ponds and the weeds at the edge. Peter said he could hear the distressed call of a cat yowling and then I saw Jesse, half submerged among the thick pond weeds. I kept calling to him and slowly he managed to get himself a bit nearer the side. But the sides of the ponds consisted of walls about 4ft high so even if he had reached them there was no way he could have got out. Jesse was getting very distressed and in danger of drowning when suddenly Peter jumped down into the side pound where he was. Luckily it was only about two feet deep and Peter quickly grabbed Jesse and passed him up to me. He then had a bit of a struggle to get back out himself as his feet were stuck in the mud beneath the water and there was nothing for him to grip his hands onto on the walls. So I ran to get a rope, but by the time I'd got back to him he had somehow managed to heave himself out. So much for a relaxing life in the slow lane, there was no chance when you had cats aboard. From then on we made a point of looking to see if there were any dangerous side ponds at locks.

Moored up, well away from any locks there were soon 4 dead mice astern and two on the path next morning and Ibley Dibley was batting around with a dead mouse in the bedroom last night, throwing it up in the air and doing back flips all around it. I was more frightened of spiders and there were getting far too many of them around the boat for my liking.

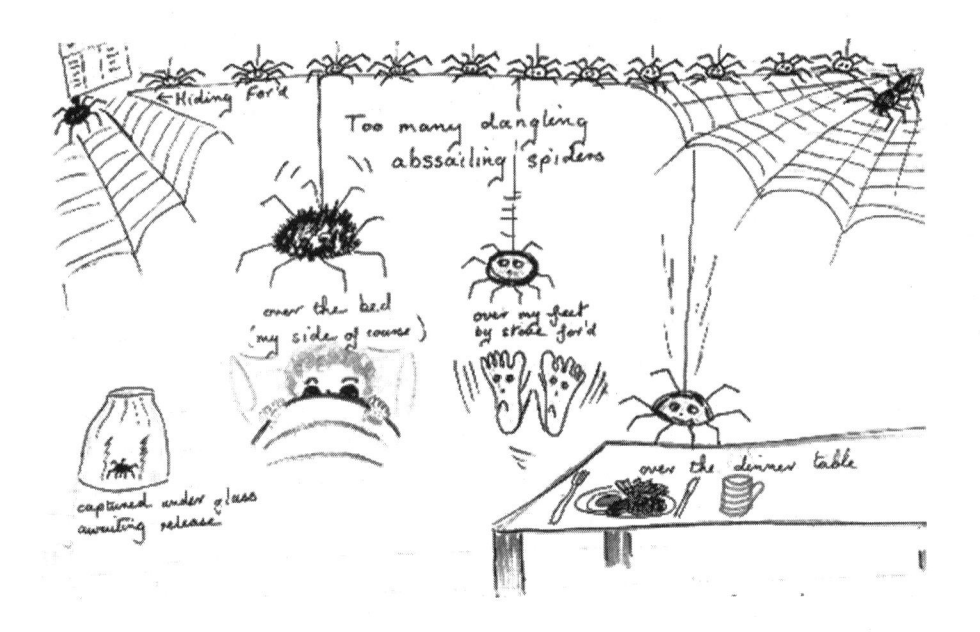

Then the boat and every other boater's boat were invaded with hundreds of flies, similar to house flies. They were everywhere and as soon as you swatted ten, another twenty would take their place. There were just as many outside as in. One boater blamed the fishermen. "They leave loads of maggots behind them and they all hatch out," he moaned. I was more interested in watching a lone mink dart along the bank on a stretch of canal between Leighton Buzzard, and Stoke Hammond and often caught a glimpse of it as we passed along there.

We made quite a few trips out of necessity to Leighton Buzzard, in particular to the bike shop there and caused pandemonium on one visit when we were moored up by the turning point, water point and the trip boat. The stern rope had somehow became free and the boat had swung out across the canal just hanging onto the mooring from her bow and quite unknown to Peter who was having a nap while I was away, shopping in Tesco. There was much shouting, hooting of boat horns as boats appeared from all directions and I don't know how a serious collision or two was avoided, but, thankfully canal boats don't travel at road traffic speeds. The rules were 4mph maximum and slower past moored boats.

It was good to be back out in the peace of the countryside and Ibley Dibley and Jesse soon had their noses down rabbit holes which were numerous on the other side of the towpath hedge. Peter found a couple of snare pegs there. We relaxed to the strains of a yellow hammer singing loudly for a 'little-bit-of-bread-and-cheese.' Later on in the evening Jesse caught a baby rabbit and brought it back to the boat, and dropped it, whereby Ibley Dibley wasted no time in pinching it, growling and running off the boat with it and dashing up the towpath when Peter pretended to be after him. Dibley brought it back and chewed its head off then Jesse proceeded to eat the body in the bedroom. At least it wasn't killed for nothing. Everything was eating everything else. The world was one big Gob.

A chap on a bike stopped by the boat next day, took his helmet off, hung his shirt up on the hedge, dolloped some deodorant on himself and sat on the path to cool off, rest and talk to us. I mentioned the mink back near Soulbury and he said that they were in fact otters, a pair, not to be talked about too much as the less people knew about them the better. He said they were along the River Ouzel near the canal. Whether this was true, or not, I don't know, but it would have been nice to think it was, though I suspect what I saw was most certainly American mink which had become naturalized along our canals.

Peter, after many hours working on repairs to my bike, eventually had it ride-able and it was good to go pedalling off on a trial run. What a difference it made to fetching shopping. We had bought a new inner tube for one of the tyres but Ibley Dibley punctured it when he pounced on it and bit into it, so that was one more job for Peter, repairing it.

While taking advantage of the nice weather we did endless painting jobs around the boat.

Then, having a relaxing siesta one hot afternoon, reading and dozing we were unaware that we had come adrift and were floating around in the middle of the canal. However there weren't many boats on the move so there was no harm done apart from one or two of the cats maybe stranded ashore.

Ibley Dibley was off colour, hiding under the bed and growling when picked up and in a few days time we decided we'd better take him to the vets as he seemed to be in considerable pain. We took him to the vets and he was diagnosed with an abscess and a temperature of 104. The vet was amazed that he was so lively and gave him an injection and a course of antibiotics and said the abscess might burst of its own accord or if not it might go away or it might end up needing to be lanced.

We had heard from the police station that no one had claimed the camera we handed in so it was ours if we wanted to collect it. Gerald had come out to see us and gave me and my bike a lift to the station at Tring, some fifteen miles away, but the camera had been transferred to Berkhamstead the day before, so it was a wasted journey. So Gerald dropped me and my bike off at Slapton and I cycled along the canal towpath, about eight miles. Peter was going to meet me with the boat at Soulbury locks. It was a very desolate stretch between Slapton and Leighton Buzzard, bit lonely for a woman on her own. Much of the towpath was rough and hardly fit to ride along on a shopper bike so it was slow going at times. Just past the Globe, the other side of Leighton Buzzard I saw a familiar and pleasing sight coming towards me. Peter, having become worried about me had set off on foot to meet me. I was as pleased to see him as he was me. On his way, he had passed two very undesirable looking men, one carrying a large net and a rope and the other a torch. Both were of an unpleasant and villainous demeanour. As we walked along together on our way back we passed them on their return and the thought of me having had to pass them alone made my flesh creep. Peter never liked me going anywhere on my own and always, if possible, went with me, or met me. He worried if I was so much as out of his sight.

The camera was sent back to Tring where we eventually picked it up and ended up having to buy a new battery for it which cost £11.

It was now mid August, still scorching hot weather. We discussed travel options and various places we'd like to go and had to decide where we would plan to over winter. Many canal repairs were carried out during winter months and it was wise to find out in advance where these operations were going to be as details were listed in advance by BWB giving information of where work and closure of locks and sections of canals would take place. So when planning routes it was advisable to make sure you reached your destination before closures took place and prevented you from doing so. Some routes would not be affected, or if you planned right, you could navigate through them before they shut down. It was now time to be thinking ahead and planning.

Part of our reasons to come down South had been to spend some time with my elderly mother and take her on the boat for trips with us, which we had done. So now we decided it was time to head back North via as many different canals as possible while the weather was still pleasant. Depending on our progress we then aimed to spend the winter months on the almost thirty mile lock free Bridgewater canal just the other side of Preston Brook tunnel so our movement wouldn't be hindered by any closures.

On hot days we were sometimes delayed for hours getting going due to cats being asleep in the grass or hedges somewhere and not responding to any cajoling measures by us to get them in. Cats pleased themselves what they did and when they did it. Free spirits for sure. Peter called me up on deck to watch a crow in the middle of a harvested cornfield which had a couple of bales of hay remaining in it. The crow was on the bale and appeared to be lying down on it, but when Peter continued to call the cats in, the so called crow jumped up in a Jesse shape and came running. "Time you had some new glasses Peter", I said.

My mother had kindly bought us a camcorder, which at that time was a relatively new and exciting way of filming and I was now able to capture our life and travels on film. As long as it didn't interfere with apple and black berry pie making, Peter said it was fine.

Ready at last to set off we made our way back through what was now familiar territory as far as Blisworth tunnel which was very busy with tourists and boaters. About a quarter of the way through the tunnel our headlight conked out and then all our internal lights went out too. All Peter could do was to yell to oncoming boats "I've got no lights," and hoot the horn. There was a boat behind us and lots coming towards us and it was unnerving to be completely in the dark, unseen by approaching boats until they were almost on top of us. I dashed down below, groped around in the blackest pitch darkness I'd ever seen, for the torch which was pretty useless compared to a headlight, but I put it on the red flashing hazard light setting and held it up for'd, hoping it would make some difference, and would be seen by any approaching boats, then propped it up and went below to fish out the two coach lamps, filled them up with paraffin, by candlelight and slotted them into their appropriate holders up on the bow. We now felt a bit safer as they were quite bright and better than the torch. Peter shouted to the boat behind us to pass us as soon as he could, so that we could follow behind them, in the wake of their lights. Quite suddenly the interior lights came on again and Peter realized that he had accidentally knocked the switch off while he was trying to find the hooter button in the dark. There were a lot of bats flying around in the tunnel that day, none of whom were quite as batty as the crew on Rainbow II. The light was soon operational again, as the problem was only a fuse.

We moored up for the night a couple of miles on from Gayton Junction. Peter made the dinner and I found some horse radish plants, pulled one up and added some of the grated up root to the sauce to liven it up, which it certainly did as it is very hot stuff.

The happy mousers were soon desecrating the mouse population. Jesse dropped one when I went up to him and let me pick it up, all trembling, but still very lively in my hands so I put it in the grass well away from Jesse. Ibley caught a little bank vole alongside the boat, dropped it behind Jesse who spun round and gave Ibley a clout which took him by surprise and he lost his vole.

Peter cut a few promising looking hawthorn sticks. The way my joints were acting up I thought he'd better be making me one first. He seemed to have a natural talent for working with wood, maybe because he enjoyed doing it so much. He made some brilliant bookshelves with scalloped fancy edges to the supports, all with just a grotty old knife, so with a set of proper tools he would, no doubt have used his skills well and made some really fantastic things, but he was happy to carry on and manage with what he had and with the patience of a saint he'd sit for hours whittling away working on a walking stick with just a pen knife.

Half past midnight, we had just fallen asleep when we were awaken by piercing cat wails, typical of a cat fight, so we leapt out of bed, grabbed the torch and ran bare foot, me in nightie, Peter in his underpants, up on deck, just in time to see Ibley Dibley scrambling up the bank out of the canal and a triumphant Jesse looking down at him from the roof of the boat, so they had obviously had a clash of claws. We would never have slept had we not gone to see what was happening, we always had visions of prowling foxes and or poachers or drowning cats. Must have been something in the air, as the following day Peter and I had a nautical nark but cooled off as we headed towards the Ashby canal and Bosworth field, scene of a much bigger battle where Richard III was killed in 1485.

We saw a solitary tortoise along the bank in the middle of nowhere and the second one we had seen during our travels, the first being up in Cheshire. Both were no doubt Garden escapees. The boat was acting up, moving along sluggishly like a tortoise too and we discovered that a formidable barrier of weeds and reeds had gathered on our bow waterline and was continuing to build up, slowing us down considerably. It was like pushing a haystack along.

The next morning being a Sunday I decided to cycle to Shenton about a mile away to treat Peter to a Sunday paper. According to the canal guide book there was a shop there but when I got there I discovered that the one and only shop that had been there had shut down about three years ago. On my way back I got stuck behind a herd of cows all in the middle of the road. Not one to be defeated I then cycled to Market Bosworth, an all up hill slog, and found a paper shop there. I had cycled a total of about seven miles just to get a paper but it was worth it because I knew how much Peter would enjoy it. He had been busy when I returned, tightening up the fan belt and other jobs.

About midday, we walked to the scene of the battle, first entering 'Richards field' where he was slain. The canal now runs along this field and a large memorial stone stands commemorating his death. As it happened, by strange coincidence I was halfway through reading a book about Richard III, so it made it all so much more interesting and enjoyable. When we reached the centre, there was a display of archery going on so we watched that before looking round the centre where various artefacts typical of the day were on display with models of the battle scenes, suits of armour, weapons, models of medieval villages etc. An extract from the famous film about Richard III lasting 16 minutes, showing the battle and his death, and starring Sir Laurence Olivier was shown, making a grand finale. We then watched the jousting tournament by the famous Northampton jousters which we found very entertaining with plenty of humour thrown in including a drunken knight and the evil black knight who drew lots of loud booing and cheering from the crowd.

Had it not been for visiting the battlefield, our journey up the Ashby canal would have been an almost totally worthless, monotonous journey with the shallow water making our progress painfully slow and laborious. Even the scenery seemed pretty mundane compared with what we had already seen elsewhere. We were glad to return to the spot where we had moored four months previous and found Ibley Dibley and wondered if he remembered it too. Perhaps we should have named him 'Atherstone the Alley Cat'.

More catastrophes going down the eleven locks spread over about fourteen miles when vibrations from the boat managed to gradually work the bolt on the for'd cabin doors free. All three cats managed to escape when we were in a lock, springing out onto the boat in all directions like mutinous Pirates of the Caribbean, but, thankfully, only Jesse managed to attempt, and succeed in getting ashore before one of us managed to climb up out of the lock and retrieve him along with the others from their various mutinous positions up on and around the boat. Peter said jokingly that they should all be given a lashing with the 'cat-o-nine-tails'. I found I had a few more grey hairs – I wonder why?

We stopped only briefly at Tamworth after hearing a few tales of vandalism and boats having been broken into and of a Dutch couple on holiday who had moored up on a quiet stretch and who had all their windows smashed in by five louts who then terrorised and robbed them. The couple had only had one of their five weeks holiday but cancelled it and went back to Holland. This sort of thing made me sick to my core and I felt ashamed to share the same nationality as those thugs.

There were no signs of any decent moorings as we headed for Birmingham where the canal ran underneath the complex Spaghetti junction motorway and on to the Tame Valley canal with its vista of thick industry. The canal water resembled black treacle, cluttered up with rubbish of every description. We had little choice but to carry on up the thirteen locks at Perry bar and just managed to reach the top at sunset and moor along a tree lined, high banked stretch to let the cats out. Having made our way up a total of twenty locks that day we were more than ready for a rest.

The following day matters became even worse with huge and endless conglomerations of industry excluding everything else for miles and rough areas that we had no intention of mooring up in and so we plodded on and on till past 10pm through Coseley, Bilston and into Wolverhampton. This was the first time we had travelled at night in the dark in unknown territory and we didn't feel at all comfortable about it. The day before, we had moored up along the Birmingham level on the approach to Dudley Port junction and watched boat after boat turning down into Netherton tunnel. We reckoned on about 700 boats being down at the Dudley rally and most would have booked moorings so we decided to stay away and look for a suitable quiet spot along the level and to go into Dudley to the rally by bus. However, it didn't work out like that and we had decided against going back and through the tunnel. We ended up navigating our way down the Wolverhampton flight of twentyone locks on a scorching hot day and with great relief found a mooring along by some playing fields where at last the cats could be let out and we could have some peace of mind. Birmingham was certainly OFF the map regards any further trips we would be making.

We met up with Gerald and Freda and they took us into the meeting held by the newly formed N.A.B.O, association and then we all went to the Bank Holiday rally site which was heaving with boats and people all crammed together like Blackpool. Peter and I were starving hungry and boiling hot most of the time and were glad to get away from the crowds and back to the solitude of our boat. Not however hazard free as Blobs almost got run over on the towpath by a motor cyclist who should not have been using the towpath. Then Peter got stung by a wasp. Happy days, never a dull moment! We were looking forward to a less stressful trip up the Shropshire Canal the next day.

- Awful day
- Depressing
- Mile upon mile of sludge filled with rubbish
- Mega NARKs
- GRAFITTI
- more depression — moan moan / moan moan — Black Country blues
- Fed up moggies
- accumulation of haystacks on bow causing GO SLOW + STOP
- bad language *+!*$0-
- moan! groan!
- STINKS!
- Nylon rope
- string vest - black
- plastic bag
- Wire
- all round propeller
- Pete had to take generator out twice to cut off rubbish from propeller via the weed box
- Too many boats going too fast! to the rally
- no decent moggy-moorings
- Too many locks
- Its the Pits!
- YUK + MUCK!
- Mutineering moggies
- long faces + miserable fishermen
- 👎 To B'ham.
- torrential rain

Chapter Five

Man Overboard

The Shropshire Union Canal was Telford's last and is a fine example of his engineering skills. It was built to provide the shortest and quickest route and with a minimum of locks and runs more direct than either the road or railway does. The Southern section contains long straight cuts through deep sandstone cuttings with high embankments, which if you climb to the top of, you are rewarded with wonderful views across the Midlands. From the Southern section there are equally fine views across the Shropshire countryside and the further north you travel into Cheshire, you will see, on a clear day, the Welsh mountains. However, for us, much of the time the views were obliterated by the steep embankments which provided ideal hunting grounds for the moggies and on our first mooring stop on the canal we counted fourteen assorted grizzly mouse remains, spread at intervals along the towpath the next morning. The mouse population must have thought it was Armageddon..

Wind was the worst hazard, particularly on the exposed embankments where we caught its full force as it blew strongly across the Cheshire plain.

Peter was almost falling to sleep as we chugged along at a steady 3 – 4mph. I often went and sat up in the bow where it was quieter away from the constant noise of the engine.

There were many pheasants around this time of the year and Peter always had the urge to re-home them in the oven, but we found difficulty in mooring up anywhere much due to a concrete sill running along the bank which kept us about three or four feet off the bank and ideally we liked to get in closer, mainly for the cats, although we had a couple of planks we could use fore and aft if need be. Often I'd be painting a butterfly or something on one side or the other of the boat, so that was another reason we needed to be moored tightly flush with the bank. Finally about 23 miles on from Autherley junction we managed to find deep enough water to moor up close to the bank.

We usually stayed put for a day or two at least when we found nice moorings and enjoyed the moment of each day as it came and realized the futility of forever chasing rainbows and the pot of gold at the end of it, when in truth the real 'Pot of Gold' existed only as 'you treasured' the moment.

August had been a perfect month and was now at an end with still nice weather.

I was busy washing and drying all the bedding and doing some mending when Peter decided to go on my bike and find a shop, the nearest place according to the map being Cheswardine. I made a shopping list for him and drew him a rough map and off he pedalled. Shortly after he left a couple came by and stopped for a chat. They informed me that the village was nearer if you went in the opposite direction to which Peter had gone. So in an attempt to draw his attention, I frantically blasted the boat horn, hoping he would hear it and do an about turn, but he didn't. This was about 4.20pm. Over an hour later he arrived back, dripping with sweat, knees caving in and no groceries. He had cycled about 8 miles, not seen a building of any description, let alone a village or shop. A farm lad told him he was going in the wrong direction and so he had turned back, other wise I don't know where he would have ended up, probably somewhere in Outer Mongolia via Australia.

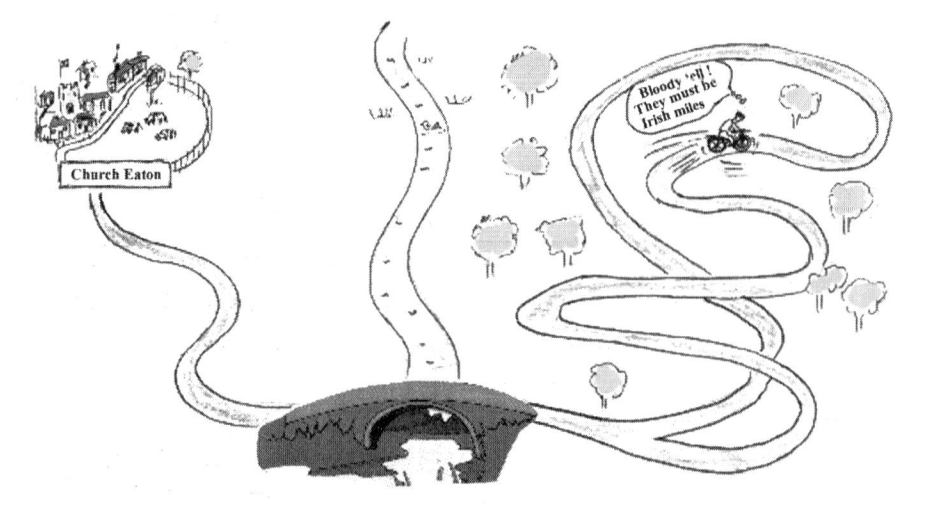

Once Peter felt fit enough we decided we would try to find the village and the pub, together, so with Peter walking and me on the bike we retraced the route he had taken as far as the canal bridge and discovered that he had then turned right instead of left, and gone in the opposite direction to the village. We were lucky enough to find a store open and walked a different way back. I decided I might have to get Peter a guide dog.

There was a locust like invasion of crane flies and fishermen, the latter of whom were in a match and took over miles of the canal bank, upsetting our plans of only travelling a short distance before mooring up. Instead, we travelled about eight or nine miles. "How far have we gone now?" Peter asked.

"Two pages" I replied. We came to relate distances by how many pages in the canal map guide book we had travelled. One page on average consisted of about 4½ miles.

Peter's hair had grown so long but he wasn't particularly worried until one day I was showing a couple who had stopped to chat to me, some photos, one of which included Ibley Dibley on top of the boat with Peter leaning over the hatch cover talking to him, with just his head and shoulders visible. They commented on the photos and the lady enquired of the one with Peter and Ibley on. "Oh is that your mother?"

I could hardly contain myself or keep a straight face, but once they had gone, I pulled Peter's leg something rotten about it. He couldn't wait to get his haircut then.

Nantwich, with its long history of salt mining was certainly worth a visit and we walked all round it admiring the many old Tudor buildings and making good use of our new camcorder. I was so impressed and taken by it all that I returned later on in the day to do some more filming.

Alongside the second lock that day we discovered a greengage tree laden with fruit and as Peter shook it I stood underneath getting bombarded with ripe greengages. We must have gathered about 5lb of them and they were beautiful in a pie or just stewed with custard and made a nice change from our almost daily blackberry and apple pie. We also found many damsons to pick and I must say that they were always my favourite even though it was a tiresome job getting the stones out of them after they were stewed.

Jesse came back with a live shrew dangling from his jaws, and dropped it in front of me, as if to say. "You can have this one for your tea, I don't like them". The shrew didn't hang around and shot off into the long grass. We were thinking of renaming Ibley Dibley "Aqua cat" seeing as he spent so much time falling into the water. I filmed him eating cat food from an open tin I had left on the table. He was putting his paw in and scooping paws full of meat up to eat. No doubt he would want an 'Oscar' for that performance!

We were now, almost at the start of our journey up the forty-six or so miles long Llangollen canal which was Telford's first. Surely it was one of the most popular canals among tourists and holiday makers and meandered its way along a very pretty winding route towards the Welsh mountains. We were looking forward to it very much

I'd been experiencing shoulder pains for some weeks which were now worse than ever, especially the left one which when at a certain angle was like being struck by lightening and would temporarily freeze me. I swung down the hatch one day and somehow hung on by my left arm as I went down and was creased up with excruciating pain for a few minutes. But although the joint was still sore long afterwards, I think the dramatic wrench might have even done it some good. Peter said it sounded like it was a frozen shoulder.

A new experience for us was operating and passing through three or four lift bridges, especially the one at Wrenbury which was operated by using the windlass and was of the type seen in Holland. We took them slowly to make sure no damage was done, either to the boat, us, or anyone else who happened to be around. Unfortunately I left and lost one of our best windlasses at one of the bridges. We lost many and rarely had the luck to find any ourselves.

It was becoming quite standard practice once moored up, for us and the cats to all go for a walk together. They followed along behind us like little dogs. If one of the cats went off on a hunting trip, occasionally they would cross a nearby bridge and end up on the opposite bank somewhere. From across the canal they would spot or smell the boat on the other side and get confused about how to get back to it. Not at all happy with the situation they would yowl in distress across the water to us. Jesse became stranded like this after he'd probably followed Peter across a bridge, and didn't return with him. Sometimes we just pushed the boat across to the bank where they were stranded, or alternatively walked down to the nearest bridge and around to the opposite bank to bring them back. When distressed cats had a distinctive deep throated yowling call, completely different to any other one they make.

There were many boats waiting at Grindley Brook staircase, with the lock keeper in attendance letting three boats up and three boats down at a time. A chap alongside the winding hole at the bottom of the locks was waving his arms and doing circular signals to us as we approached, so Peter shouted to him "Are you going up the locks?"

Instead of shouting or nodding in the affirmative or otherwise, he gesticulated with his hands, making turning round motions with them, so we assumed he was going to turn around and we passed alongside him and to the front of him, at which he started throwing a fit. Once alongside the bank, I decided to go up to him and see if he was going up the locks after all, as we had no intentions to push in out of turn. But he had lost the plot and threatened to do this and that to us; he was beyond reasoning with and got slightly up my nose, I must admit. Peter reversed down alongside his boat and coolly but firmly told him that we had misunderstood his erratic unintelligible sign language intentions and that his behaviour was very out of order. He apologized one minute then ranted on a bit more. He must have had very high blood pressure.

The lovely open countryside made up for bad tempered boaters, which I must add were a minority, thankfully. Peter lost the grease-gun (for keeping the propeller shaft greased up) over the side, and the only way to try and retrieve it was to go into the water and feel around with your feet, something I certainly wasn't going to volunteer for. My excuse being "You are taller than me Peter, so if the water is deeper than it looks, you will have more chance of keeping your head above water while your feet feel around in the mud for it". Yuk! I hoped Peter would be convinced he was best suited for the task and also hoped there was nothing sharp and nasty lurking on the canal bottom, as was often the case, for him to cut his feet on. No problem for an old war veteran who had been, as he was always telling me, up to his neck in muck and bullets on D-Day in Normandy. So, he stripped off, climbed gingerly over the side and lowered himself down into the water, first checking there were no crocodiles around. But he could not locate the grease-gun with his feet, so he took one deep breath and disappeared under the water and hey presto surfaced triumphantly with it in his hand, which was a relief, as if the prop shaft wasn't kept greased up it leaked water around it and into the boat and even just a small but constant drip could soon build up to a lot of water. The bilge pump was also very important to keep in good working order especially if you were a little accident prone like us and needed to stay afloat. As one boater reminded us when he passed us on the following Sunday and shouted out to us.

"You got her up then?"

We were a bit stumped at first by this remark to know what he meant then he added that he'd seen us when we'd been half sunk at Wigan in February.

We rested up at Ellesmere, out of necessity more than anything else, as Peter's back and sciatica were playing him up. It was pleasant to be among other boaters to enjoy the start of the Waterways Festival with boats all dressed up fancy and a small fun fair, boat trips, steam engines and lots of stalls to browse around.

We were looking forward to crossing the famous Pontcysyllte aqueduct which was surely one of, or <u>the</u> highlight of the canal. First crossing the impressive 70ft high Chirk aqueduct which crosses the river below it, was just a taste of what was soon to come.

The engineering skills of Thomas Telford and William Jessop could be seen and fully admired in the spectacular structure of the Pontcysyllte aqueduct which if you had no head for heights, would be advisable to cross it on foot on the towpath side where there were safety railings, or stay below in the narrow boat cabin. Those more adventurous and with a head for heights could navigate it from the stern or bows of their boats with nothing more than just a 12inch high aqueduct offside between them and the 120ft sheer drop to the River Dee below. The width of the top of the aqueduct is only 11ft 10 inches and runs in length an amazing 1,000ft. Neither Peter or I had heads for heights; Peter would get dizzy going up stairs. But this was one sight we just had to admire even if our stomachs did churn around a bit. The views and the experience were beyond words and not to be missed. To try to imagine what the building of it over a period of 10 years must have involved, and at such a great height, made the mind boggle. Plus the vast amount of materials required and made for it and labourers toiling away for sums on average around 10 shillings a week (50p). The cost of building it was £47,000, between the years of 1795 and 1805 when it was opened.

Back to more mundane events, we had never come across so many rabbits and rabbit holes as we did around this part of our travels. We were just in time to see Ibley Dibley with his nose down a hole and then he just disappeared down it and scared us to death, thinking he would disappear into the unknown never to be seen again. It was with relief when he showed up again none the worse for his curiosity.

Jesse had taken to sleeping out mostly, curled up in the hedges or banks among the bracken. Peter found him one day asleep like that, with half a rabbit carcass alongside him. When he was not hungry, it was sometimes very difficult to get him to come in or to find him and we had to wait hours to get on the move.

Llangollen itself, we found to be very congested as the canal becomes so narrow and in some places only wide enough for one boat, extremely limited mooring space and so many boats all heading for the same place and then having to return the same way. But the journey made it all very enjoyable and the return journeys even though along the same terrain always seemed different when going in the opposite direction.

It was now almost the end of September, so our original plans to go up to Chester were put on hold and we decided to save that for another time and instead to head towards Preston Brook. Another holiday boat came hurtling round a corner and piled into us. We had quickly stopped to lessen the inevitable blow which luckily hit us at an angle so wasn't too bad. Then towards Bunbury we were a short distance on from the staircase lock just in time to see the boat behind us hurl round the bend, pull the tiller over the wrong way and end up head first in the trees and bushes on the offside bank.

Some of these holiday boaters must have been in need of another holiday by the time they returned home, in order to recover from the experience. Most of them seemed to still be in the fast lane dashing around doing "rings" of canals as fast as they could as if their very lives depended upon how quickly they could complete them. We used to hear them discussing their progress while operating locks, and relating how many miles and locks they had done in how many record breaking hours, minutes and seconds. It appeared to be a race among many crews and we'd see them running and leaping energetically from lock to lock preparing them in advance so as not to lose any time. Sometimes crew members were so far in front of their boat it was nowhere in sight and they'd prepare locks and be waiting for when their boat did arrive. On one such occasion another boat did appear. It was coming in the opposite direction and wished to use the lock, but of course the lock was ready for traffic coming in the opposite direction. Not very good practice at all, as it was generally the rule that the first boat to arrive at a lock had priority over its use. You couldn't run ahead and reserve a lock for a boat unless there was nothing coming from the opposite direction that would reach it before your boat did.

We wondered what these "race around the rings" boaters could have found to have enjoyed about their boating holiday. Perhaps it was just the fun of a race. Perhaps they considered we were odd in such a laid back dawdle. I suppose as long as they were happy and enjoying themselves that was the main thing, and as long as they weren't ramming into our boat too often.

Between Middlewich and Nantwith, back on the Trent and Mersey canal, in the Dane Valley, there were quite a few lagoons caused by subsidence that merged into the canal along certain stretches. They were riddled with rocks and old remaining hulks of wrecked barges and narrow boats which had been dumped and stranded there. To anyone not aware of the hazards in these circumstances, and who happened to stray off the main canal route, it could be misleading and end up with them becoming stranded too. Unknowingly, they would think the water was deep enough to stray into the lagoon and in doing so would go aground on the shallow and submerged hidden offside bank of the canal.

Sure enough we came across one such hire boat, very high and dry and it looked quite funny stuck there with two male crew members standing on the stern looking hopelessly lost and abandoned. We managed to throw them a rope and attempted to pull them off and when that failed, to then to push them off with our bow without getting ourselves stranded too. However, it was no good and just as we gave up, someone arrived from the boatyard to assist them. So we wished them good luck and continued on our way.

We were both awake at 4.30 am the next morning and talked for an hour. No matter what time of the night it was, if one of us were unable to sleep, the other one would always be willing to be awake too and either have a cup of tea, a chat, or read. Peter in particular was so thoughtful and kind to me, as for many years I sometimes had great difficulty in getting to sleep. One night he suggested that he could read his book to me to see if that would help. Well it worked like magic as though he had hypnotized me and within minutes his voice had sent me off to sleep. With that discovery, little did he know what he had let himself in for, but never ever did he complain or be anything other than willing to read me to sleep, no matter what time of the night it was or how tired he was and he never even minded being woken up. Sometimes I would last a few pages before falling asleep and he'd test me out saying "Maggie are you still awake?" If I answered he'd continue reading; if not he knew I was asleep and either closed the book or continued to read quietly to himself. He'd read two or three books a week if we had a good supply which I always tried to manage to scrounge or buy from charity shops.

We had a few battles over snoring and I once almost cured him by recording an earthshaking snoring session of him when he was asleep in his chair one day, so there was no denying the evidence of that on the camcorder. The almost 'break the sound barrier' snores that I recorded were nearly grounds for divorce stuff, if it hadn't have been so funny to watch on film.

Early one morning I'd just lit the fire and started to make breakfast when three greyhounds and a mongrel ran past the boat chasing what looked like our cats. I flew out and saw the dogs in the fields and bushes nearby and a man with them. I called out to him about the cats and he replied in an off hand manner. "Its up the tree" adding "You want to watch your cats round here, there's lots of people walking greyhounds and they'll have them if they get the chance."

By this time Peter was up and dressed and through the hedge. We soon found Ibley Dibley and Jesse and put them aboard along with Blobs who was already in. We put breakfast on hold and moved the boat on a few miles to a spot we hoped was more 'cat' friendly. It started to rain, then poured down and became torrential with thunder and lightening, so the cats didn't want to go out anyway.

If it wasn't dogs chasing cats it was cats chasing mice. A little mouse suddenly ran out from the logs placed at the base of the wood stove and made Blobs, who was dozing nearby, jump. It dashed into the galley and I grabbed a cardboard box to try and catch it in but before I had chance to do so Jesse had already dealt with it and sat smugly up on the step with it lifeless at his feet.

We eventually came into the salt mining territory of Northwich on a dull, windy cold and depressing day, with both of us feeling tetchy and argumentative. We moored up for a break and not long after continuing our journey I discovered Ibley Dibley was not on board and came to the conclusion that he must have somehow got out and off the boat unnoticed somewhere. We stopped the boat, tied up and walked back along the towpath calling him and searching. A lad fishing nearby informed us that he had heard a 'splash' and a cat meow, so that made us even more worried about him and we had visions of Ibley having fallen in the water as the boat had set off and having been dragged under it in the wash and drowned or, worse, chopped up in the propeller. How one's mind ran amuck in such situations. We were consumed with horribly gloomy pessimistic thoughts for the next hour when a man came past and Peter asked him if he had seen a little black and white cat. The man walked on saying nothing but then turned and walked back to Peter and I and said that he had, after all, remembered seeing a cat like that on the stern some time ago where we now were. I continued to call Ibley and suddenly he came running out of the hedge. What a relief, I could have hugged the man. Ibley must have gone from the stern deck, down through the two gaps by the tiller bar and been down underneath somewhere and then come back up and out when we had stopped and nipped ashore without us seeing him.

In the afternoon I couldn't find Jesse and searched everywhere and walked all around the woods calling him. Blobs followed me and nearly got chewed up by a pit-bull. I grabbed Blobs and swung him round away from the dog but it kept prancing round and I visualized its jaws round my arm or Blobs. I swung Blobs up a nearby tree trunk and he promptly fell down again. The dog owners just stood calling the dog but it took no notice of them. I scrambled up the bank and told them to get it on a lead and they apologized and did so. Jesse was still missing so Peter went looking and discovered him, with the help of Ibley Dibley, up a tree, too scared to come down. No matter how much we called him or coaxed him, he just sat meowing on the lowest protrusion of a sawn off branch. He was about 15ft up. Peter climbed to within a foot of him but could get no further or reach him and Jesse wasn't budging. Peter then sawed a long branch off a tree and propped it alongside the tree and up to Jesse, but no joy. After trying all angles, we decided to leave him and see if he would eventually come down on his own. Still no sign of him later after dark, so we made a platform on the end of the boat pole and put it up to him, but he wouldn't get on it. Out of desperation to get him down we then got the broom and tried to push him off the branch down towards us, but that failed too, so it was time to bring in more drastic 'cruel to be kind' measures. Peter fetched the boathook, shoved the hook up through Jesse's collar and unceremoniously hauled him down and then quickly grabbed him. He had been up the tree for about seven hours.

CAT RESCUE PATROL

Late September we travelled about nineteen miles from Barnston through three tunnels, one 500 odd yards long and the other some 400 yards. We had to go through the first one with no headlight and Peter had a job to avoid hitting his head on the tunnel roof in places as it was so low. The generator, with which we used to run the headlamp conked out, so I turned all the internal lights on inside the boat to enable some light to reflect onto the tunnel walls, lit the coach lamps, got the torch out and followed another boat through. Navigating wouldn't have been very easy otherwise especially as one tunnel had a lot of bends in it so we couldn't see the end and it was darker than I ever knew darkness could be. I was up front with the torch, shouting to Peter 'left a bit, right a bit, you are going to hit the wall'. We did manage to get the generator going but then the light bulb blew as water had got into the light. We decided it was time we must get a more efficient light. But before that we had to also get through the 1,239 yards long Preston Brook tunnel, so we sat tight and waited for another boat to come along which we could follow through.

It was listed in our canal map book that there was a post office, garage and store on top of the tunnel about halfway along somewhere, so once the other side, safely moored up we trotted off to find it and asked another chap on a boat which way it was to the shop. He was a bit of a strange character like someone out of one of Dickens' books and spoke in very slow monotonous monosyllables and said, "W-ha-t s-h-o-p, oooooh it be gorn. Din yer know it be gorn, there aint no shop, it be gorn, f-e-ll thr-ooough the tunnel four ye-ars ago it d-i-d". Apparently part of the tunnel had collapsed and the post office and the other shop had collapsed with it. Suddenly we had second thoughts about making unnecessary trips through the tunnel. We also heard the morbid tale of a lone boater in his twenties or early thirties who had gone through the tunnel and never come out the other end and had been found drowned. I suppose there were obviously more risks navigating alone.

We learned that there were some stoppages planned somewhere along the Bridgewater canal that were not listed in the BWB stoppages list due to the fact which I had overlooked that the Bridgewater did not come under the jurisdiction of BWB so would not be included in their list. As there were no locks on it I wondered where and why the stoppages were going to be made and learned via the grapevine that somewhere along it was a section was being drained for some maintenance work to take place. I hoped it would be on the other side of Lymm in which case we would be alright. There were only 3 places along the section of the Bridgewater where we intended to over winter, where we would be able to get water between Bollington the other side of Lymm and a few miles past Stockton Heath in the opposite direction. None were suitable for mooring up other than just to take on water and if the winter was bad and we became iced in it made sense to moor not too far from an accessible water point. The one by the small marina shop at London Bridge was far too near a main road to be safe for the cats, the other by the Old No 3 pub was on the opposite side to the towpath where the canal ran dangerously parallel with the busy A56. We decided that if there was any danger of the canal icing up we would have to moor opposite the latter and if we froze up and couldn't move, one of us would have to walk about 20 minutes down and along the canal, under an aqueduct bridge, round a small hamlet and along the A56 to the pub side tap, tie the hose on a line and throw it across the canal and fill up with water that way. We hoped we were not going to end up frozen in. We could always use the beer barrels to store water in if the worst came to the worst and just ration it out sparingly.

As for now it wasn't even October and we were battling our way through rain and gales but finally decided we'd had enough and were ready to just moor up anywhere, which conveniently turned out to be alongside a huge field of potatoes. Well we had run out, so a few for tea wouldn't, we were sure, be missed. So Peter went out at dusk to dig a few up and hoped that the slimy and pongy stuff he dug his hand into was just a rotten spud and not something one of the cats had buried.

Ibley Dibley bought in a live mouse which managed to escape when we tried to catch it and disappeared behind the wood panelling at the bottom of the bed. So we now had a stowaway on board, but I didn't think it would survive long with three cats on the prowl.

We found a derelict orchard and collected an abundance of apples, and damsons and there were still plenty of blackberries about to keep us going. We were eating fruit pie most days of the week as if there were no tomorrows.

I went for a little ride along the towpath on my bike one day and came upon a fisherman all huddled up on the bank with his parka hood pulled right over his head, completely obscuring all his side vision. I slowed down, rang my bell but got no response, so continued to ride at almost stopping speed and crept past but just as I drew level with him he caught a sprat and quickly pulled back his roach pole right into the spokes of my bike wheel. Next thing I heard was a disgruntled moan and "You've snapped my bloody rod!"

"Well, I did ring my bell and crawl past you, sorry about that, is it okay?"

He examined it with a long facial expression and grumbled that he supposed he would be able to fix it. I thought that with a miserable face like that he would have been better playing poker. The pole looked to me as though it had been repaired before where part was encased in tape. And anyway, he should have considered himself lucky as he could have caused me to have had a nasty accident.

Good news from the family, a new grandson Joshua born out in Australia, making me now a granny of 3 and hoping it wouldn't be too long before we got around to seeing him and the family again. We had now been travelling for 6 months and covered some 800 miles of canal.

In the middle of October we had an Indian summer so we took advantage of the nice weather and moored up on the opposite bank to the towpath not far from a footpath into Lymm. The cats liked it as it was open but with enough small birch and oak trees and other foliage to provide them with good cover. Peter and I had enjoyed an almost summer like day, apart from the obvious autumn colours of the trees. We walked through Lymm and up to the Dam, all round the reservoir and lovely woods, predominantly of huge lofty beech trees and dozens of squirrels scampering all over the place. We sat and ate a few sandwiches before walking back into Lymm and buying 40p worth of chips which we sat and shared by the pond.

A few days later, we had been out and away from the boat which was moored up near the Old No.3 pub. We returned just as it was getting dark, and were walking along the path towards our boat when somewhere in the vicinity of the three or four other boats moored up there I thought I heard a man's voice call out from behind me. Peter was some paces in front of me when I distinctly heard the voice call out again, a rather weak and pathetic one at that. I turned, almost half heartedly, to try and locate where on earth the call had come from and in disbelief just managed to make out in the half light the shape of a man in the water, half hidden between a boat and the bank. He was clinging to the boat rope and trying to get his legs up onto another rope. I quickly called Peter and he ran back and together we tried frantically to pull the man out of the water, but he must have weighed about 16 stone and with the additional weight of his wet clothes we couldn't pull him up and to make matters worse he said he had arthritis in his arms and couldn't heave himself up or be of much help to us. The water here was a good 7ft or more deep so it was not possible for him to touch the bottom. After awhile we realized we were getting nowhere and the man was becoming very tired and cold. How long he had been in the water we didn't know, but we were pretty sure he had come from the pub. We urgently had to get help from somewhere and couldn't leave him alone as he was in danger of drowning. Peter said he would hang onto him while I went to try and fetch some help so I ran to the nearby lay-by where I'd remembered seeing a couple of lorries pull in for the night. I knocked loudly on the cab of one and told the driver and his mate that a man was in the cut and couldn't get out. They soon dashed to the rescue and helped Peter to pull him out to safety. We bundled him up onto and into his boat with orders to "get dried off, warm and sleep it off". The lorry driver told us that the previous year a boater had come back from the pub all tanked up, fallen in the cut and drowned there. So this man was lucky he hadn't ended up the same, as had I not heard him when I did, it is very unlikely anyone else would have been that way in the dark and heard him in time to save him. His boat was a large cabin cruiser called the Admiral something or other but I think "Whiskey Galore" would have been more appropriate.

The resident mouse was still with us and somehow managed to get into the oven and nibble the pie crust on the egg custard pie. It also polished off every last sultana in the packet that was on the work top, so War was declared.

Peter and I became weary with aches and pains in our joints and muscles and put it down to the weather and old age creeping on. We walked to meet a chap at a pub where he'd said he would be waiting with two rabbits for us but he didn't turn up, so we stayed for a drink and walked back in the dark.

Much of our time now over the next months would have to be spent finding and logging wood to keep us warm all winter, regardless of aching joints. Peter's neck and shoulder were giving him some sleepless nights. We decided it might make life a little easier for us if we were to fetch Peter's car that had been left in safe keeping with the family, and try and find somewhere safe along the canal to park it where we could access it now and then. We managed to find a few obliging pub landlords strategically placed along the canal and left the car parked in their car parks. It wasn't at all convenient at times, but on the odd occasion it was a Godsend, especially at this time of the year. There was always risk involved leaving it and this caused us considerable worry.

Come the end of October we were beginning to become addicted to porridge, including Jesse who could hardly wait to lick the plate. He would sit opposite me and my bowl and when he thought I wasn't paying attention would quickly shoot out his paw and dip it into my porridge for a taste.

We soon ran completely out of logs and reluctantly had to resort to using the small portable gas fire, but this was the reason why we'd bought it, to use when we were cold and out of wood. We knew it was only temporary and that we would have to go down to Preston Brook and through the tunnel where we'd still be able to find plenty of wood to log up, but I didn't want Peter sawing wood while his arm was still so painful. As if to emphasize the need to go for wood even more, the gas bottle for the fire ran out. We were just nice and comfortable and there was a gale blowing outside, but Peter had to lift the 5 gallon barrel of beer off the top of the fire to remove the empty gas cylinder, then go up on deck to get the full one which was stored under the deck boards. At least with the gas fire lit, when there was a gale blowing, we didn't get smoked out as we did when the wood stove was burning with the wind blowing down the flue, creating billowing clouds of smoke blowing into the cabin.

Peter made me laugh when we went to the supermarket in Stockton Heath, where a young lad working there was stripping leaves off cauliflowers and throwing them into a box. Obviously the leaves were going to be thrown away, so Peter asked if he could have some for his rabbit and the lad told him to help himself. "Is the rabbit called Peter Rabbit?" I said to Peter, laughing. We always had our eyes open for anything going to waste and were still picking blackberries, even some big red ones we found. Peter found some quite dirty and partly bruised apples lying in a lane where they had fallen off a tree. I washed the mud off and cut out the bad bits and stewed them with the red berries and made another lovely pie. The potato fields had all been harvested but around the edges of some lay a lot of spuds that had been missed and left, so we had a lot of spuds aboard, stored everywhere, under the bed and bagged up, on the roof where we would have to watch out for any signs of frost or they would be ruined.

Before we left Stockton Heath, I'd popped into the boat and left Peter on the quayside taking on water, when he suddenly spotted Jesse sitting under a parked car by the boat shop. He went into a cold sweat and called Jesse to him and tried to coax him out but no way would Jesse move and then a dog came along and dashed under the car and the cat shot out towards Peter who grabbed him up into his arms. The woman, owner of the dog, apologized and spoke a few words to Peter and he then realized that the cat he had hold of had a yellow collar on and wasn't Jesse at all. But to save face he pretended it was until the woman was well out of sight, then released the confused moggy back to its surroundings.

Sometimes when taking on water, if we didn't keep a check on it, the tank would fill up quicker if the water tap flow was fast, or slowly if it wasn't. We were caught out now and then and the tank would be full and the water would spill over into the boat bilge for'd at first and then gradually work its way down to the stern. This happened when we were down near the small holiday boatyard at Preston Brook and had moored up for the night in a nice quiet spot but where the water was very deep and wide. I casually mentioned to Peter that we seemed to have an offshore list, but nothing more was said till I went into the galley to make a brew about 11.30pm and found water on the floor, deeper on the sink cupboard side of the gangway than the offshore side cupboards. Peter shot up on deck and lifted up the deck boards to look below into the bilge compartment and discovered there was a lot of water there so pumped it out but it filled up again. I removed all the wet stuff out of the cupboards and from under the bed which luckily was mostly alright apart from a few wet bottomed cardboard storage boxes. My mind was racing around trying to plan what I would salvage first if we were going to sink and decided that it would be 'women and cats' first if we did. We thought that perhaps we might have a leak, but had not taken into consideration the fact that when we had taken on water and allowed it to overflow into the bilge, the water would have taken its time to seep from the bow down along into the stern and collect in one place. So even though we had pumped out the water, there was still more running down the bilge to replace it. It was very unnerving at midnight in the pitch darkness, with wind and rain adding to our problems. Peter untied the boat and pulled it back some way, mooring nearer to the boatyard, thinking that if our predicament worsened at least we should be able to get hold of a powerful pump and some help there.

We resolved to be more careful when taking on water and not to overfill the tank.

Once the clocks went back and we lost the precious hour of daylight in the evenings, what daylight we did have became all important. The lighting inside the boat wasn't very bright, just a small fluorescent tube overhead and another one on the side. It was very restricting when I was trying to do any painting on dark evenings so Peter said he would try and fix up a better light for me.

Regards finding wood, our luck was in when BWB workers did some clearing along the towpath, lopping branches here and there and letting us more or less help ourselves to as much as we liked. I determined to pull my weight, sore shoulder or not, and together with Peter, dragged as many branches as we could and stored up on top of the boat. Peter sawed up the bigger ones and I spent over an hour sawing up smaller ones and was glad it was my left shoulder and not my right one which was sore. The following day we set off for Preston Brook, hoping to find enough wood to log up and be able to fill our fore peak hold.

The stowaway mouse was still living in the vicinity of the oven and Peter was worried that it might nibble and chew the plastic water pipes and cause a flood and because there was no way it could get out of the boat or we could catch it, and neither could the cats. We reluctantly decided we would have to buy a trap. I tried to make it an escape route by putting one end of a length of wood into the oven and the other end up the steps to the stern doors, leaving one of them open in the evening when all was quiet in the galley. I put some bread on the piece of wood, hoping it would be tempted, but it didn't seem to want to escape, given the chance to do so. With three cats onboard it wasn't going to survive long one way or the other anyway. I moved all perishable food to a secure cupboard on the other side of the galley and made sure I washed saucepans and everything before use. We discovered that the wood around the back of the cooker was scorched brown and when the cooker was on it was red hot, so considered ourselves lucky it had not set on fire. Peter knocked all the wood around it out and we planned to replace it with something more heat resistant.

My bike developed a buckled wheel and three broken spokes. I missed it desperately, and hoped we could soon pick up another somewhere to replace it. On examining the wheel Peter accidentally stabbed himself in the hand with a screw driver and when I opened up the first aid box, six earwigs fell out. How the little blighters got in was a mystery.

I saw an advert for a shopper bike and rang the owner who agreed to bring it down to London Bridge for us to have a look at. It was dark when he arrived so we couldn't really see it properly but it looked in good enough shape so we gave him £20 for it. We had no working headlight at all now so often had to navigate without one in the dark, which was not ideal but kept us on our toes hoping we wouldn't meet another boat coming towards us. On our way up to London Bridge a canal worker who had been thinning out trees, gave us a shout, so we pulled in to the bank and loaded up the roof with branches which, had we not done so, the chap was going to burn. We gave him a few bob for a pint and swapped bow saws with him as his blade was better than ours. We thought it would be a big help if we invested in a small chain saw, as the way things were going with our painful arms and shoulders we wouldn't last the winter. We were both waking up half the night, dosing up on tablets and getting up just to move about and alleviate stiff joints. No doubt the damp conditions didn't help.

Peter found some nice looking mushrooms with lilac blue gills and a beige brown top, shiny with a slight bluish sheen, so we looked them up in the little mushroom book and were pretty sure they were 'wood blewits' and edible when cooked so decided to try a couple for breakfast. I lightly fried them with the rest of our breakfast and sat down with Peter to enjoy the meal. Glancing at Peter's plate I saw his mushrooms were already gone.

"You soon polished them off", I said tucking into mine. No sooner had I eaten my mushrooms, than he lifted up the edge of his fried egg with his fork, to reveal his mushrooms hidden there, laughing cheekily as he did so and said that he'd let me try mine first and if I had keeled over he would have known they were poisonous.

Chapter Six

A Runaway and Stolen Bike

A couple called Kenny and Jackie, of about our age, who we'd first met when we bought 'Rainbow II' in Skipton, were on a boat called Salamander, and often passed on their boat and gave us a wave, or moored in the same areas as us and we came to the conclusion they were also wintering along this stretch of canal. We became friendly and shared a chat and a drink with them now and then, either on their boat or ours. Kenny also had his car parked down a lane not far from one of the bridges we moored near, but we thought this was a bit too risky and preferred to have ours in the pub car park even if it was a considerable distance of a few miles away and meant we had to go there in the boat if we wanted to use it, which we didn't very often. It was mostly too much too-ing and fro-ing, time consuming and a nuisance apart from the few times when we wanted to go and visit the family and then it was appreciated. In the New Year it developed serious problems so was once again put into mothballs.

We still hadn't got a headlamp sorted out and although there was little, if any, boat traffic moving during the daytime, let alone after dark, it wasn't good practice to be without one, even though we almost knew the canal between Lymm and Preston Brook like the back of our hands. This point was proved one night when heading back in the dark from Stockton Heath to moor near Thomason's bridge, I went down below to light the fire, leaving Peter steering the boat in the wind and rain. On hindsight it is something I should never have done while he was navigating this completely blacked out and particularly heavily wooded stretch. Suddenly there was one almighty crunch and I lurched forward and fell onto the cabin step. Our engine cut out and we had obviously hit something. I scrambled quickly out onto the bow to find a huge tree some 60ft tall across the canal which had obviously been blown down very recently in the gales. I suppose we should have considered ourselves lucky that we had not been in this particular spot at the time it had come down. Luckily we'd only been creeping slowly along in the pitch dark and the water full of leaves was making the boat even more sluggish. So there we were trapped and with little choice but to try and turn the boat if the canal was wide enough to allow us to do so. From the towpath we heaved it back a bit on ropes and managed after a few futile attempts with her bow (nose) catching on the far bank, to finally pull her round manually and journeyed back to about a mile the other side of Stockton Heath. It was such painfully slow going in the dark and I stood up on deck with Peter, in the driving rain, as we needed 'all eyes' not 'all hands' on deck. By the time we got there my wet gloved hands were so cold they were burning and I struggled to pull on the mid-ship rope and hold the boat alongside while Peter knocked the mooring pins in. It was about 9pm before we managed to get out of our dripping wet soaked to the skin gear, re-light the fire, get warm and have our dinner. We hoped that the Water board would not waste any time moving the tree and unblock the canal so we'd be able to get back to our familiar mooring. This so called pleasure cruising boating lark was proving to be not quite so in the winter months.

The next day, Wednesday, we decided to go back in the afternoon to see if the tree had been cleared, but it was still there and in the daylight we were able to see just what a size it was and once again felt lucky that we had not been in its path when it had fallen. Kenny's boat and a cabin cruiser with a young couple called Gary and Heather on were there and they told us that they had rung the authorities who said they would be arriving within the next hour to clear it. An hour later they rang again and were told the boat was on its way, but by 3 pm there was still no signs of anyone and before long it was going to be dark and we could see us all being stuck there indefinitely. One of us suggested we might be able to saw through the top part with a bow saw and make a wide enough gap for the boats to get through, which sounded all very simple in theory, but using a bow saw from moving boats and at awkward, bordering on impossible, angles was insanely optimistic. We unanimously decided to have a go though and Peter climbed on the bow of Kenny's boat with the saw. At first they attached the tree to his boat and reversed hoping to pull it back, but that didn't work so Peter started sawing. But it wasn't just a case of sawing through the main trunk as before he could do that he had to saw his way through all the obstructing branches around it in order to reach it and he had at times to almost become a saw wielding contortionist to achieve any successful results. Anyway, with much determination and effort, the men all took turns to keep sawing while Heather and I kept the tea and coffee flowing and after some hours a seven foot gap was cleared. But there were still some submerged branches and others that had to be shoved clear with the boat poles. By this time it was dark and the bank was a complete quagmire of churned up slippery mud. We tied a rope to Kenny's boat and from the bank helped guide it through the gap and with Kenny going full speed ahead he managed to manoeuvre it through, followed by the cabin cruiser Andante and finally us. All three boats moored up together near Thomason's bridge for the night. The remaining tree was still there across the canal on the Friday, until it was removed later that day. I was never very happy about mooring under big trees from then on, and it wasn't the last lucky escape we had from one.

We found a snug, somewhat sheltered little mooring by a small copse and a grassy glen set back in a bank where I was able to tie a washing line and hang some washing out, and maybe would also be able to hang up some nuts for the birds as we'd be able to see them from the boat windows. There was a little path at the top of the bank that ran along through the bracken, bushes and copse, so it was ideal for the cats.

The canal was blocked off with two large iron girder type constructions, preventing us from now going down to Preston Brook, or through the tunnel or down to Runcorn. We asked a workman how long they would be working there and blocking off the canal and he said probably up to Christmas. Well that wasn't so bad and we were glad that we had gone for wood before the restrictions had come about.

We had no mobile phone then, so our whereabouts and welfare were always a bit of a mystery to the family. However when we did receive some mail c/o Poste Restante, from the post office at Lymm, we found a nice letter and invite to spend Christmas with them.

Blobs and Ibley Dibley seemed to have become very friendly, snoozing cosily together on the bed with Ibley often giving old Blobs a good wash. Blobs often almost set himself alight when I turned the gas fire on full. He'd sit right in front of it if it was on and start to singe but never bothered to move. He had three really dark ginger singes on him that matched his ginger markings. He also took to sleeping up on the roof, wrapped around the chimney stack for warmth.

Ibley Dibley

Ibley Dibley (bright eyes) was growing bigger and didn't miss anything. When he was up on his shelf he'd pull the curtain open with his paws so he could see out. He liked bits of crumpet with syrup on and he and Jesse both liked trifle.

Jesse started to disappear down towards Thomason's bridge and, we thought he was also going across it to the other side of the canal. Sure enough, he was and one evening there he was stuck on the far bank, yowling across to the boat, so Peter untied the boat and took it over to pick him up, which was easier than walking all down to cross the bridge, and then along the far bank to get him.

Our stow-away mouse was still with us and had not taken advantage of jumping ship and using the escape route I'd made for it, so he was doomed and duly executed in the oven by mousetrap. He had escaped it the first time Peter had set it, and we heard it go off and fully expected to find mousey snuffed out, but the bait had gone and so had he along with it. I felt quite sad when he was finalized.

We managed to pick up another little second hand bike, for Peter to use and enjoyed a couple of short rides, one over the ship canal to Moore Nature Reserve, where Peter was sure he had found the footprints of a BIG CAT, a puma or something such. We decided another day to cycle up to Daresbury to see if the canal was still blocked off but had only gone a few yards when Peter's bike chain broke and fell off so we made do with a little walk instead.

Wait Mag! me chain's come off! an I've got a puncture so it's Plan B "we're walking"

c'mon Pete it'll be dark soon

Speedy Gonzarles

There was a little robin that used to come and sit on the tiller bar and was no doubt eating the cat food we put out. I hoped that he would not end up as cat food too. Peter found a dead mink by the boat, which we think might have come onboard to eat the cat food left out on the stern and been attacked by Jesse or Ibley. Then on the following Saturday night Peter saw two small eyes shining in the dark in the direction of the towpath. Ibley

Dibley had seen or heard it too and was all eyes and ears, but whatever it was soon disappeared. We often heard scurrying sounds on and off the boat at night and were not worried as long as it was not two legged visitors. We also heard owls and even saw them now and then at odd times during the daylight hours.

A young lad of about sixteen came along the towpath one Sunday and stopped to ask Peter which direction Runcorn was. He looked very dishevelled and was wearing, jeans, trainers and a tartan shirt which was torn a bit and had no buttons on the cuffs. I started to talk to him and realized that he was in some kind of bother. He told us that he was running away from boarding school because they had forced him to go to church and he had been bullied and held forcibly. We invited him onboard, gave him a drink of tea and talked to him and listened to what he had to say but it was difficult to build up a true picture of him. But we couldn't help but empathize with him regardless of the circumstances and truth of his plight. He looked very young for his age and as if he could have done with some kind of parental help. He was worried about the school authorities coming after him and picking him up and said he was making his way to his Dad's at Runcorn, which he later changed to 'his mother and step fathers place' He had no money so we gave him £3 towards bus fare and told him that he would probably be able to get a bus at Preston Brook. We emphasized to him that he was not to spend the money on things like cigarettes. We gave him some chocolate and peanuts and a pair of Peter's socks too as he had none on and it was cold. He then set off on his way, stopping every now and again to give us a cheery wave, till he was out of sight. We half expected him to turn up for refuge later but he didn't and we hoped that things would work out alright for him.

By 11th December there was 1½ inches of ice on the canal and we spent most of the day slowly breaking it up, making our way in the boat to Stockton Heath. It was hard going and Kenny was also making his way there, so as his boat was more powerful and bigger than ours we tied up abreast of each other and cut through the ice together, managing to break our boat pole as we struggled along, often having to grind to a halt and break up large stubborn slabs of ice. As we broke our way through the ice, the fresh unbroken tracts before us exploded under pressure and ricocheted like pistol shots up the canal in front of us and the boat shook and juddered with vibrating shocks. We had to be very careful when passing any moored fibre glass boats, as ice breaking around their hulls was capable of putting a hole in them. Many boat owners took the precautions of breaking the ice around their moored boats but of course this wasn't always an option for them.

There was also ice inside the boat, a thin layer on the washing up water in the sink and the flannels were frozen stiff. Sitting on the loo was like sitting on an ice berg and sitting in bed reading I had to wear my gloves as my hands were so cold. We were almost out of wood by now and cut off from the woods the other side of the tunnel at Preston Brook.

Wood and water were now both on ration.

Then out of the blue a boat came along and pulled alongside to see how we were doing. It was Maureen and Hornby, from Burscough, a couple we had met on our travels, and they were on their way to the Llangollen canal. We exchanged news and Hornby fished out some wood for us to use for kindling and some other bits he could spare and helped Peter to saw it up. Wood was becoming like gold dust. We probably had enough to last just a couple of days.

Due to the frost we had lost many of the potatoes we had stored on top of the boat but managed to rescue about 20lb and find room to store them inside the boat.

With my bike having yet another puncture, I used Peter's to go to the shop, but didn't get far before realising that too had a puncture. I think we should have been in the Guinness book of records for punctures, mostly the result of thorns this time of the year. Peter intended to fix them the following morning but we didn't like the look of Jesse who had been unwell for a couple of days, not wanting to go out, seeking warmth, off his food and very sick one day. We thought he had developed another abscess as there was a bad smell, so we carted him off to the vets who soon discovered the problem was a rabbit bone stuck in his mouth causing a puncture wound that might have caused an infection as well as making life very uncomfortable for him.

On our return to the boat Peter only had punctures to fix on his bike as mine had been stolen. We came to the conclusion that it had probably been taken the night before, Friday, by someone making their way home from the pub, and we had not noticed in our concern and rush to get Jesse to the vets. I was very attached to that little bike, and it was so comfortable to ride for me, so I felt quite sad and also cross with the selfish thief. However, I also knew that if we forgot to lock up things we left outside we were inviting trouble. Ironically, we could take the trouble to lock something up for weeks on end, then forget for just a few minutes and in those few unguarded moments it would be gone, especially bikes, no matter how old they were. One consolation was that whoever had stolen it would have had a very uncomfortable ride with a puncture.

"Hope they fall off into the canal" I muttered grumpily to Peter, who grinned and agreed and proceeded to spend about four hours repairing the punctures and gears on his bike, with the patience of a saint. I cooked him a curry for dinner, wrapped up Christmas presents for the family and we spent a nice peaceful evening watching an entertaining programme of comedy shows such as Morecambe and Wise and Hancock's Half Hour. One thing we were never short of regardless of what happened was being able to laugh.

Christmas was next on our list but even that looked like being a disaster. We were up at 7.30 am Christmas day, and ready at 10 am to take the boat up to Moore where it would be overlooked by a shop and a row of houses with the shop keeper promising that he would keep an eye on it for us. But, there was no sign of Jesse anywhere and he did not respond to calling or clanging on food dishes. He had gone out about 6.30 am and we felt sure he would soon be back in for a meal before we left. By 10 am he still had not appeared and we walked up and down the canal towpath calling and looking for him, then went further a field to look as recently he'd taken to wandering off somewhere right down the canal past a bridge where he must have found some attraction. By 11 am still no Jesse so we continued walking around and must have walked about three miles by 12 noon by which time we were both thinking the worst as there had been a lot of shooting going on in the area of late. After a long fruitless search we returned to the boat, weary, worried and resigned to cancelling Christmas and the family gathering. Jesse came trundling up the towpath just after midday and we were so relieved and happy to see him and also that if we made haste, Christmas would still be "on". We dashed off and although Christmas dinner was put on hold for two hours, it was served up to perfection and we had a wonderful day, followed by more of the same on Boxing Day before returning to the boat in the evening, happy to find the cats safe and sound too and with a nice bag of turkey scraps for them.

For the best part of two days we had been spoiled by the luxuries of hot baths, endless amounts of un-rationed water and electricity, wonderful TV pictures without having to go outside and adjust an aerial, instant gas fires, flush toilets and all the other comforts that before living on the boat we had taken for granted.

New Years day began for Peter with burnt toast and lemsips, after which he returned to bed while I made him a little fresh toast and left him to rest. We were both under the weather, feeling more like a couple of old shipwrecks, with aches and pains all over and fit for nothing much. Outside the wind was gale force and endlessly buffeted the boat around like a cork. Peter got up later, before it grew dark, to check that the mooring pins and ropes had not worked loose and were still secure and at the same time fished out a couple of nice fence posts from the water and sawed them up. Often during wind, objects would get blown down or up the canal and become lodged alongside the boat, mostly rubbish, but occasionally something useful, such as an odd fender.

It was well into the season of soup and dumplings which by now we should have been expert enough to make blindfold. We purchased a huge marrow bone for a few pence and simmered it for a soup stock in a saucepan that was bigger than the pressure cooker but I forgot to put the lentils and barley in with it. They say too many cooks spoil the broth and I think on this occasion it was the case. Peter transferred the stock from the bone to the pressure cooker and added the dried ingredients which I'd omitted and before long we had burnt offerings and a black pressure cooker. Peter took about half an hour cleaning it and I salvaged some lentils and barley etc, added some spuds, vegetables and dumplings and hoped the end product would be edible. Talk about 'Marathon stew'. I burned the porridge the next morning when trying to light the fire at the same time. Peter suggested we start up a 'charcoal business'.

Now desperate for wood we decided to head up towards Lymm and our luck was in when we came across a load of felled branches that had been dumped on waste ground. After loading them up we purchased a few bargains from the charity shop and acquired more bones from the butcher Peter examine the big marrow bones, and was really intrigued by some with moveable joints and suggested he might have a go at doing hip and or knee replacements with them. Or even start up a spare 'new bones for old' shop. We finished up laughing hysterically and singing 'dem bones dem bones dem dry bones'.

After almost a week our forepeak was just about full of logs again so we set off back to Thomason Bridge. It was about this time that I seriously decided to start writing a book about Peter's life. I'd listened intently as he told me so many stories about himself from his childhood living in poverty on Merseyside to joining the Navy and taking part in the D-Day landings, his various jobs after the war and years working on the ferry boats from being a seaman and over the years working his way up to Captain. I started to scribble down notes which at first were all over the place, in no order at all, but I was determined that if I could keep the stories flowing from Peter I would in time have enough to collate into some kind of book form. It seemed a good time to start with so many long dark evenings on hand. It was slow going though and I wished that I had kept up with the shorthand I had learned when I was sixteen. I could still remember a little but regretfully not enough to make it useful, so I scribbled away as fast as I could while Peter related his life stories and sometimes I would type on my portable typewriter as he talked. I could still type about 60 wpm so sometimes it was easier than writing by hand. Then I had to re-write it all, refresh on incidents and facts with Peter and put it all into some kind of order of events, re-write, add to and draw little illustrative sketches. As the pages and chapters grew, so did my determination that I would write this book for Peter however long it took me. Also I enjoyed hearing all about his life, as neither of us had known anything about each other or the places we had lived, until we met. We had a lot to tell each other and had the time to listen which sadly, many couples when younger and leading busy lives working and bringing up families, often didn't have that quality time to spend with and for each other. We rather complimented each other, as Peter had the gift of talking and describing the events of his life but was unable to write it down, while I had the ability to write, but I could not adequately express myself the same in conversation. I knew I lacked confidence in that respect and always had done. I was terrified when, in my Secondary school years, the head mistress had discovered I could play the piano and she'd included me in the Christmas concert programme and put me down to play the grand piano in front of the whole school and parents. If only she had known the sheer torment I suffered the week before that event, she would not have put me through it. I think it must have been through sheer all consuming fright that I somehow managed to rattle off "Rudolph the Red Nosed Reindeer" on the ivories that day. Peter said he felt the same about being able to write and that he couldn't even sign a cheque or write with anyone watching him and that he would just freeze up. He attributed this short coming to his childhood days when one teacher would stand behind him and frequently cuff him round the ear and belittle his efforts as soon as he attempted to write anything. He had a poor education but a great love of books and reading which in many ways compensated for the poor quality of his school years and gave him an inexhaustible appetite for knowledge.

Talking about tales to tell, on our way back from Lymm we bumped into a local man near Moor where we had often noticed a flat white stone along the towpath with undecipherable wording on it, just the odd number and letter and a cross roughly engraved. He told us that it had been placed there by someone local in memory of a chap called Ken who had roamed around the area for years, a vagabond who used to sleep under Walton bridge until vandals started throwing stones and tormenting him and then he had moved down near Moore and used to sleep along the towpath there under a large fishing umbrella. Eventually people there grew to like him and used to take him food or clothes and blankets. They tried to help him in other ways but he was very independent and refused much that they offered him. He was said to have been in the army, an ex Desert Rat! One winter a farmer told him that he could sleep in his barns in the warm but he still continued to sleep in his usual haunts. The man we'd met told us that many of the then youngsters remembered him with affection and that he taught lots of them how to fish. How interesting his life story would have been, had someone written it.

The evening we arrived back at our mooring we passed a farm field where I noticed a sheep lying down and a little lamb tottering unsteadily on its legs. Its mother stood up and we could see the umbilical cord still attached to her. As it was almost dark and a frost in the air I made a detour to the farm and told the lady who answered the door. She was pleased that I had taken the trouble to call in and said they would bring the sheep and lamb in for the night and put with the other lamb and a set of twin lambs they already had inside. We spoke to the farmer the following night and he said that we had done him a favour as the ewe gave birth to a further lamb during the night.

I was never cut out to live like an Eskimo, as was obvious when I went to bed clad in layers. Peter had, more for a joke I think than anything else, rescued a long pink pair of knitted pantaloons from an assortment of clothes down at the tip, which I washed and found deliciously warm to wear in bed, to Peter's great amusement. He called them my 'astronaut pants'.

We became friendly with the young couple Gary and Heather who we had met at the time the tree fell across the canal. They were very easy going and helpful and nothing was ever too much for them if we needed anything and we were the same with them, real shipmates. They had a cabin cruiser called Andante. Gary and Peter shared the same wonderful sense of humour both being from Merseyside and we would sit talking and laughing and having a beer or two, for hours together. Gary borrowed our bow saw one day to take back to their boat which was moored down at Preston Brook and the next morning when I opened the stern doors I found a large bag full of sawn up logs, which was a nice gesture, typical of Gary and Heather.

My brother Gerald and friend Freda had planned to come and see us for a few days to see what life was like on a boat during the winter months. "COLD" we had told them. Not deterred they arrived towards the end of January in Gerald's ancient old bus of a van which they intended to sleep in even though it was not fitted out or equipped to accommodate any but the most robust of campers. The only luxury I think they had inside was a small heater of sorts. We offered them space in our fore cabin which stayed warm for some hours into the night until the fire died down and they could have kept it going if they'd wished to, but they decided on the van and also thought it would be safer with them in it than left on its own, parked up in the country lane. At around 8.30 am the next morning they had a number of police knocking on their van and demanding to know who they were, where they were from and what they were doing and also had to show their documents. We weren't a bit surprised as Gerald's van looked suspicious 24/7.

The canal froze over again and we decided to break through the ice to keep a channel open as far as Stockton Heath in case it became too thick to break through. On reaching Stockton Heath to top up with water we found the water tap there was frozen up so we had to return with what little water we already had which was about a third of a tank full. We kept the wood stove blazing away, consumed endless bowls of soup and dumplings and crumpets, talked non stop and enjoyed a musical evening or two, playing tunes (or attempting to play) on harmonicas, penny whistle and yazoos. Much hilarity, singing and laughing and surprise at how little of the words to the well known tunes we all knew apart from the choruses which we sang with gusto, especially as the night wore on and the home brew went down.

Ibley Dibley caught and killed a large rabbit the next day and came running back to the boat with it only to have it quickly confiscated by Gerald who soon had it skinned and ready for the pot minus the head which he rewarded Ibley with. Ibley chewed away at it voraciously then shot off up the bank with it when Jesse became interested. When Jesse came back he ran off under the bed with some of the skin and fur and Blobs ate the liver so in all it became quite a communal meal.

Gerald and I went up to Stockton Heath in the van to see if the tap was still frozen up and it was. Another boater told us that he'd been lucky enough that morning to get some water by passing his hose up into a first floor window where someone had connected it to an indoor tap for him to fill up from. We still had just under a third of a tank full so were not desperate yet.

We all enjoyed rabbit stew, courtesy of Ibley Dibley and Gerald and Freda went to look at a boat down at Preston Brook before they left on their journey back home.

Gary and Heather walked down from Preston Brook to see us and said they had seen a brief case, cheque book and papers strewn on the ice in the middle of the canal AND, that they had also seen a bike at the edge of the water further down near the Red Brow under-bridge steps leading to the housing estates. They said they could see the bike in the water under the ice and that it had a white saddle and handle bar grips. We decided we would have to go and have a look for ourselves later on. Meanwhile Gary spent an hour or so fixing up the head lamp my son had given us for Xmas. We thought we would try and get the boat down to Preston Brook and take Gary and Heather back, but the ice was too thick so we walked back with them. The brief case and stuff with it had been recovered somehow and as we neared the lane by Red Brow Gary pointed the bike out but by this time it was dark and we had to use a torch. Peter and Gary broke the ice and lowered down a grappling hook, caught and pulled up the bike which I didn't think for a minute could possibly be mine. But it was, so I was thrilled to bits and somewhat amazed to have it back again. We left it covered in mud with Gary and Heather who said they would bring it down the next day when they had some transport. The water tap in the marina was frozen so we couldn't hose it down. Gary and Heather got busy filling hot water bottles to put around their butane gas cylinder to keep it from freezing up and then made us a nice dinner of jacket potatoes, chops and peas with cider and lager to wash it down. The next day Gary brought my bike back in his sister's car, spick and span and with the puncture repaired.

Returning to visit the family gave us a good excuse to enjoy a soak in the bath. I went in first and was in the middle of a relaxing wallow when the extractor fan in the bathroom blew up with two warning blue flashes then an almighty 'bang' and all the light in the house went out. Peter, ever the hero, soon came dashing upstairs to the rescue. It seemed whether on dry land or water problems just seemed to follow us.

When we returned the canal had thawed so we took the boat down to the wide part of the canal where it joined the Runcorn arm and moored just outside the marina. Gary and Heather joined us in our boat for the evening and we played cards over a drink or two. I'd been mentioning to Peter, on and off for hours, ever since we'd tied up at the mooring that the boat seemed to have a more pronounced list than usual and which was becoming progressively worse as the evening wore on, but nobody else seemed to notice. Perhaps if they had they put it down to the effects of the home brew or Gary's bottle of whiskey. Even when the bottle slid off the table and we all lost our balance every time we tried to get to our feet, no one was concerned. That is, not until I went into the galley and started paddling about in two inches of water. I flew to the stern, yelling "bloody hell we're sinking" as I ran and automatically switched the water pump on. Rather dramatically, from then on it was 'Action Stations' all night with about 300 gallons of water in the engine compartment below deck. I have never seen people sober up as quickly as they did that night. Gary spent the next two hours down the bilge in almost virtual darkness, bailing out and mopping as the water continued to fill up and seep in. We hoped his 'eyes' would stay in (contact lenses). Heather was always joking and telling him he could take them out and give his eyes a rest.

Just where all the water was coming from we didn't know but on the trip down we had experienced a fair bit of wind and rough water and Peter was inclined to think that we still had a drainage hole or two that was too low and close to the canal surface and into which little wind blown waves could be whipped up high enough to lap into, but we couldn't comprehend how it could have done so to such an extent in such a short a time. However, we didn't have time to analyse the situation, we just had to get the water out.

Everything under the bed was sopping wet and as fast as we mopped and squeezed into buckets, water appeared again. By 5 am I was asleep on my feet and making brews to keep everyone warm and awake. We were all frozen and Gary and Peter were still up on deck until 6 am when they came in for a warm before Gary went back to his boat and Peter and I finally went to bed, glad to still be afloat on what was a particularly deep and wide part of canal. It was a good job we had not gone to bed early before the water had seeped into the galley as we would never have noticed it and we could have ended up in 'Davy Jones Locker' as a submarine class narrow boat. We both slept comatose until 11 am.

Chapter Seven

Tragedy Strikes

A week into February found us moored once again, just the other side of the tunnel, not far from Dutton Stop lock, waiting to go into the small dry dock there in a few days time. We felt very at home and relaxed along this part of the canal and made the most of some unusually pleasant weather, taking walks and strolling along the towpath where we could smell the warmth of the earth in the air, and witness the impending nearness of Spring in the bright fresh green leaves of new plants. Dark spotted, arrow shaped leaves of Lords and Ladies, the olive green heart shaped leaves of celandines, fresh tight clumps of sprouting bluebell leaves, many hidden beneath last autumns fallen leaves, cow parsley unfurling themselves and pushing through the earth and dogs mercury in abundance, already showing off its rather insignificant yellowy green flowers, along with white dead nettle. All these were encouraging signs of more to come. We loved examining hedgerows looking for suitable sticks for Peter to cut for making walking sticks with, which was easier during winter months when the hedgerows were bare. We ambled around together taking in and savouring all that nature threw our way, often watched kingfishers down by the stream or darting along the canal banks and flocks of lapwing and gulls following behind a tractor where on the previous day we had watched dozens of wagtails feeding among the soil that the tractor had churned up. New daily discoveries provided endless topics of conversation and opportunities to discuss the merits of nature and the whys and wherefores of life in general. What made it all so perfect was the deep intensity of happiness we shared through a special and magical all consuming bond of togetherness. At all levels it was about communication and without that in a relationship I don't think you have a chance.

It was now staying light in the evenings until about 5.30pm and getting lighter earlier in the mornings. At night we listened to the owls hooting and sometimes watched a silvery moon glide silhouetted behind the tall skeletal branches of the trees. Ibley Dibley and Jesse were frequently out on the prowl hunting together under cover of the night. During the day we watched them at a distance as they scampered around the woods together, stalking and jumping out at each other and it was lovely to see them enjoying themselves freely in natural surroundings. They were real scamps at times too, seemed to work in pairs and encourage one another in deeds of mischief. We had been given a small fridge by a boater but didn't really want it. However, we fitted it up under the bow side seat where it was out of the way and didn't take up much room. We stored some turkey legs we had bought in it but Jesse and Ibley had smelled them and managed to get the door open and pull them out. The rascals were thoroughly enjoying themselves chewing away on the legs when we discovered the rogues.

Ibley Dib fell off the boat waterside and swam like the clappers round the boat, as fast as an otter, scrambled up the bank unaided, then ran off and hid at the base of a tree. He soon came back in and dried himself then sat on Peter's lap as if he needed a bit of comforting.

We walked down to the Weaver Navigation, Dutton locks, huge in comparison to the canal locks. Ships from all over the world used to journey here but few and far between did so now, but we were lucky to see the German cargo ship 'Pinnau' carrying soda-ash back to Sweden from Northwich. The working narrow boats used to carry the cargoes but now one big ship could do the work of about 40 of them.

Gary and Heather often called in for a chat over a brew and a snack of whatever was going, be it toast, hot crumpets, soup, and we were always made equally welcome on their boat. Jesse seemed to make a point of getting stuck up trees when Gary and Heather visited, call it attention seeking if you like. He was stuck up one for over an hour and nothing would entice him down, which we knew by now was a waste of time trying anyway. Peter and Gary came up with various rescue plans and finally put plan 'G' into action, which was to drive the biggest nails I had ever seen into the tree trunk and use them as footholds. Gary who was smaller and lighter than Peter then climbed up on them sufficiently far enough to be able to grab Jesse, unceremoniously by the scruff of his neck and pull him down.

Little did the cats know that shortly their freedom would be curtailed for a few days when they would have to be confined to the boat while we went into dry dock. When it was time for the boat to go in, we rounded them up and shut them in with two nice fresh litter trays, which Jesse wasted no time climbing into, dug a hole and was promptly gazumped by Blobs who came along and took it over, squatted, and with so much as a 'kiss my a---' to Jesse, who just sat and watched looking quite 'check mated' by Blobs usurping catty behaviour. Blobs gave a few feeble paw scraping, cover up attempts when he had finished with the hole and moved off with an air of "I'm Senior Service", I can get away with it!

Once the dock was drained of water the boat was left sitting high and dry on chocks, like a big old broody hen on a perch and we literally had to walk the plank in order to get on and off her. We had two planks, one forward and one astern, both leading out across the dry dock to the sides. Everywhere around and beneath was extremely muddy and it was a constant battle to keep the inside of the boat clean and also to keep the cats from getting out as they were so quick and ever on the alert for the slightest opportunity of making a dash for it. Jesse did manage to get out briefly but was soon re captured. They probably would have been alright but we didn't want to risk it just for the sake of a few days confinement.

We had to run sink water into a bucket and empty it away from the boat so as to prevent water from running down the hull while it was being cleaned and painted, also in case a worker was underneath in direct line of fire. We went down into the dock to see how the work was progressing and watched the new prop shaft put in. Peter and I decided that once she was re-launched we would find a quiet spot and spend what was left of the rest of the winter working on the superstructure, rubbing the paint down completely and repainting all, the sides olive green and the roof black and also remove the name boards and paint a large butterfly each side in their place. I'd paint a rainbow on the bow sides and two smaller name boards to place in the port and starboard windows. We also planned to replace carpet with cushion floor which would be so much easier to keep clean and Peter would do many outside jobs such as re-fixing deck board edging strips and putting a layer of fibre glass along the gunwales with a sprinkling of course sand to prevent them being so slippery' for us and the cats to walk along. In all, more than enough work, weather permitting, to keep us busy until it was time to plan another new journey, which would be left entirely up to me to decide on and plan.

We had found a temporary parking place to leave the car, which we still occasionally used, up by the cottages on the tunnel. Peter had been having difficulty getting it to start and one day an old chap marched out from one of the nearby cottages, stuck his head under the already propped up bonnet and started undoing this and that while cursing the automatic choke. He got his spanners out of his toolbox which he had brought out with him. All Peter could do was stand there immobilized in disbelief as the old boy continued to SORT THINGS OUT, but Peter didn't know if he knew what he was doing or not and was desperate to stop him before he completely dismantled the car on the spot. On hindsight, he should have been more grateful and given the chap more credit as the car engine was soon bursting into life, but the chap didn't hang around to receive any grateful thanks, he just disappeared as quickly as he had appeared.

However, the car still continually proved to be more trouble to us than it was worth. Starting it became a nightmare, a case of will she or won't she. More often than not the answer was a decisive 'no she won't'. One day we tried to push it from the sloping canal access path up onto a flat part where we would be able to manoeuvre it more easily. Peter took the handbrake off while standing firmly alongside the car, shoulder against the door frame while I got my shoulder on the bonnet at the front. As soon as the hand brake came off, the car began to roll slowly forward and somehow I managed to jump aside and avoid being flattened as it began to gain speed. Peter grabbed the wheel with one hand, door frame with the other and put all the strength he could muster from his body into holding the car back. But it was not for being held back on such a steep slope and he ended up with his legs doing the one minute mile on the spot as he fought to defy all the laws of gravity and stop it until he was running alongside it as it continued to roll uncontrollably onward towards the canal. I think, for a split second he was going so fast that he just momentarily disappeared into the next century, but by a miraculous feat of heroism or unique rush of supersonic adrenalin, he somehow managed to leap into the car as it careered on its suicidal mission and brought it to a halt. We later wondered if he should have just let it run away into the canal and save us the job of selling it or spending anymore time and money on it. No wonder our medication for arthritis didn't appear to be having any beneficial results, not surprising the way we were mistreating our bodies. I fully expected Peter to suffer another collapsed lung, as it had only been a couple of years since he'd had the last one and been told to avoid any strenuous work, especially lifting. He had always been a physically strong man and still was, but unfortunately he had weakened and damaged his lungs through years of smoking from an early age and now had lung disease and bouts of breathlessness and suffered from bronchitis and miserable chest colds in the winter months. But, since living on the boat he had lost a lot of weight which had been beneficial and had felt better for the exercise and the healthier lifestyle. However, life was never all a bed of roses and there were times when we fell out, were moody and low in spirits. Peter had said that at times our past lives would surface and throw us off balance awhile, probably without us even being aware of it. He also knew and understood that as a mother I worried at times about my family and that of course I did miss being with them. I sometimes felt guilty for going off and leaving them, even though they were all now grown up and living their own lives independently. It was difficult after thirty years of being 'mum' at the centre of the family, suddenly not to be. Plus the inevitable scars left from a marriage break up and difficulties for Peter too after his happy forty year marriage with Beryl (Bess) had come to such a tragic end.

But Peter didn't sink to the depths and analyse everything as I tended to do, he accepted them and got on with it but at times I did feel the depths of his sadness over losing Bess and we would talk, hold hands and comfort and share the pain in each others souls. Sometimes a song or piece of music would promote a quiet tear. However our deep love of wanting so much to ease the hurt for each other saw us through those agonizing times. I encouraged Peter to remember and tell me about Bess and their lives together and to keep her fondly in his memories and as I continued to write his life story I also grew to know Bess too and was happy that she and Peter had had such a wonderfully happy life together. When Peter and I eventually married many years later I suggested that inside his wedding ring which he had continually worn all those years and would continue to wear through our marriage, we should have it engraved with three names, "Beryl, Peter, Marge" and this we did. I felt very warm towards Beryl and sad that she still couldn't be with Peter, but I hoped that I made him happy even though I never ever wanted to or believed that I could in anyway replace her. I just wanted to carry on where she had left off. Peter said that she and I would have got along very well together as we were very alike in many ways with our love of nature and the countryside, sense of humour and earthiness as Peter would put it.

Some days my body seemed on fire all over with pain and the shoulder would wake me up early and have me making tea at unacceptable hours. I'd get out of bed to move around and shiver with the cold. I'd had it now for five or six months and wondered if it was going to be permanent. Peter said that frozen shoulders often just went away as quickly as they had come. I hoped he would be proved right and SOON.

Unintentionally and very stupidly I almost blew myself up, into smithereens for sure. I had decided to take the rubbish that had accumulated, out onto the bank and burn it, as we had nowhere to take it while we were stuck the other side of the tunnel, so I piled it all up and picked up the petrol can that we kept just for the generator, opened the cap and poured a little on the unlit fire, then lit a piece of paper and threw it onto it. There was one almighty booming explosive WHOOOOOF! from the fire which blew me backward off my feet, my eyebrows momentarily meeting up with my hairline in shocked surprise. I lived to tell the tale with singed eyebrows and hair and certainly learned a lesson from it. I think I absentmindedly thought I was using diesel, which was still a stupid thing to do, but it wasn't as volatile as petrol.

"You've been framed" has nothing on us.

Peter always enjoyed a game of darts so now and then we'd make a point of finding a pub with a dart board and maybe he would get a good game with one of the locals, rather than with me who he could beat blindfold. He'd played in darts teams and won many trophies over the years, especially during the time when he had lived on the Isle of Man.

We met up with Kenny and Jackie on Salamander when they went into dry dock to have their hull painted with black bitumen. We caught up on news over a few beers and I went along to see Jackie. Ibley Dibley followed me and leaped around on top of Salamander playing with all the ropes there. He liked to nose around looking at things on other boats, especially under tarpaulins and looking into windows whenever he got the chance. Kenny also had plans to strip down the outside of his boat and repaint, so we thought it might be a good idea to find a suitable place and moor up near each other when the time was right to start the work. We did just that at the beginning of March, along another quiet stretch, down towards Saltersford by a small wood. Gary and Heather often moored up with us too.

Hey Mag. There's a couple of rogues gone in the woods with suitcases and a torch. Keep down so they can't see us, and lock up for'd. Bloody IRA get everywhere

Get the gun Pete

One evening, after dark, Peter called me up to the galley where he was having a sneaky look out of the door with the light out. He motioned me towards the door with a big SHHHHHSING finger action on his lips and whispered "There's two people gone into the wood carrying a suitcase and flashing a torch around." and "What do you make of that Mag?" I wasn't sure what to suggest but it certainly seemed that whatever they were up to wasn't anything good, creeping around in the dark like that. At times like this, one's mind was apt to run away into the realms of fantasy. "Perhaps they've got a body or body parts in the case and are disposing of it", I suggested in my best Crime novel detective voice. One dramatic notion ran away with another and we soon made sure both ends of the boat were securely locked up while we kept a quiet and low profile inside the boat in the dark until we heard the muffled voices of the couple as they returned past the boat and went to wherever they had come from.

The following day we related the tale to Gary and Heather and asked them if they had seen or heard anything suspicious, at which they rolled up laughing hysterically, and when they eventually stopped they told us that it had been them sneaking into the woods with their look alike suitcase porta potti, to find a suitable spot to bury it. Good job we hadn't called the police out.

That evening was dry and cold and we all decided to get together and have a nice warm cosy bonfire on the canal bank. Unfortunately about two hours into our evening round the fire, we heard the unmistakeable sounds of a wailing fire engine siren approaching, so we quickly doused the fire out and retreated to our boats. There were some nearby houses across the canal and I expect they thought it right to report a fire as they weren't to know it was being supervised and safe.

We spent some happy times playing cards in the evenings with Gary and Heather who I think were the best friends we had during all the years we spent on the canal. But sadly in time we lost touch with each other and they sold their boat and we think went ashore somewhere in Runcorn.

By the end of March we felt that we'd once again survived another winter and a particularly cold one at that. Early signs of Spring continued to be evident and rewarded us with ever more magical sights of various forms of its rebirth. I'd already seen a small tortoiseshell butterfly flitting among the top catkins of willow trees and while stopping on my bike to watch it I'd lost my balance and toppled into a big heap under my bike. The only compensation, as the butterfly disappeared from sight, was to see a carpet of delicate wood anemones down in the wood below, their white star-like flower heads spread all along the woodland floor like a miniature Milky Way. Had I not toppled off my bike I probably would not have seen them. It really did pay to be tumbling along in the slow lane of life. All the blackthorn bushes were in full bloom, snow white blossoms like the bridesmaids of Spring. By May their petals would all be fallen and lay like confetti as the arrival of the new May Queen of the hedgerows, the hawthorn, came, festooned in thick creamy white blossom.

With the arrival of British Summertime our spirits rose – it was so good to be alive. We'd worked hard when the weather had permitted and kept busy working on the boat, inside and out and as soon as one job had been finished, two more seemed to have taken its place. But, it was good to be busy and the boat was looking very smart with a new Buckingham green coat of paint. "She looks like a big green caterpillar" laughed Peter. "Of the aquatic variety"

Once the major jobs were complete we concentrated on the smaller ones and Spring cleaning took off in earnest, including a trip to the launderette with various articles of bedding, consisting mainly of three sleeping bags and an assortment of seat covers, curtains etc. We needed four machines for it all.

Then suddenly and typically of UK weather, Spring seemed to be on hold while winter returned with a vengeance of rain, snow, cold east winds, hail and forecasts of thunder storms. We debated going back into hibernation but our interests were kept occupied now, even when confined inside the boat, as so much was happening and coming to life out in the natural world for us to see. We often saw a large old mink ambling around the banks near the boatyard. He had somehow acquired an injury to one of his back legs and limped along about his business. It amused us to see a 'high rise' moorhen's nest some 12ft high up in a hawthorn bush along the banks of the canal, complete with proud hen sitting on it. She obviously wasn't going to risk being washed off her nest by any high waves. But I wondered how the chicks would get on when it was time to leave the nest.

Peter developed a nasty chest cold so I confined him to bed dosed up with tablets and flu powders plus ample supplies of reading material. I always worried about him getting chest infections and developing complications and ending up with possibly yet another lung collapse. So, I cycled to Preston Brook and rang a Health centre and a Doctors surgery to enquire about getting a doctor out to see him. The Health centre informed me that we were not in their area and that I should phone Frodsham, which I did and was given yet another number to call. Just as well I had taken a good supply of change with me. I spoke to a doctor who told me to "bring him to the surgery if possible". So I said I'd bring him in a taxi the following morning as long as when we got there he could go in and be seen straight away. On my way back I bumped into Gary and Heather and Gary said he would ring the surgery at Runcorn. I'd just arrived back at the boat when Gary appeared and said that a doctor was on his way. Gary wasn't having any excuses and had insisted "I want a doctor to this man now." The doctor was very understanding when the arrived at the boat of my concern for Peter and of calling him out to see him in the circumstances. He examined him fully and gave him some tablets to tide him over till I could get a prescription the following day. He also prescribed lots of rest. It wasn't easy keeping Peter confined to rest and after a few days he insisted on getting up to tackle a few jobs which he didn't like seeing me struggling to do. Plus we'd soon have to move to take on water and gas.

Mid April, now Easter and with Peter still chesty, coughing and very slowly on the mend, we made our way up to Lymm and were able to emerge from our green tin cocoon confinement when suddenly the weather took a turn for the better. The isolated towpath became alive with walkers, many of whom stopped to have a chat to us. Peter sat out on deck while I finished painting the rainbows on our bow.

It really was time we got going, we were getting itchy feet to be on the move, so I decided to plan our next journey. Out came the maps and books and eventually I had a written agenda starting at Preston Brook down to Lower Heyford in Oxfordshire, some 263 miles, 116 locks (69 up and 92 down). In fact it turned out to be 300 odd miles as we went on to Leighton Buzzard. Add to those miles all the to-ing and fro-ing up and down parts of the canal for water, supplies, sanitary stations, wood etc and many more miles were added to those of the actual estimated journey. We felt excited at the prospect of travelling into new territory and were eager to make a start.

However, fate had other plans for us for some weeks yet. That afternoon about 4.30, while I was still out painting the bow and Peter was sitting astern, he suddenly saw two men with shotguns approaching the small copse nearby. It unnerved him and rang alarm bells to see them so near the towpath. They disappeared from sight and shortly after we heard two very loud initial bursts of gunfire followed by more. Peter shot to his feet almost as quickly as the men suddenly reappeared and walked along the fence dividing the canal from the field back in our direction. Between them, the fence and us, was quite a wide area of rough overgrown ground. Peter, now more than worried, shouted to the men who stopped by the fence and one bent down as if to tie a shoelace and seemed to mumble something to the other man. Peter angrily yelled to them about shooting so close to the towpath and that we had cats out nearby. Both men looked uneasy and one shouted back to Peter that "we are only shooting wood pigeons." They then hurriedly made their way off in the direction of the small village of Bollington

We dashed around, calling the cats to check they were all alright and Jesse soon came running in. Blobs was already aboard but no sign of Ibley Dibley. We spent ages searching and calling him and were very worried but also knew that he would only come in when he was ready and all we could do was hope and pray he was okay and out there somewhere enjoying himself, full of fun and life as he always was. Once it grew dark we were unable to search any longer.

Friday 24th April. The day our rainbow faded away. We'd known in our hearts that Dibley was not coming home when he didn't turn up all night. At first light we put our waders and heavy gear on and went out into the cold wind, down the steep bank, through the hawthorn hedge and undergrowth to the marshy little glen where the kingcups and first of the 'may' flowers were growing. Sometime into our search Peter shouted from the shallow bank of the ditch like stream and confirmed our worst fears. Little Dibley lay shot in the back at the edge of the ditch. Peter was so angry – it all tied in with the men shooting around 4.30pm the day before. They had already shot Dibley when Peter approached them. We put dear little Dibley into a bag and took back to the boat. We were too upset at that moment to do anything else. Knowing how friendly Dibley was, he probably ran out to greet the men, thinking it was us as he so often did.

Later on we walked towards the small village of Bollington, the way Peter had seen the men go off and spoke to a lady living there about it. We thought about going to visit the local pub "The Swan with Two Necks" at lunch time to make some enquiries but decided it was best to just get away from the area. I felt quite frightened to think what Peter might do to either of those men if he got his hands on them. Arriving back at Lymm we called in at the police station to report the incident and were surprised to find the two officers there gave us so much attention and showed sympathetic concern. They said they would contact Altringham and get the area watched and let us know if anything came of it. Joe, who lived on a boat and moored at 'The Old No 3' was disgusted and said he would pass word round the other boaters and the pub and keep a look out himself for the men. The reporter from the Warrington Guardian came to the boat and interviewed us and we hoped the subsequent article would prick some ones conscience but doubted it as the lowest of the low have no consciences. I also contacted the Stockton Heath Cat Protection Society a week or so later as we thought about going to rescue another lively young cat to fill the gap. They told me that I should have reported it to the RSPCA investigations department, so I did and they took all the details and said that if we found out anything further, emphasizing the anything, we should let them know, adding that if they knew the identification of the culprits they would be able to prosecute them. Word was spread around by other boaters about the shooting and one couple with a cat who were on their way to moor near the scene were glad to be forewarned and find an alternative mooring.

In very low spirits we travelled back to Preston Brook to bury little Dibley along the towpath bank near the Preston Brook/Shardlow milestone. It was hard to come to terms with the cold blooded, deliberate and wicked slaughter of just a little innocent cat. It was heartbreaking. Living as we did in such close proximity onboard with our cats, they were a great part of our existence and much of our days and nights revolved around them. Ibley Dibley had filled a large part of our past year on the boat, given us so much pleasure with his antics, bright eyes and cheeky mannerisms. He had such a comical look on his face at times and used to weigh everything up very intelligently. It was such a waste of a beautiful little cat in the prime of life. We would miss him so much and forever feel the deep hurt and horror of the way he had so unnecessarily died.

That evening Jesse went ashore up and down the towpath, stopping now and then and calling to Ibley Dibley in a strange tone between a loud meow and yowl of distress. It was quite obvious that he was calling for him and this was something new we learned about cat behaviour. They had become hunting pals, the old wise Jesse, cool calm and collected, almost akin to a feline Clint Eastwood, and young brash impatient Ibley in need of a swipe or two from Jesse's paw to curb his eagerness in bringing the chase to a rewarding pounce on some unsuspecting prey.

Our enthusiasm was on the wane, even when the first swallows appeared, our spirits failed to lift with them as they rose up into the sky. Our sorrow even seemed to be etched in the very lace like veils of the cow parsley flowers that smothered the banks and hedgerows. And, as much as we loved the woods we were now permanently on edge moored near them and were becoming nervous wrecks every time we heard a gunshot. We decided to confine Jesse to the boat during the day and only let him out after dark. Blobs was no bother as he didn't wander far or have any interest in hunting. However, keeping the doors permanently shut and confining Jesse was easier said than done and ten minutes after we discovered he'd gone absent without leave one day, we heard the dreaded sound of a shotgun blast and immediately panicked into thinking the worst. We dashed into the woods, searching and calling in all directions but to no avail and after almost an hour we were visualizing yet another tragedy unfolding. Every still dark shadow had our minds playing tricks on us as we assumed it was him. Another dark shadow came into view as we peered through the woods to the edge where there was a small access road to the railway line. The dark shadow became a cat shaped blob sitting there patiently waiting for rabbits to appear and was far too engrossed than to have his fun spoiled by responding to our frantic cat calls. Jesse nonchalantly sauntered up to us as we approached and rubbed affectionately round our legs, oblivious to the trauma he had caused us for the past hour.

The next day we moved away from the woods, but not before Jesse was confined to being shut in the boat while Peter watched Liverpool –v– Sunderland play in the FA cup final. Nothing was priority over that, even if the boat had been on fire and sinking. Peter was on cloud nine when Liverpool won 2 – 0. I was secretly glad too but always pretended to support the opposite team just to enjoy a bit of banter.

Our new mooring overlooked the Weaver Navigation with extensive open views across the countryside and no woods to worry about. Peter lost his footing going along the offside gunwale and just saved himself from going into the cut by twisting around and quickly grabbing hold of the grab rail, but pulled a muscle or stretched a ligament or two in his side and was in a lot of pain for a considerable time. I spotted him down the bank one day in a nice quiet spot with Jesse asleep on his lap and they looked a picture of restful peace and tranquillity. Not for long though as a boatful of holiday makers on an Anglo Welsh hire boat tied up astern of us and asked for a loan of Peter's bike so that they could get to the nearest phone box to phone the boat hire office to inform them they had broken down. Peter, ever one to oblige pumped up the bike tyres and one of the crew took off on it. Not many people had mobile phones at that time.

I had never met Peter's sister Edith who was a few years older than him and who lived in Wallasey, but he'd told me a lot about her. We decided that it would be nice to treat her to a day on the boat with us and to arrange it as soon as possible before we set off on our journey south. The day we fetched her couldn't have been more perfect in every way and she and Peter sat reminiscing and laughing about their childhood days while I kept the tea and cream buns flowing plus the odd glass of sherry and ale. We took Edith for a trip up the canal and then for lunch at The Horns Inn and she seemed to really have enjoyed every minute of it all. We had too and it was especially nice to give her a special day as she was the sort of person who never asked much from life, or who had ever received it. Towards the end of the day, a holiday boat passed by and an excited young lady shouted across to us "We've got a week's holiday aboard, how long have you got?" Peter a little smugly replied "Forever". The girl was rendered speechless but her face said it all with a look of 'oh you lucky things,' and as if she couldn't imagine anything more marvellous.

Peter often sat astern for hours, either fishing or day dreaming, watching the world go by and saw many interesting aspects of nature that I missed as I was usually busy, occupied doing daily chores or eyes down painting. He called me up on deck early one morning to watch a fox sitting in full view down in some tractor tracks in the cornfield opposite. After awhile the fox ambled up the tracks before disappearing into the foot high corn, then reappeared running in leaps and bounds across the field towards the hedge where we then glimpsed him in hot pursuit of a rabbit which he continued to chase along the edge of the field before finally disappearing through the hedge and leaving us guessing as to the outcome of the chase.

By the end of May, regardless of anything in our way to deter our plans we decided to up anchor and GO. It was fond farewells to Gary and Heather – till we met again which we were sure we would.

Chapter Eight

Saga of Red Bull Basin

Now journeying south our first stop was just short of Middlewich big lock by the River Dee. We took advantage of the shops and stocked up on stores before continuing on our way early the next day in a real heat wave (up to 100degrees) in some parts of the country. It was a hot slog doing the 9 locks but we swapped around to give each other a break from steering the boat to doing some locks each and finally moored up about 3.30pm at the 'flashes' near Sandbach. It was slow going but we were in no rush to miss all the wonderful scenery as we travelled along and once I spotted butterflies, time stood still while I attempted to film them. However, try as I might to capture some 'wall browns', as soon as they settled they closed up their wings and deprived me of seeing them in full display. Even though not one of our most colourful butterflies, it was nice to see them open winged. I had no luck when trying to catch the unmistakeable very bright crimson coloured 'cinnabar moth' which un-moth-like flits about during the day and lays its eggs on the yellow flowered ragwort plants. The eggs hatch out into eye catching colonies of yellow and black striped caterpillars, all chomping away on the plant till it truly does resemble a raggy ragwort. The caterpillars' colours announce to all would be predators that they are very poisonous.

Travelling on towards Harecastle tunnel, 14 more locks away, we had a job to find suitable moorings where we could safely allow the cats out. So we decided to make a detour up the Macclesfield canal a few miles, hoping to find somewhere up there. But, after 4 miles there was nothing so we had no choice but to keep the cats shut in all night. They were desperate to get out the next morning so we settled for the aqueduct near the Trent and Mersey junction and Red Bull Basin, which wasn't ideal but better than anywhere else we had found. We had promised to contact Gary and Heather when we got to the tunnel as they were keen to come down and navigate through it with us, but one phone call after another led to much hassle, wrong numbers and a trip to the library to look in a phone directory. From what should have been a few minute phone call became an all around the world fruitless expedition and we were not happy hanging around the area which had an unpleasant and uneasy atmosphere attached to it. But we had promised Gary and Heather and needed to know if they were coming or not. After trying our utmost to contact them we decided that all we could do was to leave a message for them at the Preston Brook marina and that if they were coming we would meet them at 6pm in The Tavern and go through the tunnel at 7 pm. It wasn't that simple though as after cycling down to the entrance of the tunnel just to check the times we found out that after 4 pm no one could go through, so it was back to the phone to amend the previous message left. But we couldn't get through. So after being out on our bikes for the best part of about 7 hours we felt it was time to give up trying to make plans and just get back to the boat, which we did about 8.30, very weary in mind and body. I also had a stinking migraine headache so we just piled aboard, bikes and all, stowed one astern, one on the bow. The boat was moored a few feet off the bank with boarding planks out, as the shallow water prevented us getting any closer in. We always locked the bikes up, but the one time in a hundred that we hadn't done so that night, thieves struck and both bikes were stolen sometime after dark. Whoever had taken them must have been very light on their feet getting on and off the boat on the planks and getting both bikes off without rocking the boat or making any noise, all in the dark, unless we'd both been extremely comatose in deep sleep. In our three days there, we learned that the area was rife with thieves and we had picked up on those uncomfortable vibes ourselves on arrival. It was a necessary stopping area for boaters waiting to navigate either the tunnel or the locks and other boaters and local people agreed with us that notices should have been put up warning boaters to be extra vigilant.

Well, one bike stolen would have been a bitter blow, but both of them were a disaster as they were so important to us. We trundled up to Kidsgrove police station and I made out a report, then the sergeant said that as it was quiet he would run me round a few areas on the off chance of spotting the culprits and the bikes, but no luck. I met Peter back in The Tavern and we got talking to the local window cleaner Fred, who had a drink with us and bought us a sandwich. Everyone we spoke to seemed to have had a bike stolen and a lad that I talked to had seen the bikes on our boat and even remarkably knew one was a pink/mauve Raleigh Mustang! As we left the pub about 1.30pm, about to cross the road, I stepped back as two lads whizzed past on bikes almost knocking me over. My eyes almost popped out of my head, as I recognized the last bike ridden past us was none other than Peter's. We both shouted and started to pursue the boys on foot and they turned to look back at us but soon disappeared from sight round a corner and by the time we reached the corner they were half way up the main road. I attempted to hijack another innocent biker who happened to ride by and I was so wound up and keen to catch the boys I excitedly ordered him to "quick chase after them, they've stolen our bikes." When he didn't respond, I felt like grabbing his bike and chasing after them myself but the lad was so taken aback he didn't comprehend the urgency of the situation. So Peter and I left him gawping and we took off in the direction the boys had disappeared in. We came to a grinding halt at a crossroads with traffic lights and were stumped as to which way the boys had gone. Feeling that we'd lost out on the chance to retrieve our bikes and nab the boys, we turned and retraced our tracks and came upon a group of lads. On the off chance, we asked them if they had seen two boys in shorts on bikes, told them why we were interested to know and nearly fell over in shock when one replied, enquiringly. "Is one a pink Raleigh Mustang and the other a blue and white shopper?" It seemed that everyone on the planet knew all about our bikes. We couldn't believe our luck when the lad went on to tell us that he and his mates knew who had them and where they lived. We informed the police and they came out in minutes and took one of the boys in the police car, we assumed to the homes of the boys who had stolen the bikes, but when the boy was returned and got out of the car he told us that the police had driven past the homes, not stopped and made enquiries or anything. When we paid another trip to the police station to find out what was happening, we were told that the incident had taken place on police force boundaries so the report at Kidsgrove would be sent on to Alsager-Crewe and take a few days to get there. The officer added that they would do all they could to get the bikes back. We found all this hard to comprehend. It was like something out of a Carry On film. Apparently we didn't understand much of the futility that surrounded all this petty theft. Peter and I sat in the park opposite the thieves' house for hours on the Saturday, just hoping and waiting for one or the other of the boys to appear and if we were lucky enough perhaps with one or the other of the bikes, so we could catch them red handed and retrieve our bikes. One of the cocky lads strolled home to the house later on but with no bike. I recognized him as one I'd seen on our bikes and we considered going over to the house and having it out with him and his parents but one or two locals that we had spoken to told us that he lived with his mother who was no good and that we would only get verbal abuse from her. We were also told that the boy's brother was in prison and the boy himself had recently come out of remand home or such. We were getting nowhere and all we wanted was our bikes back, as there was no chance of any 'justice' being done for the crime, not a cat's chance in hell. So we continued to wait, hoping the boy would come out again and we could then follow him. We could see him moving around in an upstairs room. There was only a side and front entry so we knew he could not leave without us seeing him go. After waiting an hour we were frozen, as where we stood, concealed from view, it was like a wind tunnel, so we decided to call it a day. On our way back we passed the other boy's house but there was no sign of anyone or the bikes there either. The woman in the chip shop who we spoke to said she knew, without volunteering names, just who had stolen the bikes and said that one boy was known to get up in the night to go out stealing anything he could including milk money people may have left out. He had broken into the shop to steal cigarettes and the police had even found mince pies etc from the shop in his house but he'd got away with it. Peter and I both agreed that the best thing that could happen to these two young criminals who seemed to be beyond the law would be for them to get caught up some dark alley one night and given a good hiding, with a threat of more to come if they didn't change their ways. Something they would understand and definitely needed.

The following day I went up to the house again and saw one of the boys, a tall thin spotty faced specimen. I followed him and his mate down towards the canal but think they knew I was following them as they disappeared at the bridge. Apparently, one of the thieves used to live on a boat so he would know the ropes regards getting on and off and stealing from them. One of the men in the boatyard said they were plagued by youths, vandalism and theft. He told us that one night at about 2 am a nearby resident heard the locks being operated and thought perhaps a boat was being stolen. She alerted the police and they discovered the lock being vandalised. On another occasion they'd blocked the weir and flooded the area and another time had put huge stones under one side of moored boats where it was exceptionally shallow, trying to capsize them. Yet, first impressions of the area all seemed pleasant and rural. After a few days we knew differently and heard more and more incredulous stories. One boater told us that he fished out a brand new looking mountain bike, phoned the police and was told to just "leave it there". The young criminals in this area seemed to be getting away with everything and were encouraged to flaunt the fact in the face of the law. The men in the boatyard said youths often stood nearby shouting abuse and jeering at them and that it was an ongoing job to protect the boatyard from break ins.

However, we felt that if we stayed around long enough we'd perhaps get our bikes back but it was miserable hanging around an area like this and no place for the cats either. We'd watched five youths brandishing air rifles go sauntering past the boat like vigilantes one afternoon and I heard

Peter shout angrily at them "Don't kill the bloody birds". He said they were firing at the song birds and one of them was aiming at a blackbird up in a tree. The youths just arrogantly sneered at Peter and went on their way. I dashed out to look for Jesse who was fast asleep all curled up in the nearby undergrowth. He wasn't too happy to be disturbed but it was somewhat in his best interests to be brought inside. I thought I ought to have gone to the pub and phoned the police to report the youths but our experiences over the past few days put me off – there seemed no point. Twenty minutes later a man walked along the towpath and started chatting to Peter who mentioned the youths to him. The man wanted to know all the ins and outs about them and which way they had gone and said that he'd been after getting them caught for ages as they had been shooting all the young ducks.

Back at the pub the landlady said that her son had his bike stolen when they had first moved in. It was a custom built one that he used to race on. She said that it had been locked up and kept in a spare store room inside the pub but someone had managed to steal it all the same. One customer made us laugh as he said. "If you stay around long enough you will probably get your bikes sold back to you." We had a drink with friendly Fred the window cleaner and he promised he would keep a look out for our bikes. He bought us some chicken sandwiches then his son gave us a lift into town to the hole in the wall and then to the police station. On the Sunday we had lunch in the Tavern with Fred and invited him back to the boat, so we all piled into his car only to find that his radio had been left on and flattened the battery. So a friend of his gave us all a lift back in his van and we swapped his flat battery for one of our charged up boat ones. We had a chat and Peter gave him two of his walking sticks as a parting gift and Fred gave us a bottle of whiskey. It was a tonic to meet this friendly, hard working father of eight and grandfather of nineteen, especially so at a time when much of our faith in human beings was at a low ebb.

In a happier frame of mind than we had been for the past few days we at last set off through Harecastle tunnel about 9 am the next morning. Headroom in this notoriously low 2,926 yard (2676m) tunnel was virtually nil for a six footer such as Peter. The tunnel operated on a one way system to a timetable, so at least you knew that once you were in it you'd not be meeting any boats coming in the opposite direction. I always felt slightly uneasy and sealed in as it was a very claustrophobic tunnel and a large noisy ventilation fan at the southern end made me feel as though we were in the dungeons of hell, especially when entering the southern end to travel north. It is the fourth longest navigable canal tunnel in the UK.

Travelling all down through the potteries of Stoke-on-Trent, Peter did most of the donkey work opening up the tough wide lock gates. We moored up briefly near the Wedgewood factory at Barlaston before moving on to find a more suitable mooring before dark and found a pleasant spot by a field with a horse in who we nicknamed Dobbin and he proved to be quite an attention seeker, noisily kicking the fence nearby. He relished a couple of porridge oat butties that we gave him.

Having no bikes was a great loss and inconvenience to us. We decided to put an insurance claim in for them, in hopes that some compensation could be put towards buying two more, albeit second hand ones. Already experiencing very sore joints from all the extra walking and lumbering around with shopping bags, there was an increased intake of pain killers on the agenda.

One of the more pleasant aspects of travelling was to never know who we might meet along the way. We met and chatted to so many people as we waited for locks to be made ready, stopped to take on water or use the sanitary stations, or when moored up, to passers by on the towpath. I started to keep a list of names of people we particularly found interesting and or friendly. I remember one such elderly couple on a small cabin cruiser, who haled us as we approached the locks at Fradley junction and asked us if they could share the locks with us. We had already seen their boat "Jonazar" way back at Shugborough and they had only just been out a week due to problems with health. They were Una aged 72 and Fred almost 83 and they'd had a few years experience on the canals and we really enjoyed their company, even though it was short lived, as we turned off onto the Coventry canal while they continued down the Trent and Mersey. While Peter moored at the junction to fill up with water I bimbled off down to the next lock to help Una and Fred through it. I learned that they had celebrated their Golden Wedding anniversary the previous year, so I dashed back to the boat an ran back with one of the walking sticks they had been admiring and a little painted pot and gave to them. I hoped we would meet up again when we were both more stationary and could spend some more time together, perhaps sitting out on the towpath sharing a yarn or two. Briefly we had touched on the subject of 'families' and I felt very sad to learn that they'd lost their only child, a son of twenty-three, killed in an accident.

When we reached Hopwas we relaxed and found a nice spot overlooking a sea-blue field of flax. After days of travelling and the constant banging in our ears of the engine, it was nice to enjoy some real peace and quiet, to hear the sounds of nature all around us and the quiet lapping of the water against the hull of the boat and to settle down to enjoy a meal. Then maybe

Peter would sit out astern to fish awhile as the last of the day faded away. After which we'd read our books or talk about things and often end up laughing at something till our sides ached.

We hadn't however been moored up long before Jesse leapt onboard with what I thought was a big mouse hanging from his jaws. Whatever it was squeaked dramatically in distress and Jesse scuttled off with it, raced astern past Peter and onto the towpath. Peter, who'd dozed off, woke with a start and managed to corner Jesse and coax him to drop the bundle of fur which turned out to be a baby rabbit, its big eyes staring up in terror. I grabbed Jesse and shut him in the boat and Peter gently put the little rabbit down and it ran off none the worse for its ordeal. The next day another baby rabbit hadn't been so lucky as all that was left of it was its back legs. Jesse then brought a mouse onboard and proceeded to throw it up in the air and it landed alive on Peter as he sat astern fishing. As a consequence, Peter spilled his tea and got an eyeful of it, by which time Jesse had sprung back into action and the mouse was dead.

Jesse was truly a 'hunter' of the first degree, but he lost a few and one in particular that he briefly dropped on the towpath was quickly snatched up by a rook who had been eyeing up the situation. Jesse looked quite indignant.

As May departed with all her fresh and delicate shades of colour, in came brassy June, bringing dreamy poetic thoughts to mind;-

> 'Now where nodding coltsfoot once stood along the banks, there's none at all
> Now tangled stands of reeds and rush, umbels of keck and dropwort tall
> All scramble in competitive confusion, strangled by vetches and bryony's twine
> No gentleness now that Spring's in her Autumn, her freshness and grace in decline.
> For summer she comes rushing in, ablaze in gaudy sheen of rainbow reds, greens and blues.
> Such a knowing maid of little virtue, flaunting her tempting bee lined hues.'

With now being able to have a good break from constant wooding we were able to get on with some other jobs, aided by a spell of dry warm weather. I started to paint a monarch butterfly, midships, which I first outlined on a large sheet of Perspex before Peter cut it out so that I then had a nice template. This butterfly was going to be the biggest one on the planet some 3ft x 2ft approximately. I spent most of the day kneeling on the bank painting it onto the boat side while Peter worked ashore making his walking sticks and two small shelves to put my paint pots on. It was a relief not to have too many boats passing or Peter onboard rocking the boat as it was difficult to paint the detailed and intricate parts of the butterfly on a moving canvas. Of course, I often had to manage, but when it came to the extremely fine lines such as the antennae, which required not only a steady boat but a very steady hand and 100% concentration, then strict orders for Peter to "abandon ship" were introduced. I always dreaded this final part of painting the butterflies, as usually after holding my breath and getting one antennae just right, it would take numerous unsuccessful attempts to line up a second exact and equally matching one. Then once complete I had to think about doing the whole butterfly again on the other side of the boat.

Peter took the stern deck boards up and got to grips with the really dirty job of cleaning all the grease and oil out of the bilge and doing an oil change. What a mess he was in when he'd finished, covered in gunge. He stripped off to his underpants out on the bank while I brought out and filled a large dhoby tub with soapy water and he scrubbed himself down then tipped the lot all over himself. I refilled the tub with fresh water so that he could rinse himself down. Half an hour later at 5 pm we were on our way up the 11 locks to Atherstone, remembering as we did so our little Ibley Dibley who had joined us here about a year ago. It was 10 pm before we moored up for the night and had our supper. No messing about for Jesse, he was straight out and back in again with a rabbit for his supper, but he just appeared on deck by the galley door with it held in his mouth, (as cats would hold kittens), poked his head in at the door, looked at Peter standing there and made a little greeting noise as Peter held out his cupped hands and talked coaxingly to Jesse who then just dropped the baby rabbit into his hands as if to say "it's for you". Peter passed it to me while he confined Jesse aboard and I took it some distance from the boat and released it into the field where it quickly shot off.

For the first time since leaving Preston Brook we lit a fire and decided to try and fit in some time here and there on our travels to gradually get some wood stored up.

Grey skies, drizzle, and spoil heaps as we came into and soon left Nuneaton for Hawkesbury junction where we strolled up to the nearest pub to make a phone call. There was a good atmosphere there, with music and locals singing out of tune so we stayed awhile and played two legs of crib. Needless to say I won both legs, by just one hole much to Peter's disbelief.

Nearing Hillmorton we came across a large brood of moorhen chicks which were all spread out in a line along a low branch that ran down into the water to their nest where just one solitary black fluffy chick sat as if to say "It's Sunday and I'm not getting up just yet." After we moored at

Hillmorton just outside Rugby, a family of nine tiny mallard chicks came swimming along. Peter fed them some bread and we wondered where their mother was as there was no sign of her. We hoped she was around as Peter had seen a fox roaming around in a nearby field.

The next day we came across a dead duck down the canal and assumed that the little group of chicks we had seen were her now orphaned family. They showed up again later in the day but this time there were only six of them. We gave them lots of food and hoped they would hurry up and grow bigger in order to stand more chance of surviving all the dangers they'd face in their infancy, especially at night when they were ashore unprotected by mum. There were so many predators constantly after them, such as water rats, herons, pike, mink, foxes and cats. Everything in nature was competing for food, even the likes of Jesse who was fortunate enough to have it provided for him and didn't need to catch any. He caught a mouse and left it a few yards away on the towpath as a crow flew down nearby and strutted around eyeing it up while Jesse simultaneously eyed him up. The crow swooped up and quickly back down onto the mouse and flew off with it.

The family of surviving ducks dwindled down to five and then we didn't see them for a few days but when they reappeared they were much bigger and whereas before, the older ducks would chase them, now they could hold their own more. It was comical to see them, still so small in comparison, chasing away full grown drakes, and going like the clappers of hell after them when they competed for the food we fed them.

Peter wandered off looking for wood and returned with some good fallen branches and went off for more but returned with no more wood and limping badly. He'd been sorting through a pile of stuff that had been dumped in a field and trodden heavily on a plank of wood with some long nails sticking out of it. Some of the nails had gone right through the sole of his plimsoll into his foot and the worst one had gone deep into the arch of his foot. He soaked his foot in a solution of diluted Milton and put a dressing on it to keep it clean. We had no choice but to stay put as the foot became very swollen and too painful for Peter to stand on, though he didn't complain or moan, just hoped it wouldn't turn nasty as puncture wounds could easily do. I'd booked a ticket to go to Lancashire in a few days time to sort out a few things back there but decided that if Peter was still immobile I would cancel it. However, by then, he was hobbling around a bit so I made sure he had plenty of food and he just had to stay put until I returned. Easier said than done, as where Peter was concerned even if I'd left him wrapped up in cotton wool it would not have guaranteed his safety as he was more accident prone than an accident.

By the time I left the boat, his foot was almost healed but I'd only left the boat and gone on my way for about an hour when he decided to refill the grease gun on the stern. He filled it up, pulled himself up on the grab rail, but his greasy hand just slid off and he did a back somersault into the canal. I think he must have been in competition with Blobs to see who could fall in the most. After scrambling out, cleaning himself up and changing his clothes he decided to transfer the beer from the ferment bin to the barrel. After doing this he left the barrel of beer on the low topped galley sideboard and went to check out where Jesse was. A boat went hurtling past, rocking ours violently as it did so and sent the barrel crashing to the floor, spilling out about twenty pints before Peter returned and salvaged what was left. After that little escapade and cleaning up all the mess, he poured himself a much needed pint and sat down for a rest just as another boat tore past and in jumping up to shout at the chap on the stern, he caught his knee under the table and sent his pint flying all over the place.

As if that wasn't enough for one day he had a surprise visit from Gerald and Freda who were on a cycling holiday and in the area. So Peter took the opportunity of borrowing Gerald's bike that evening to cycle to a phone box in the village and phone me. Halfway through Newbold tunnel he heard a great clattering of hooves and came to a grinding halt as out of the gloom of the tunnel he made out the shapes of about eight goat like beasts charging full pelt towards him. The tunnel was about 400 yards long with a rail separating the canal from the very narrow towpath to afford some safety to pedestrians. With the beasts fast approaching in stampede mode, Peter's survival instincts quickly set in and he leaned the bike on the rail and climbed over it, feet placed firmly on the path edge below the rail and hands firmly hanging onto it. One slip and he'd be having another good dunk in the canal but some old chap had gleefully related a tale to us of 'flesh eating zanders' (a cross between a perch and a pike I believe) living in the tunnel water, so true or false it probably helped Peter to hang on while the escapee goats charged past. After he phoned me, apart from being amazed that so much could happen to him in such a short space of time since I'd left, I just felt some relief to know that Gerald and Freda were now there to keep an eye on him before he managed to get into the Guinness book of records for having the most accidents in one day. On my return a few days later, we all enjoyed a musical evening down at The Barley Mow.

We couldn't afford to hang around much longer though as we had a deadline to meet up with my mum at Lower Heyford and take her on a holiday cruise with us. We filled up with red diesel (now £1 a gallon) and a new 19k gas bottle and headed off for Napton on the S.Oxford canal. It was so hot that we couldn't stand bare footed on the wooden deck boards or touch the steel parts of the boat with our hands. With all the heat, the inside of the boat was extremely hot too, even with all doors and windows open and if there was no breeze it was a bit like being cooked alive in a tin at times. It could be 80 degrees outside and 90 inside. The cats were fine, they just slunk off into some nice cool foliage and slept till the cool of the evening.

Arriving at Napton lock we couldn't believe how many cats were running around and soon learned that Sue and her husband the lock keeper, lived in and ran the small lock side shop. At the side was a barn full of hay and a comfortable looking old three piece suite to accommodate the numerous feral cats who came and went as they pleased and whom the husband fed each day at noon. We were told that many of the cats had found this haven from where they had previously lived in the nearby brickworks, and some were inevitably not in good health through inter breeding and living the hard uncared for life of feral cats. This feeding time was something we couldn't miss so we were there when the lock keeper arrived to feed the cats and they all came running in all directions but stayed at arms length, not wanting to be touched. We couldn't believe our eyes when we saw a lot of young black and white ones and one with almost identical markings to Ibley Dibley. "That's Trevor" the lock keeper informed us, adding that we could have him if we wanted. So we said we'd think about it and might pick him up after my mother's holiday had finished, as it would be impossible and a worry trying to keep him confined in the boat, get him used to a new life with us and look after mum at the same time. We also wondered if it was wise to try and replace Ibley Dibley with a replica moggy and perhaps also a bit unfair on Trevor as we'd surely be making comparisons all the time. He'd also be a constant reminder of Dibley, so we needed to give it some serious thought first.

We still had three days to spare before meeting mum and a journey of about 35 miles and 28 locks so weren't in a particular rush as we set off from Napton and worked our way up nine locks to Marston Doles where the canal became distinctly chalky. The lovely countryside tempted us to moor up early and enjoy what was left of the day. Lots of happy boaters passing and Peter gave one a cheery wave and the chap turned, waved back and promptly ran aground with his bow stuck on the opposite bank. Perhaps Peter's new Gabby Hayes whiskered look had given him a fright. I wrote to the Ministry of Defence enquiring after Peter's Campaign medals from the last war, with a view to recovering them. He'd make a joke of it all and said I should have them for living with him.

Down to just two days to get to our rendezvous with mum we made an early start after leaving a trail of burned toast behind us and before the day was out had travelled some 18-19 miles and thirteen locks so we were making good progress, helped out by some fine weather which changed dramatically the next day when it just poured with rain all day. But we were committed and resigned to whatever the weather threw at us and by 5 pm we had completed a further ten miles and seven locks, one of which was so deep I thought someone had pulled the plug out of it. Even our thick water proofs couldn't keep out the rain, or our boots and we squelched around like very water logged soggy sponges. Normally we would have had time to stop and look around at any places of historical or other interest such as at Cropredy famous for the battle Cromwell had there fighting the Royalists in order to access an entry into Oxford but he had been defeated. We felt as though we had been in a battle ourselves by the time we moored up and got out of our wet gear.

We now felt that the cats were safer when we managed to moor up alongside fields of grazing livestock until a farmer whose horses were in a field nearby, stopped to chat to us and told us he had three cats. He also said that he had to keep a keen eye out for those getting up to no good with air rifles and had caught some youths firing at his cattle one day. He'd given them what for and later on the police visited him saying that he could end up on charges of assault. But he told them he would continue to clobber anyone illegally on his land or damaging his property or livestock because if he didn't no one else would, including them.

We rather admired him for standing up for 'common sense' and old fashioned 'clout round the ear' measures of justice. Peter and I were beginning to feel that life was more like living in the Wild West than on Britain's quiet waterways.

Torrential overnight rain transformed fields of grazing cows into lakes of floating ducks. We had no urge to be up at the crack of dawn and were a little ahead of schedule so we stayed in our warm bed reading and dozing. A few boats had gone charging past but we were oblivious to all outside until Peter saw an unfamiliar tree through the window, a moving one at that which just disappeared. He got up and took a good look out of the window to discover we were not moored up anymore and were just floating about adrift in the middle of the canal at a horizontal angle across it and heading sideways for a bridge about 30 yards from our original mooring. The heavy rain on the soft sandy soil plus fast moving boats had gradually worked our mooring pins at an angle and allowed the ropes to slip off, or perhaps even pulled up the pins. There was a boat approaching to our stern so Peter had to look sharp and get up on deck to quickly manoeuvre us out of the way and back to the bank. Luckily none of the cats were stranded ashore and none of our mooring pins were lost. The type of metal pin with the additional enclosed ring at the top for a rope to pass through was the best type to have but even then the rope could come loose and slip through.

The chimney funnel broke off it's hinge so Peter removed the old part and put another hinge on but it didn't work so we settled for sticking it back on upside down and as the song goes – 'the smoke went up the chimney just the same.' But we had to remember it was not now on a hinge and make sure when travelling it was lowered or we'd risk it being ripped off going through a tunnel or bridge hole.

On the morning of our rendezvous with mum I had a quick clean up and final sort out ready for her arrival and we moved the boat up the remaining lock which meant having to intrude on a fishing match and two nearby rather irate fishermen who were slowly coming to the boil watching our seemingly deliberate anti-fishermen tactics. I decided to explain the situation before "fish wars" erupted, and once they knew our reasons for mooring up near the lock bank they were fine.

We met mum and duly piped her aboard and settled her in, leaving the fishermen in peace as we set off, but only did two locks before the weather turned nasty so called it a day. Just as well as we all had lots to talk about and relaxed over a nice meal. Our luck changed the next day as we headed for Banbury and found a nearby supermarket and soon filled a trolley full of groceries which we wheeled right to the boat and unloaded. A friendly chap on a boat named "Legless II" kindly offered to return our trolley to the store for us. Mum and I took a little walk around Banbury and left Peter in charge of the painted canal-ware I'd left out for sale, all displayed on top of the boat. On our return there was quite a queue of people at the boat, all handing in small pots and cauldrons that had blown off the boat in the wind and been floating around in the canal. I considered stopping all shore leave for Peter for neglecting his duties on watch, but decided that would be tougher on the rest of us than on him.

Back out in the countryside, with Peter fishing, mum relaxing and repeatedly informing us that she could hear voices and that a boat must be coming. Peter turned his hearing aid up full and I tuned in my 'bat ears' but still we couldn't hear any voices or a boat coming. We realized that what mum was hearing was the baa-ing (voices) of all the sheep 'talking' in the surrounding fields and if nothing else, that we were all in for a good laugh at least.

Every time I descended down into the stern cabin I invariably caught my clothing on one or the other of the bungee clips that hung there and thought if I didn't soon move them it would only be a matter of time before I was caught up and catapulted into the canal or up in a tree. I'd just found a new home for them when a group of people on the towpath stopped us and asked us if we'd do them a favour and give a disabled friend of theirs a lift to their boat which was a few hundred yards up the canal past us. It would, they said be easier for them than having to put the chap into his wheelchair and struggle up the bumpy unmade towpath. He'd had muscular sclerosis for ten years and appeared to be in his late forties, a jolly faced chap with a cheerful disposition. We were happy to be of some help.

Napton was a nice place for mum to spend some time pottering about and talking to people, something she missed out on living on her own. We enjoyed watching the cats being fed at the lock cottage and kept checking to see if 'Trevor' was still among them. The lady in the Folly shop took some of my canal ware and Peter's walking sticks to sell on a sale or return basis and I also sold quite a few items from the boat.

The village of Napton, as I found out when I went to post a letter, had a peaceful homely atmosphere and was spread out in a spacious and unconforming way on and below the hill, among trees and winding lanes. The focus of the village was the windmill on top of the hill and the square church

Bradwell Windmill

tower to the right of it. A row of eye catching pink 'chocolate box' cottages, swathed in rambling roses and other floral delights lazed timelessly in the warm sun. I was tempted to explore an enticing footpath that meandered up between a row of cottages near the "Crown" pub but thought I better save it for another time and perhaps Peter and I could explore it together. As I ambled back I could smell the sweet honey scented creeping thistles along the roadside verges, smelling even sweeter after a little rain and now invaded by dozens of nectar seeking butterflies and bees.

That evening we treated ourselves to a meal in the Folly and sampled some of their home made pies. Peter had 'cow pie' – a huge affair consisting of over a pound of beef under puff pastry. Mum and I had a more modest choice.

Our next port of call was Braunston and we had no choice but to stay put as there were lock restrictions to save water and no more boats were allowed through that day.

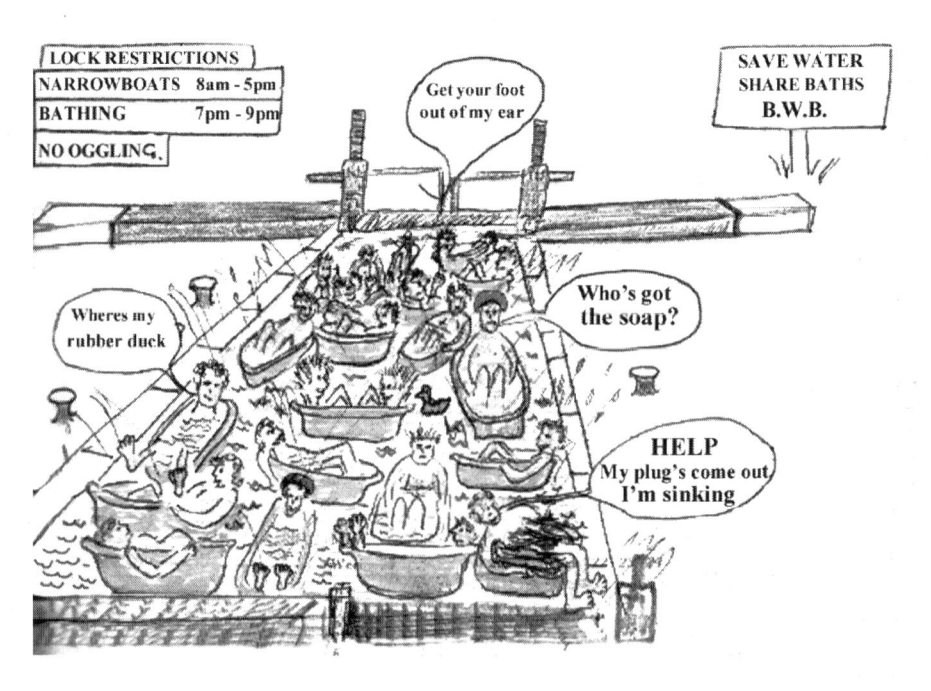

We got into discussion about how many baths per day over a period of ten years could be obtained from a lock full of water. Rumour had it that the water would be enough for one person to bath once a day for ten years. Peter thought it more likely that 50,000 people could bath each day for ten years which would use about one billion seven hundred and sixty million gallons of water. So on average, how much water did a lock hold?

We ended up splitting our sides with laughter as we envisaged the scenes. More laughter as Peter opened the top of the pressure barrel and volumes of frothy beer shot out like a fire extinguisher. He managed to re-seal it before flooding the forward cabin and the whole boat had a lovely brewery like aroma to it.

With the lock restrictions in place from 9am – 4pm Braunston was very congested. We doubled up with a weekend hire boat and they were happy to do most of the lock paddles, all being in the holiday spirit of things. Peter helped with some but it seemed a long process going up the seven locks to the almost mile long tunnel. (2,042 yards; 1867 metres).

One day mum decided she would do a little bit of fishing off the stern deck. Apparently she had, in her younger days, been quite an expert at fishing with her cousins in Canada on lakes up in the Laurentian mountains. Not for a minute did she think she was going to catch one on the canal and she was completely taken by surprise when she did and not at all happy with the poor little fish on the end of the line gasping for breath. She wasn't happy till Peter unhooked it and gently plopped it back into the water and didn't ever want to do anymore fishing.

I think mum was glad when we were finished with going through tunnels too and Blisworth was the last one of the journey, coming out at Stoke Bruerne, ever busy with tourists and boaters. We opted to move on quickly from there to the more peaceful moorings opposite the derelict Isworth Farm, one of our all time favourites.

All panic at 7 am the next morning when there was a loud gunshot bang. Peter shot up out of bed, me in hot pursuit to look for Jesse who was the only one missing. Much to our relief he strolled out of the hedge and we realized the bangs were from a bird (gas cylinder) scarer, not a gun. That was one way of getting us all out of bed early. Most mornings we took our time, had tea in bed, talked and read or did a crossword which sometimes could be hilarious with Peter up in the fore cabin separated from us by the bulkhead to our cabin plus both him and mum being hard of hearing. As we read out the clues they were interpreted in all but the true format and so the answers were completely irrelevant and it all got so funny and impossible to do.

Peter would say for example "First clue = small fry".

Mum would reply "Yes I could eat a stirfry" and I would exclaim "stirfry?!!!"

Peter would then say "No! sorry I mean small FLY?"

"Ah yes" says Mum "A nit"

"A nit, exclaims I.

"Who's a twit?" asks Peter and "Oh and two down must be 'tart".
"Whose done a fart?" pipes up Mum.
"Not fart – TART, cloth ears" says I in exasperation.
Needless to say not much of the crossword got done.

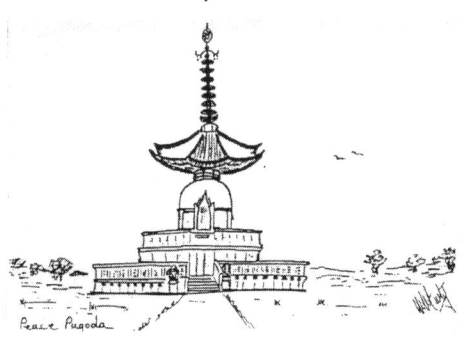

Travelling through Milton Keynes we had time to visit the Peace Pagoda which was founded by a Japanese Buddhist monk called Nichidatsu Fujii who worked with Mahatma Gandhi on peaceful ways of opposing wrong doing by governments. After the Second World War he campaigned against American and Russian plans to fight future wars by killing huge numbers of civilians with nuclear weapons as the Americans had done to Japan. He said "Civilization has nothing to do with having electric lights, airplanes, or manufacturing atomic bombs. It had nothing to do with killing human beings, destroying things or waging war. Civilization was meant to hold one another in mutual affection and respect." He lived to be 100 and his movement built eighty Peace Pagodas all round the world to remind people of the need to seek world peace and peaceful means to resolve arguments. Near the pagoda there are a thousand cherry trees and cedars which was a gift from Japan to remind us of the victims of all wars.

Mum's eighty mile canal trip ended at The Globe, just outside Leighton Buzzard where we waited for Gerald to pick her up and for her to get her land legs again. We hoped she would have lots of happy memories of her journey and all the fun we had had together.

Chapter Nine

Bigfoot Aboard

Some good news came from the Insurance Company saying that they would pay us £240 for the two bikes we'd had stolen, so now we'd be able to buy ourselves two new or good second hand ones plus two good strong 'D' locks to go with them.

Late on in July Peter picked some early blackberries and we had our first apple and blackberry pie of the year. He romantically brought me quite a bower of long twining honeysuckle which I placed in a large jar on top of the wood stove and trailed all around the chimney flue and wound another piece all around the window. The next morning I drew the curtains and disturbed a very large 'Old Lady Moth.' It was about the size of a red admiral butterfly' and flew out of the honeysuckle whizzing around in all directions. I shot into the bedroom, dived under the bed covers to hide and in doing so accidentally smacked Peter in the face. He thought I'd gone mad. I'd had an aversion to big furry bodied moths since childhood and remember hiding under the covers terrified and my kind old grandmother coming up the stairs saying in her broad London twang, "Don't worry I'll get that old morf".

Peter enjoyed watching the Olympics which were held in Barcelona and our first gold medallist was Chris Boardman whose grandfather Billy and his brother Eric had both worked on the ferries with Peter.

We sweltered as a real heat wave set in and one morning it was hot enough to set the boat on fire when a very pungent smell of burning hit our noses but on investigation it turned out to be Blobs taking a short cut across the cooker and burning his tail on the gas jet as he went. I'd never seen such a singed looking moggy. His fur was a patchwork of original ginger blobs mingled with a deeper ginger assortment of singed ones. He just didn't care one jot.

Don't forget to put the cat out Mag

On our way to the Dolphin Inn later we saw a terrapin on a sandy bank of the canal, just one of many that unfortunately ended up being dumped in the canal once their owners realized there was more to looking after them than they'd bargained for. As we sat in the bar of the Dolphin we wondered what had happened to the noisy minah bird that was missing since our last visit. When questioned about it the barman just shrugged his shoulders and said in a matter of fact tone "It ate too many cigarette butts."

By the beginning of August we were back in Fenny Stratford which was a handy place for everything plus good moorings to be had for the cats but one day we tied up on the other side of the stop lock opposite a house which obviously had a passion for water fowl as there were squawking ducks and geese all over their canal side garden. One tiny white duck amazed us when it opened its beak and omitted a loud volley of record breaking high decibel quacks, more suited to a duck the size of an ostrich. We nicknamed him 'klaxon beak' and were glad when we were able to move on to quieter moorings.

Never did two days pass the same and we were forever looking at sights we'd just never have seen when living in a house. Glancing out of the stern doors early one morning I spotted Jessie doing a flat bellied snake-like slow motion cat creep towards an unsuspecting heron perched one legged on the bank, standing stock still, frozen in time, his beady eyes watching the water for a fish. Jesse stealthily inched his way up to within an arms reach of him and then sat still and they both stared hypnotically at each other. I don't think it was a case of love at first sight. Maybe Jesse was just curious to find out how the heron managed to catch fish so easily, or perhaps he had a more ultimate motive and was intent on doing a bit of 'fish snatching' should the opportunity arise.

For sometime we'd discussed the pros and cons of bringing the car down South if we were going to spend the winter on the Grand Union canal, one of the main reasons being that it would enable us to visit and help my mother out more often. She lived in the small village of Kensworth just the other side of Dunstable.

The landlord of the Bridge Inn had no problem with allowing us to park the car in the pub car park, so we made the necessary arrangements for it to be taken to Preston Brook Marina, left with Gary and Heather, where we would pick it up. We left the boat well secured along with the cats shut in with plenty of food, water and litter trays and caught a National Express coach to Warrington which only took two and a quarter hours to get there. Gary and Heather were there to meet us and we went back to their boat and had dinner and caught up on each others' news. It was great to see them again and when it was time for us to leave we hoped that their plans to swap Andante for a narrow boat would materialize so they would be able to leave the marina and go travelling, hopefully in our direction so we'd be able to meet up often. I left a little painted plaque with Gary to give to Heather on her birthday and we said our farewells and left about 7.30pm and under 3 hours driving we were back in Fenny.

We went to visit my mum and tackle a very overdue hedge cutting job for her. The hedge went around the back garden and had grown so much that even Jack of Jack and the beanstalk would have found it daunting. It was so high that the sun had long ago given up showing itself for very long in the garden, apart from when it was high in the sky directly overhead. I don't think my mum's neighbour had seen mum over the garden hedge for many years so she got quite a shock when the hedge was finally reduced from about 10ft to 3ft high and mum yoo-hooed herself over the hedge at her and with a wave said "hello Alice where have you been for the last ten years?" Alice replied somewhat sarcastically, "Are you having a coming out party?" Daylight and neighbours at last!

Hot humid weather brought a terrific electrical storm which raged all of one night, lighting up the sky, while torrential rain clattered deafeningly on the roof and the boat was buffeted around like a cork in the water. During one such storm around 3 pm., there was a terrific flash overhead followed by an almost immediate ear splitting crack of thunder. I looked out and just 50 yards or so away across the canal all the top of a big sycamore tree had been struck and was scorched brown like beech leaves in autumn. Normally we'd have been moored in a spot opposite the tree for shade, but we had learned from experience to avoid such big trees in stormy weather.

Peter had been fly tying and living in hopes of finding somewhere affordable to do a spot of fly fishing and we'd toured around many areas looking for a fishery without any luck.

With the car it was now easier to look and we went off around Milton Keynes and came across quite a few lakes but none for fly fishing. Then quite by chance we came upon a fishery sign pointing up a dirt track so we followed this and kept on the lookout for anyone we could ask about trout fishing in the area, but the place seemed quite deserted. Then way across the field we spotted a lake and on the far side we could see two green fishermen's umbrellas rigged up on the bank. Peter didn't need any more encouragement as he started striding out towards them with me trying to keep up behind him. As we neared the umbrellas there was still no signs of life until we were virtually on top of them and then we saw two old chaps who must have been in their 80's or even 90's by the looks of them, fast asleep under the umbrellas. One woke up with a start, looked up and frowned at Peter. "It's the bloody bailiff again – what do you want?"

The other old boy who had a full set of dentures placed neatly on a handkerchief on the grass alongside him, smiled gummily up at the sky and said,

"You were here yesterday" and the other old boy snapped back at him saying.

"No 'e wasn't cos we weren't 'ere yesterday."

Peter interrupted and asked, "Is there any fly fishing around here?" To which the same old boy snapped back,

"Fly fishing! Do I look as though I'm fly fishing?"

However, once they both emerged from being half asleep they were more amiable and politely gave Peter directions to a small private fishery which we subsequently visited.

Never a dull moment, back at the boat Peter took the back off the TV to see if the faulty speaker connection was an obvious one. We had no sound on the TV and soon realized that lip reading wasn't one of our talents, but neither was sorting out the conglomeration of electronics that appeared inside the TV. So we did the most sensible thing, put the back on again and looked for a repair shop in Bletchley. But the only one we could find wanted a £5 deposit on the estimate which would take them 14 days to quote us a price and be forfeited if we did not agree to accept it. On principle we decided to look elsewhere and I could almost hear what Peter was thinking about the 'offer' which was something about monkeys and nuts.

On the way back to the boat we stopped for some chips and Peter spotted a porta potti left outside at the back of the chippy and made enquiries as to whether it was wanted. The lady serving in the chippy made a phone call and then told us we could have it for £5, so we agreed and were very pleased as it was a nice big and newer loo than the one we had. Our happy bargain mood soon disappeared when we discovered that it was far too big to fit into our toilet compartment alongside the hip bath. There was simply no way it would fit in and the only option if we wanted to keep it was to knock down the bulkhead between the tiny closet and gangway, remove the louvre door and go for the 'open plan' no privacy in the privy look. All would certainly be revealed if we opted for that which did seem to be the solution and to be honest it really was a squash as it was, almost like sitting on the throne in a straight jacket, wedged in tightly between bath and bulkhead. So Peter demolished the bulkhead and I rigged up a curtain for some privacy and retention of modesty, mainly for anyone brave enough to visit or stay with us. I soon discovered that the flush compartment of the porta potti wasn't as easy to fill as the old one, and was also more cumbersome and leaked out when carried by the handle to fill with flushing water and was not as easy to use. We had to sit on it with one foot on a pedal set in a shallow recess halfway up the potti in order to slide open the potti flap and 'GO'.

It was most uncomfortable and felt more like being on a motorbike than a loo.

Peter was in his element as we headed off towards Draycote for a day's fly fishing, but not before we'd turned the boat upside down and spent ages on a witch hunt looking for his fly box. Then a tail back on the M1 set us back an hour and we got our access point to the lake wrong so it was 1pm before we arrived. It wasn't a suitable day for fly fishing, too calm and hot and not a rise to be seen. All of the fish were no doubt having a siesta on the bottom of the lake. We fished from the bank, but after a couple of hours decided to have a motor boat out and try our luck around the lake where there might be a bit of breeze and ripple. Even though the water was like glass most of the time we still enjoyed floating around trying to tempt a fish or two with various flies. Peter managed to catch two good sized rainbow trout and also thought he'd caught a whopper when he cast a fly which caught in my hair, while I only had one bite but was not quick enough and lost it. Being a novice I still had a lot to learn. It was almost dark when we came off the lake and no-one seemed to have been catching much fish, but fish or not we'd had a perfect time.

On a mission to go shopping before the shops shut, we were all ready to leave but Jesse was missing. We walked up and down the thick hedgerows searching and poking with sticks as he was usually curled up in a nice cosy place hidden in the long grass. Being black he was more difficult to see. One and a half hours later I heard a meow coming from a pollarded willow tree and there he was dramatically meowing "I can't get down". The trunk of the tree was thick and stumpy and very gnarled, throwing up masses of slender branches like thick spines among which Jesse was weaving in and out and getting himself continuously tangled up. Peter put a pallet against the trunk to enable him to get a foothold and get higher up and in reach of Jesse but Jesse moved out of reach. I fixed a pouch of mince to the end of a hiking stick, shoved it up through the branches till it was under Jesse's nose and slowly tempted him down to within Peter's grasp. I held my breath as Peter made a grab for him and got him by his collar but success was short lived as the collar snapped and Jesse was about to climb up again. But before he could, Peter swiftly grabbed him by the scruff of his neck and unceremoniously hauled him down. The shopping was postponed.

In late August my friend Shirley invited me to spend a week's holiday with her at Kessingland where she and her husband had a caravan. I was torn between leaving accident prone Peter to his own resources and having a lovely holiday with my friends on the coast. I decided to live dangerously and risk it and Peter assured me he would be fine and that I must go. My nephew Adam would perhaps be able to come and spend a few days with him, so that made the decision easier. In fact I think the pair of them had a whale of a time without me around, just fishing, playing pool and sampling ale at the Bridge Inn plus home brew on the boat, the latter of which Adam had been most impressed with.

By now the nights were drawing in and getting dark just after 8 pm and also chillier. Blobs moved in off the draining board which had been his summer quarters to the warmer step alongside the woodstove in the fore cabin. Wind and rain and clouds of smoke billowed out of the fire doors into the cabin. Winter league of Crib games started and with extreme luck Peter managed to win the first game and then by a fluke he won the second game. He was after my crown for sure.

Although we had the car parked in Fenny Stratford we still missed the bikes when we were some miles distant on other parts of the canal so when we saw a notice saying there was to be a second hand bike sale to be held in Bletchley we made a point of being there early at 9 am, to see what was going. We came away with a Raleigh shopper and a Raleigh mountain bike plus two good locks. It was marvellous to have towpath transport again.

Leaving Fenny we decided to journey to Campbell park near Willen Lakes to join the gathering taking place there – Waterways For You exhibition – over the first weekend in September. The weather wasn't too good but when it brightened up quite a few people stopped to chat, look at our boat, canal wares and walking sticks and buy a few things. We enjoyed the atmosphere, displays and demonstrations of arts and crafts in the marquees and musical entertainment. Among the many stalls was one in aid of the Milton Keynes Wildlife Hospital and it was interesting to chat to the lady and her husband who ran it from their home. In the future we were to seek them out on one or two occasions when we required help and advice regards animals and birds we rescued and they were never too busy to refuse help although they were run off their feet night and day. Another person I talked to was Iris Bryce, the author of Canals Are My Home, which my friend Shirley had bought me for my birthday and which I was actually reading at the time. We enjoyed chatting and sharing our experiences, and identifying with the many pros and cons of living on a canal boat.

Towards the end of the day we decided to go for a little bike ride and see if we could track down the apple tree we'd spotted earlier near bridge 89 but it turned out to be a rather large species of sour crab apple which Peter discovered when he bit into one. It was a wonder he hadn't poisoned himself by now as he was always picking things off trees and bushes and sampling them. We cycled around part of Willen lake – Peter stopping to taste a large red oval shaped fruit (not a plum) off a tree which he said tasted 'sweet'. I had visions of him flipping over onto his back, legs and arms quivering in the air as he went into 'dying fly mode'. He took off on his bike down a rough path across a field and suddenly flew up in the air as the front wheel of his bike hit a rut and threw him up like a bucking bronco, over the handle bars. He landed in a big rugby scum type heap, just missing a sloppy cow pat. I hoped he was alright as I hurried towards him. "How on earth did you manage to do that? What were you doing going off the path like that?" "Easy," he replied and added with a grin, "I was looking for mushrooms the hard way." "Better than any human cannon ball stunt" I laughed. "Can I have an action replay?"

Mushrooming the hard way!

We never managed to find any mushrooms but picked some damsons, so pie was on the evening menu. The wind got up to almost gale force and the cats were very comical chasing around and pouncing on things blowing about. We'd noticed before how they suddenly became very animated and playful when it was windy. Old Blobs joined in and it was funny to see him chasing around too as Jesse sprinted two or three feet up and down bases of trees.

Jesse had us in stitches when he spotted a small grasshopper which he watched with intrepid curiosity. He slowly inched his nose closer, sniffed at it and got a shock when it leaped up in the air and landed a few feet away. Even more mesmerized he followed it around and somehow it ended up, still alive, in the boat, alongside the bed, so we caught it in a glass and put it out on the bank.

The oldest of the two pressure barrels was leaking around the tap, and when the pressure built up we had to twist the tap into upside down position or put up with a puddle of sticky beer running over the floor and down into the gas fire which the barrel stood on. The fire smelled like a brewery when it was lit and the drips of spilt beer would start to burn as it grew hotter and it smelled a bit like toffee apples.

We did a run over to mum's to pick up mail and give her dog Goldie a very overdue bath which took three of us to do and I think I ended up wetter than the dog. Before the bath I volunteered to comb and look for any doggy fleas. I was left on my own to tackle this Nitty Nora mission while everyone else evacuated to the opposite side of the room. I soon discovered why as I found a veritable flea city within her fur. I must have sat combing through, finding and annihilating dozens of fleas one by one for an hour or more and Goldie just lay there enjoying every minute. On completion of that and her bath she must have felt so much better and I felt rather guilty that we had not sorted her out sooner but we had no idea she was such an old flea bag. Mum could not manage to bath her on her own and her failing eyesight was too far gone to attempt looking for fleas.

By now, as Autumn leaves changed colour and began to fall, there was a distinctive air of desolation on the canal. Fungi was popping up everywhere and we picked some "shaggy ink caps" also known as "lawyer's wigs" to cook with breakfast the next day. But overnight they started to turn inky so were soon off the menu. They really had to be picked and eaten a bit younger before they started to open up.

I used quite a few of the crab apples Peter had picked, mixed in with blackberries and a small cooking apple, then stewed and cooked them in a pie which turned out surprisingly tasty.

There was so much rain that even the frogs were coming aboard to shelter and the fields began to resemble the Lake District and grazing cows gathered together marooned on small grassy islands.

Gerald and Freda came to visit and we all went to the local Leisure centre in Bletchley and had a swim followed by an energetic game of table tennis then Peter and Gerald had a game of snooker while Freda and I watched some bowling. Early the following morning Gerald and Freda decided to try out the metal detector but they might have had more luck if they had gone fishing as the previous week a fisherman had hooked a holdall full of jewellery and loot out of the canal near Fenny Stratford Bridge.

While shopping in Tesco, Peter decided to leave me to it and go back to wait in the car and read the paper. He found the car but couldn't open the door and as he struggled with the key a man's voice said "eeyar try this one" and a hand passed a key over his shoulder. Peter spun round and said "How do you know that will fit"?

"Oh don't worry" said the chap "it'll fit, it's my car!" I think Peter wished the ground would swallow him up as he realized our car was parked right next to this exact same model belonging to someone else.

Once before he had parked his car in a very large crowded car park and gone off into town, come back later to find it had gone so had called into the police station to report it stolen. He then went back to the car park and found it was there after all.

We got to know many people who used the canal towpath on a regular basis and would stop for a chat including one Irish man who often came stumbling along on his way home from the local pub as he did one day in his usual pretty sloshed state. He stopped to talk to Peter, leaning on the boat as he did so and getting himself further away from the bank as he continued to lean and push the boat on its slack ropes away from it. Peter grabbed him a few times to stop him from falling in but eventually he slid down between the boat and bank up to his knees in water. Peter heaved him up and pointed him in the right direction home and we hoped he stayed on the path and got there alright. Sadly we knew of others who on return from the pub had not been so lucky and had drowned.

Bike theft seemed to be rife the length and breadth of the country and the twelve year old son of the landlady at the pub actually had his mountain bike stolen from him while he was with it in town, snatched off him and ridden off on by a youth of about sixteen. My son came down for a flying visit and in the short space of time he spent looking for us his mountain bike was stolen from the back of his car. From a nation of shop keepers we seemed to have become a nation of thieves. We were more careful about locking our bikes up now although there were far better bikes to be stolen we were sure. Peter's gears had a mind of their own and one pedal kept coming off.

With signs of winter fast approaching, bringing cold wind and much harsher weather, smoke increasingly billowed out of the wood stove giving us the 'Al Johnson' look. We felt restless for pastures new and to get on the move so after discussing 'where to go' we opted for Napton to see if the little Ibley Dibley lookalike cat was still in need of a home.

Northward through Milton Keynes and across the aqueduct to Cosgrove with its unmistakeable row of tall poplar trees along the canal and the fascinating dark little pedestrian tunnel beneath it, just wide enough to cycle through and years ago to take horses through to be stabled at the Barley Mow pub. Here too ran the Buckingham branch of the canal, only ten miles long originally and with two locks. But it was abandoned in the 1950's and the busy A5 by-pass now ran across the long dewatered majority of it, leaving just a short section at Cosgrove used for mooring boats.

Approaching Isworth Farm we caught a glimpse of a rather wild and furtive vagrant like character scurrying along the hedgerow like a frightened rabbit as we came into view. He reminded me of Catweazle, tall and hunched up with long straggly hair and beard, wearing a loose flowing duffle coat. He was heading for the derelict farm and stared incoherently at us as we passed. No doubt he would be sleeping rough there probably for the night. I couldn't help but think how much he would probably like a hot bowl of our soup.

On leaving Isworth the next day we did the seven locks up to Gayton Junction with a couple on a boat called Dragonfly which they had only had three days. The locks up to Stoke Bruerne could be quite a slog with the heavy gates needing some strong muscle to open them and the paddles on the top lock were quite unbelievable to manipulate. An elderly man came to assist me but gave up after a few turns. We moored for the night at a lonely spot just on from the Junction and Peter fished for a short time and as it turned to dusk both he and Jesse saw a strange silent shape move quickly among the bushes and trees on the opposite bank. Surely Catweazle couldn't have got that far since the day before. Peter said it could have been a domestic animal or perhaps a poacher. What or whoever it was, we made sure the bikes were well secured and the doors. It was a nippy night with frost in the air and Blobs was almost in the wood stove, sitting on a stool in front of its open doors and wouldn't have surprised me if he'd got in to get even warmer. Smells of singed cat mixed with cooking emanated from the galley – Peter duty chef and me chief stoker keeping the fire well stoked up with logs. We were warm as toast and cosy as dormice.

After reaching Weedon and mooring for a night, we arose early with no chance of further sleep as the over enthusiastic bell ringers in the nearby church battered our eardrums. Peter suggested I do a bit of cycling so he was left on the boat while I pedalled along the mostly non existent tow path which in places was so non existent as to have collapsed into the canal, plus much of the path that remained was thick in mud which my shopper bike tyres and small wheels delighted in skidding on. I pedalled like fury getting nowhere fast while Peter added insult to injury by jokingly shouting verbal abuse (unrepeatable) at my expense. I stopped and pelted him with a load of fallen crab apples but he caught most of them and threw them back at me with a more accurate hit rate than I'd had but I managed to duck most of them. At each of the following seven locks I parked my bike and opened the paddles and gates while Peter took life easy on the boat. Age Concern definitely was order of the day. I walked and cycled some five miles to Norton Junction but didn't see much along the way as I was too busy trying to keep my bike wheels going on track. Inevitably I fell off while negotiating a rough uneven stretch between lock pounds but luckily fell towards the hedge and not the canal side which was a three foot drop into the water. After that I informed Peter that I was putting in for a draft to the Royal Yacht!

We came across two large boxes of apples left outside a lock cottage with a notice to "please help your self". We didn't need much encouragement to do just that and it was nice when people actually picked their fruit instead of leaving it to rot. Though the birds also enjoyed them whether still on the trees or on the ground. Berries were colourful and plentiful, from dark purple sloes to the bright reds of woody nightshade, holly, lords and ladies, and black bryony to name a few. Many flowers still hung on to their summer blooms defying winter chills. The small but eye catching orange balsam, hardy herb Robert, common mallow as bright as ever, yarrow, purple heads of tangled straggling tufted vetch and clumps of somewhat faded Michaelmas daisies.

At Welton when we were ready to leave I called Jesse and we watched him come out of a wood right across a ploughed field and run down the edge of the wood in response to our calls, in particular to my high pitched squeaky ones which Peter couldn't match and which the cats could pick up on at quite long distances. They also responded to the banging of a fork or spoon on the metal hatch covers. This particular area was worrying as there were lots of pheasants around and probably gamekeepers too so not a very healthy place for cats to be.

From Braunston and a brief uphill slog of a bike ride to Daventry for essential groceries, followed by yet another puncture repair, we set off mid afternoon in a cold northerly wind and rain, heading for Napton. Peter had tightened the fan belt to see if that was the cause of our batteries not charging as efficiently as they used to and I split a few logs and prepared the fire ready to light later on and also scrubbed Peter's jeans with a view to hanging them outside once we reached our destination.

While Peter was up on deck steering, I prepared our evening meal and cleaned up. He called down to draw my attention to a pair of very long tailed woolly sheep who looked like two AWOL escapees from the flock, who had been living wild for some time on a very overgrown, thickly hedged and pathless stretch of canal, where they could easily exist unseen except by boaters. Along this remote part of the canal much of the towpath did not exist and the area was very unpopulated apart from a few isolated farms. In two days we didn't see one person, with or without a dog, walk past us which was quite a nice change. Flocks of lapwing mingled with odd numbers of starlings in the fields and there were numerous sightings of kingfishers darting low along the canal.

At Napton the lady in the craft shop at the Folly had sold six of the nine walking sticks we'd left with her, which after commission left us with a nice amount of £25. We had another nine sticks to leave with her but before doing so we would have to make a two hour return to Braunston and back to pick up a mail package containing a supply of ferrules in order to fit some on the sticks to be left at the shop.

I walked up to the lock shop to see the couple there who had all the cats, plus some new ones of about 8-12 weeks old and decided that it would be less traumatic for us, Jesse and Blobs and the new crew member if we adopted a kitten rather than "Trevor" the older and wilder cat we had previously said we'd come back for when visiting in July. So the lock keeper showed me the cats and kittens in the barn and I chose a tiny fluffy tabby that we'd taken a liking to earlier and said we'd collect him in the morning. He was to be new crew member Able Seaman "Oggie bottom lock".

On a cold and frosty Friday 16th October our new shipmate of around just nine weeks old joined ship and was officially named "Yetti". I'd cycled up to the shop in Napton to buy some fresh milk for him plus a donation of tinned cat food for the lock keeper's large family of cats and kittens. He managed to catch our chosen one at feeding time when Yetti was not managing to get a look in at the food put down as it was a free for all and the mostly larger than him youngsters kept his nose out of it. He was even smaller than he looked as his fluffy fur was deceiving to the eye and made him look bigger than he was. He felt so scrawny and light when I held him and bundled him down into the warmth and safety of my padded shirt and conveyed him back to the boat. The chosen name of Yetti referred to his very large white and tufted (between the foot pads) abominable snowman like feet in proportion to the rest of his body apart from his large ears and big eyes. He had a white bib and chin and sometimes his facial markings looked as though he had a bit of a moustache. His tail was like that of a squirrel but bushier and the tufts of fur on his ears made him look like a real Norwegian forest cat. His feral mother was of mixed colouring, partly tortoise-shell but he was a beautifully patterned grey and black tabby.

We had watched the mother cat a few days ago across the lock in the yard with two other kittens, one of whom had a mouse. One was ginger and white and the other white and tabby with a bit of ginger and both were short haired. There were still a lot of the black and white ones about too.

So much for us thinking a kitten would be 'easier' to initiate into life aboard with us. How wrong we were proved to be. I cleared a space under the bed and blocked half off so he couldn't squeeze under any small gaps and disappear in the many 'kitten unfriendly' spaces such as under the bath decking or behind the tongue and groove and all the other hidden inaccessible areas he might be tempted in fear to retreat to. As much as possible we kept him with us on our laps and carefully watched him while all was so very new and terrifying to him, as it obviously was. He was so scared it was pitiful and he hid behind boxes much of the time that day when we were unable to nurse him. When I retrieved him later on from the boxes and gently stroked and talked to him and then put him snugly under my shirt between it and my jumper he settled down more and as the evening wore on he became less scared and had some milk and cat food. All too good to be true we relaxed and when we eventually decided it was bed time we realized that Yetti was absent. We soon discovered that there was a small gap some 3 by 3 inches in the tongue and groove panelling down by the side of the woodstove and that, as there was nowhere else for him to go, that he must have squeezed through it and was now somewhere in the vast unknown between the steel hull and the tongue and groove panelling of the cabins and worse that there was nothing to stop him working his way all down the boat, or of knowing where he was. Without two thoughts about it, Peter just ripped off a strip of tongue and groove leading from the hole and made a lucky grab at one surprised fluff ball before he could escape further. Peter replaced and repaired the panel temporarily and secured the hole.

By day two Yetti was getting more confident and getting onto our laps and making a fuss but still nervous of sudden movement and noises and constantly wanting to get out which I suppose was his motive for getting into any available holes. He was eating as though there was no tomorrow and licking out the remains of our soup bowls and his little belly was as fat and firm as a football.

Disaster struck again that afternoon after Peter had left on his bike to go to the shop and I was in the galley washing up, having left Yetti secure in the fore cabin, or so I thought. On going back into the cabin I wondered where he was hiding or sleeping and checked my padded shirt which was on the seating, as he'd took to crawling into it like some warm refuge or surrogate mum cat substitute. No Yetti anywhere and I felt uneasy knowing that in such a small area of some 7ft x 8ft of the cabin it didn't take much to work out that he had definitely disappeared. To where? That was the question. I was glad when Peter soon arrived back and together we discovered that the little rascal had once more dislodged the temporary repair over the hole and disappeared into the void behind it. I put my arm through the hole and felt around and shone a torch in, but nothing and not a sound. Visions of Yetti working his way along confined spaces and around obstructions of all kinds and trapped somewhere ran horribly through my mind. Could he even fall down into the bilges or astern under the deck boards into the engine housing and water that collected there? My mind started running amuck imagining the unimaginable as minds do at such times and not helped by the fact that he must have been so very frightened. We dislodged more tongue and groove all along as far as the bulkhead between the fore cabin and the bedroom and sat quietly waiting to hear a noise which would give us some indication of where he was. Nothing, so at 7.30pm we took off more panels further along on the bedroom side of the bulkhead. 11pm and still not a murmur and I felt sure that we should have heard something as much of the space between the panelling and steel outer structure was filled with polystyrene and insulation material and when disturbed polystyrene makes a squeaking noise. Had he got himself trapped behind or among all the pipes or somewhere freezing cold as he was such a tiny scrap of flesh and bone? All we could do was sit and wait, for the time being. It was awful.

Peter went to bed around midnight and I stayed up in the fore cabin in the dark and quiet, straining my ears in the hopes of hearing some noise from Yetti and now and then I thought I heard him. But at times like that ones mind played tricks.

Peter came out again to sit with me as he couldn't sleep either and just before 1 am we both thought we heard faint scuffling noises between the bedroom and fore cabin panels. I pulled a panel out and could feel a pipe with lagging on which Yetti would perhaps be able to get onto. Peter loosened the adjoining panel in the bedroom a bit more and I poked food in which was instantly met by a kitten sized growl so we knew he was there and felt such a wave of happiness. We turned out the lights and sat quiet and Yetti resumed scuffling around trying to find a way out no doubt, which he really did have to do as if we approached with our hands, he just retreated in fear. We didn't want him going off into the wrong directions and hoped he would soon get out but after what seemed like hours of more scratting around and not coming out we took further drastic action and removed yet another panel lower down in the bedroom. The boat was slowly being demolished. Maybe we should have called the fire brigade, or better still learned not to recruit more felines. 4 am and suddenly two big ears appeared level with the bed and Peter made a grab for him, missed and Yetti disappeared again. We finally and determinedly grabbed him when he was squashed down behind the lower panel where it narrowed to a V shaped space. What chaos to be caused by such a tiny ball of fur. At 5 am we eventually crawled into bed with Yetti secured for the rest of the night in a plastic storage crate with a piece of wood on top to stop him getting out until Peter could repair all the panelling the next day and make sure there were no more Yetti sized holes left for him to get through. I hoped he would hurry up and grow quickly so he couldn't access small spaces. He soon became a real little fuss pot, very playful and as fat as butter. He was using his litter tray and settling down well but Jesse and Blobs were not at all amused with his antics and there was much growling and hissing going on.

Yetti had taken up enough of our time and our next priority was to get on the move to find wood, lots of it, as we were down to the last of a few logs.

Quite by some miraculous accident, and all too good to believe, while we were moored up some miles out of Napton, we came across a lot of long straight rounded posts some 4 or 5inches in diameter lying half hidden in long grass in a field alongside the towpath They had obviously been there a considerable time and were in the early stages of decay and rightly or wrongly we decided it was a waste to leave them to rot when we could put them to good use and before long we had them stowed aboard down in the 2ft wide gangway between our bed and the boat's side. With these wet and slimy posts came a community of disturbed residents of the creepy crawly variety. I was glad that Peter slept gangway side of the bed and would hopefully provide a human barrier to any would be creepy travellers that strayed off the logs. The sooner we got them logged up the better as it was difficult getting along the gangway clambering over them.

Next day after travelling on, we finally stopped on a wide area of bank and logged up the posts which half filled the fore peak space under deck and then we found a lot of off cuts of branches where some hedges had been thinned and laid. We felt very pleased with ourselves and as it was a lovely sunny warm day we sat out and enjoyed a snack. Jesse kept disappearing into a wood which was some way off and there was also a busy road in the vicinity so we moved on to a more deserted area for the night. The only person we saw all next day was a chap on a bike who said he was cycling to meet his wife who had left Braunston about an hour ago and that he was heading for Napton. He had been on the roads and just found the road bridge that joined the canal and assumed he was heading in the right direction. We told him that he was going in the wrong direction so he did an about turn and 10 minutes later we saw him and his wife pass by on their boat.

Yetti was now allowed to explore more of the inside of the boat and was not as nervous. Blobs and Jesse still growled and hissed at him and Jesse was really put out by his presence, so much so that after giving him more black looks he went off in protest to sleep in the cupboard under the sink.

We found the body of a weasel lying by the boat the following morning, no doubt the unfortunate victim of Jesse. Attention seeking or what? He also knocked the remains of the soup off the cooker, most of which landed all over me in my nightie, thick cold sloppy lumpy stuff. Jesse got a splattering of it too and he shot off like a scalded cat.

Then the batteries went flat so the engine wouldn't start but it didn't take long to charge them up enough to get us going again. Meanwhile Peter fixed my back bike brake but on my next trip out on it I found he'd made it far too tight and as a result I had to even pedal going downhill.

Chapter Ten

Jesse Goes Missing

By late October there was far too much condensation forming everywhere aft so I wiped all around the windows and wherever excesses of moisture and green mould were forming including droplets on ceilings before they grew to drip down size.

Between sharp showers I hung washing out on the rotary line and hedges and started splitting some logs but another heavy downfall put paid to that. Peter sensibly called it a day and watched snooker on TV.

It was nice to have a few days to relax in and catch up on jobs, plus find time to paint some butterflies on plaques for Xmas presents. Peter worked up on the stern deck when the weather permitted and enjoyed watching the world go by. He was watching the antics of two squirrels running around one day when loud gunshots shattered the moment and he quickly called Jesse in. The shooter appeared and chatted to Peter for sometime and said he was just taking random pot shots at any pigeons that happened to fly over and that he'd frequently had a few ducks. Then he informed Peter that he'd also killed a couple of swans to eat! How **terrible!** Quite against the law of course too. I think Peter would have punched him if it hadn't have been for the fact that by now he realised the man wasn't quite 'a full shilling' and said things to make an impression. The point was rather proved when he fired his single barrel shotgun, looking backward over his shoulder and up in the air as he did so. We kept Jesse in till gone dusk.

It was hot in the fore cabin that night even though British summertime was due to end. Not surprisingly though as when I glanced at the thermometer it showed 92 degrees farenheight. (some 31c). It was a wonder the wood stove didn't explode with the heat it generated sometimes. In comparison back aft in the galley it was about 40f. (6c) On many mornings I was now having to get up around 5 or 6 am to walk about, wash up, make tea, or feed the cats, just to ease my joint pains. Not the best place to live with arthritis.

Running short of petrol for the generator and completely out of water we had no choice next day but to move on to Braunston for more and a new gas cylinder while we were at it and then moved on up six locks and through the tunnel with an elderly couple on a boat called 'Sherbourne'.

We now had to make sure we travelled past Buckby locks before the winter stoppages started and certain locks and stretches of canal were closed to boaters in order for repairs and maintenance work to be carried out on them. Peter wasn't in a rush and was mesmerized with the appearance of pheasants everywhere and watched one come flying out of a nearby copse where it had gone to ground. It shot up in the air with a noisy explosion of urgency, probably disturbed by the big fox which Peter had seen in the same vicinity. No doubt Mr Fox, like Peter, was itching to get one on his dinner plate too. Peter disappeared at dusk and came back sometime later with a pheasant tucked under his jacket. It was soon hanging in the WC compartment over the hip bath where Jesse tried taking a few swipes at it, but it was safely out of his reach. It was the first pheasant Peter had caught in 2 years and he soon got down to sorting it out the next day to the strains of "I am a pleasant pheasant plucker".

We moved on to moor up alongside an open field with sheep in. Blobs and Yetti were both sitting up on the shelf together and earlier in the day all three cats were asleep on the bed together. We spent the last hour of daylight sitting out watching three terns and two crows swooping back and forward over the canal, all vying for a small fish. It seemed a dead certainty that one of the terns would get it so we were quite surprised when one of the crows swooped down and successfully caught it in its beak and flew off. Then we caught a quick glimpse of a mink scurrying along the waters edge with quite a large fish in his mouth. He soon made himself scarce and disappeared under the overhanging bushes. There was always something of interest to enjoy looking at.

In the morning little Yetti was all curled up in the bed with Peter. We hoped to find a suitable place to let him go out as soon as possible and felt confident that by now he would want to always return to his home on the boat. We hoped too that if he fell into the canal he would not get too waterlogged with all his long fur so as not to be able to swim or scramble out. The 30th October was designated to become the day for his first run ashore and the doors were opened for him. He gingerly made his way out and then went leaping and bounding exuberantly around the towpath, playing. He didn't go far and we kept an eye on him BUT, when he leapt aboard for the approximate twentieth time he misjudged his step and fell down into the water. But Peter had him out in a flash – one little drowned rat. Later on we let him out again and he was springing around then disappeared and we spent an uneasy and frantic half hour looking for him as he seemed to have just vanished into thin air from the towpath. We were getting quite despondent until Peter lifted the stern deck boards and the poor little mite was crouching on the generator. He had gone down the stern deck gap and into the engine compartment, so that was another gap we would have to block off till he knew his way round these sort of obstacles. Well we calculated that he had now had about three of his nine lives.

Halloween and Jesse caught a mouse and dropped it in front of Yetti like a token of peace. Yetti grabbed it fiercely and growled at us if we so much as went near him. He ran up the towpath with it hanging from his jaws and compared to the size of Yetti the mouse looked huge hanging there. Yetti jumped aboard with it and spent the next half hour throwing it around and pouncing on it before he finally scoffed the lot, tail, feet and all. He then leaped up onto my shoulder and perched there with front paws on the window, having a good old nosey out.

Blobs was very congested, having a job to breath through his nose so we really did need to get him checked out at a vet's as soon as possible again.

Jesse disappeared around 6pm and was still not around by 10pm. By midnight we were up and dressed and walking up the canal calling him. We couldn't understand it as the area was mostly open fields either ploughed or for grazing sheep, with just a thin low hedge between the towpath. We stayed up all night, dozed a bit around 4 am, then at first light we resumed out searching up and down the canal bank calling in the hedge and across the fields. We met an extremely understanding fishing bailiff and he assured us that it was a safe enough area. Our minds started to ask the usual anxious questions. Had he got lost, drowned, killed by a fox, or stuck up a tree? All were extremely unlikely. We tramped off through a sheep grazing field and a long way round the perimeter of a huge ploughed field calling and calling against the strong wind which cut our calls short. We checked the overflow and stream and then crossed a farm bridge adjoining the fields on the far bank, walked along the edge of a field to the railway line and along a small road running alongside a wood where we had heard shots fired some half hour or so ago We asked a man walking an Alsatian dog if he'd seen a black cat and he said there was one in the road up on the bend. Even then, at first we dismissed it as not being Jesse, he wouldn't go off that far! Also when we came across the dead black cat on the verge at the side of the road it had no collar on and its tail was all bushy and I told myself it wasn't Jesse. Peter said it must be and that a killed by a car dead cat would not look the same as a live one and it was too much of a coincidence that it could be another black cat and not Jesse in such a deserted area. But he didn't have Jesse's red collar on I argued so it can't be him. Peter reasonably suggested that someone may have removed it so as to get in touch with the owners. A possibility I agreed. Halfway back to the boat I decided to walk back with Peter and have another look at the unfortunate moggie. So we did and although there was just something about the body that didn't convince me it was Jesse, until I looked at the beautiful eyes that unlike the body still seemed to shine with life, and accepted that it was Jesse. Devastated we carried him back to the boat.

We were now too upset to stay around this area and almost akin to a tribute as we left it five swans flew up the canal, their wings whirring like a swansong to Jesse. Later on a young swan locked down two locks with us as he couldn't yet fly. He placed himself up for'd between our bow and the gates. On the second lock he got impatient and as the lock water flooded to the top and over the gates he took a plunge with the cascading overflow of water and floundered over and down the gates into the canal below.

Travelling on through Blisworth and Stoke Bruerne we stopped opposite Grafton Regis and the little manorial settlement across the canal overlooked by the church tower and directly in line with the opposite towering spire on the distant horizon of another church. It was here that Peter buried Jesse over the fence on the bank of a sheep field – like one of the flock Jesse was now called home to rest. I left a red paper carnation on the fence post and a bit of my heart with it. Later on I painted a stone and placed it at the spot in his memory and it was there for many years. We also sent local postcards to the shops in the Bugbrooke area asking for information from anyone who might happen to know anything about the accident and whereabouts of the collar to contact us. It was a long shot at the time when we didn't know just how important it would turn out to be in the future.

Moored up at Cosgrove we fed a very thin and hungry greyhound type bitch, who had obviously recently had pups to feed. She had no collar and she devoured the tin of cat food and a pint of milk that we gave her as if there was no tomorrow.

As we left the picturesque and rather pastoral olde worlde scenery north of the aqueduct across the river Ouse we approached Wolverton, which in contrast had an oppressive and gloomy air to it as towering derelict blocks of factory and warehouse buildings loomed up at the waters edge throwing dark cold and sinister shadows across the canal. Immediately within yards of the towpath ran the railway line which had once been the heart of Wolverton's very existence. Those massive workshops and maintenance sheds covered a large and intricate area where so many trains had once served their purposes, including none less than 'The Royal Train' which had been based there. Some many years later when we'd become reluctant land lubbers, we were neighbours to the widow of one of the fitters who'd been assigned to travel with the train as and when he was required, often at short notice and at all hours day and night to make sure the train was in 100% running order. His widow Gertrude told us of the sad day for him and his family when while working on a particular job with another man he was involved in an accident resulting in two of his fingers being trapped and cut off. Sadly for him it was the end of his job on the Royal Train, but Gertrude proudly showed us the framed certificate he had been awarded acknowledging his services.

Near Campbell Park we stopped briefly to let Yetti out. He was still very nervous. We fished out a brand new packet of football shin protectors from the canal and found a sports bag on the bank which contained a brand new pair of soccer boots and just one Adidas trainer, the other one being a few yards further on with a towel and pair of new socks.

As we continued on our way, Peter committed the unforgivable when he forgot to haul in the stern mooring rope and as a consequence it became all wound around the propeller so we had to stop while he hacked it all off.

A boater hailed us as we neared Fenny Stratford to tell us that a chap had been asking after the whereabouts of a boat with butterflies painted on it. The boater said he remembered us more for the rotary washing line we had up on our bow than for butterflies. Not far away we saw Gerald walking down the towpath towards us, glad at last to have located us and ready for a hot mug of tea.

Freda also called in during the week and while she was with us we had a visit from the thin greyhound bitch that we had fed up at Cosgrove. She had such a lovely face and such sorrowful pleading eyes, so I gave her a whole tin of cat food, a bowl of milk and some Go-cat biscuits. She then settled down on the stern deck and was shivering with cold. Only the presence of the cats prevented me from bringing her into the cabin for a warm.

After Freda left we decided to move out into the countryside away from the hustle and bustle of Fenny and found a nice spot near Stoke Hammond. During the night we heard something on the stern. It sounded like an animal and on opening one of the stern doors just enough to peep out, we glimpsed a small dog sized animal which quickly ran off up the towpath. We noticed that the spare rib bones we'd put out earlier had all gone, so later on I put a saucer of cat food out and watched from the kitchen for further signs of the hungry creature but nothing turned up. Not surprisingly however, in the morning the food had gone.

Our minds were still uneasy with unanswered questions regarding Jesse's collar and as the car was still available at Fenny we decided to go on a sad mission back to Bugbrooke and search the roadside verge for it in case we had missed it at the time. Once there, we walked along the road to the bend and searched as thoroughly as we could, moving the leaves and foliage on the bank with our sticks but to no avail, nothing! We checked that the postcards were in the local shops and spoke to a couple of locals including one along the towpath where we finally walked along to the mooring we had been in when Jesse disappeared. I even found myself calling him and pictured him coming running out of the hedge to us. Why did we torture ourselves, giving in to remote inclinations of the mind, especially in my case as something I just could not understand was eating away at my thoughts?

Towards the end of November, a young man in his twenties cycled past the boat. He pitched his small tent up by the bridge, cursing the wind as he did so, unpacked his gear from off his bike then came along to the boat proffering a tin mug and asked if we could spare him a couple of spoonsful of coffee. "Bit expensive coffee, don't you drink tea?" I joked. "No I only drink coffee" he replied blandly. So I gave him a good heaping of coffee which would provide him with a few mugs of coffee and offered him some milk which he declined. He looked as though he'd been roughing it for awhile, with a dishevelled, un-ironed look, dirty hands and generally grubby appearance and the arse out of his pants, and he was very cold. In an ideal world, a more trustworthy situation, if there could have been such a thing those days, we could have invited him in for a warm, but it was not that sort of a world unfortunately. I think maybe that had been his motive as he seemed reluctant to go back to his dome shaped tent. Said he was waiting for friends on a boat to pick him up, supposedly 10 days ago. With "safety" in mind that night we made sure all lump hammers, iron pegs, and the axe were brought into the boat.

Thinking back to the days when the canals were being built, the people living in the nearby towns and villages must have experienced great anxieties from such close proximity to the navvies working on the construction of them. The navvies were housed in special camps and on pay nights they took to drinking and brawling on a large scale. Many poorly paid farm labourers were tempted away from working on the land to join the navvies. This loss of labour on the land caused havoc at harvest time and as a result in 1793 work on the canals was banned during harvest time. I wondered what those navvies would think if they could see the results of their hard labour now.

By the end of November we were mostly to-ing and fro-ing between Leighton Buzzard and Fenny Stratford. Leighton Buzzard was handy for shopping with a supermarket adjacent to the canal. We collected our mail from the Post office at Fenny and enjoyed mooring along quieter stretches. There was a lovely little card and letter from my six year old grand daughter which brought a tear to my eye as I read the words – *"Dear granny, I am sorry to hear Jessy has died. I love you very much and do not like you being upset. Please get smiling again soon. Love Joelle x"*

Mooring up near two 'smokey stover' boats I noticed a black cat with a red collar on and the following day I just had to get off our boat to go and have a closer look at it. My mind still played cruel tricks. The cat looked up at me with large Jesse type eyes and meowed, and I felt quite choked up. Scrambling quickly back down the hatchway of our boat I caught my jacket on the saucepan handle of a pan of potatoes boiling on the stove and it tipped up and poured the water down onto my foot. I did a good impression of an Indian doing a war dance and threw my leg up onto the sink and ran cold water over my foot. I sat nursing a sore foot which even though it had been protected with a sock and footwear produced a large sausage shaped blister.

With nothing better to do I scribbled an ode to Jesse:-

Don't go near any roads Jesse when you're out tonight
Stay away from the road Jesse, where you'll be alright.
Don't go near any road Jesse where you hadn't oughta.
Stay away from roads Jesse, safe by the boat and water.
Don't go up to the road Jesse, tonight when you're hunting prey.
Don't cross over the farm bridge Jesse, away oe'r the fields don't stray.
Please! Don't cross the road Jesse, into the woodland there.
Watch out! Watch out! The car! Quick run. Too late Jesse dear!

★ ★ ★

The next morning I was up and chopping wood at 8.30 while the Captain snored on. Blobs disappeared and I panicked as three lurchers and a black dog came down the towpath but reassuringly the owner put them all on leads before reaching the boat and Blobs in the meantime safely appeared. Once Peter was up we finished splitting and cutting all the logs up but not before the axe head flew up off its shaft and disappeared into the water. Peter managed to locate it with the strong magnet we had on the end of a line but lost it a second time and did not get so lucky. Too late to kick himself for not putting a new shaft onto the axe once it became loose.

We decided we would nip up to Leighton Buzzard to fill up with water and as we approached the disused swing bridge we were hailed by what looked like an eccentric lepidopterist frantically waving a huge net. As we slowed down and drew nearer we recognized the young tall bearded lad Tony from off the two moored boats along from 'The Globe'.

"We're trying to catch a duck" he yelled and there then appeared a uniformed RSPCA officer also equipped with a large landing net and yet another officer in a canoe driving two ducks, a large white Aylesbury and a colourful mallard drake up the canal towards the nets. According to Tony they had been after the drake for about a week now as it had a plastic four holed can holder over its head caught and pulled tightly between and around its beak, preventing it from feeding.

Tony asked if we could block off the narrow gap between the swing bridge with our boat, so I scrambled for'd and tied the bow rope to the swing bridge, with the stern across the other side where Peter then pushed the stern off a foot or two so that once trapped, the ducks would make for the only exit left between bank and boat where the nets would be waiting. The canoeist proceeded to paddle to and fro forcing the ducks towards us while Tony crouched alongside the swing bridge next to our bow with his net at the ready, plus an officer with his net ready by the gap astern. Once or twice it looked as though the ducks were going to quickly slip round the canoeist but his manoeuvres outwitted theirs, aided by a few loud slaps on the water with the flat of the paddle. Nearer and nearer they came and suddenly, in a flash, Tony swished his net down and yelled "got it!" as he followed suit with one hell of a splash into the water and momentarily completely disappeared as the water was unusually deep at this point. Moments later a frenzy of boiling water erupted with frantically splashing Tony kicking out with his legs with net raised aloft in the air and much to our disbelief still containing the duck. We were all full of admiration as we hauled them both aboard and the duck was given priority attention, while Tony shivered with cold, as one of the RSPCA officers cut off the plastic can holder, quickly assessed the duck and returned it to the water where it scuttled of quacking noisily. All sympathies were then transferred to Tony's sorry state as it wasn't the ideal time of the year for a dip in the canal. We soon had him warmed up and off back to his boat for a change of dry clothes.

The towpath all along the stretch to Leighton Buzzard was mostly water logged and a quagmire of oozy mud, not at all fit for cycling along. So we made a detour onto a nearby road and then onto pavements for the best part of the journey which was very handy coming back as we had no lights on our bikes. We always felt safer away from built up areas and at this present time I was glad we were not in Milton Keynes as during the past few months about seventeen women had been attacked and only recently a young girl had been dragged off a busy walkway and raped in broad daylight.

We'd often bump into a few boaters we knew while shopping at the Leighton Buzzard super market which was conveniently adjacent to the canal and it was always nice to meet up with friendly faces that we'd not seen for awhile. It was interesting to hear what they had been getting up to, where they had travelled to and to catch up on canal 'grapevine' gossip. One such well travelled elderly couple were on a boat called "Ours II" and we exchanged many humorous experiences with them. By the time we'd met up with them and other boaters we seemed to have spent more time chatting than shopping, but time was one thing we didn't have to skimp on.

The couple who lived on "Monkey Business" were not at all happy about having to pay £20 a week to BWB for a horrible muddy and not at all private mooring. In fact BWB was very high on the boater's 'moan list'.

We waved to "Lady Melinda", the 'duck' boat as we called it, complete with it's additional crew of large Aylesbury ducks on the stern deck. The lady skipper was chatting away fondly to them as she steered the boat, and gave us a friendly wave and indicated she was on her way to Soulbury three locks. If my memory serves me right she made some beautiful lace.

Often parked up in the small remote car park at bridge 110 there was a young chap living in an ex BT van. It had a stove in it with a chimney in the roof which gave it away as being lived in, but sensibly had no windows.

A fisherman who regularly chatted to us enjoyed a hot bowl of our stew which we shared with him one very cold day. He sat and ate it on the bank where he was fishing and when he had finished he said it had gone down a treat and warmed him up. He and Peter got onto the subject of ducks and geese and the rumour, be it true or false, that many a fisherman goes home with a duck or two for his dinner?

I had a hospital examination appointment at the beginning of December up in Lancashire so as we were going to have to leave the cats shut in the boat we had to plan on a real flying visit of a trip. We left plenty of cat food, water and litter trays out for them when we left at 11pm on the Wednesday night and arrived at out destination at 3 am Thursday. We were absolutely ready to fall into bed, or as things turned out to be, with me on the settee and Peter on a camp bed which promptly tipped up and threw him backwards into the fireplace when he sat down on it. We were not too tired to find that hilarious.

We managed to see most of the family even though it was a very tight scheduled visit. When we drove up to Mark, my youngest son's house, a black cat ran across the road, past the car and onto his front door step. It was raining hard and as he opened the door the cat tried it's hardest to get in. Mark said it was a stray and that one of his friends had been letting it in and sometimes fed it when it was around but that it did the rounds up the street and no one seemed to know where it had come from. It was out in all weathers and always trying to get in and always hungry. Mark was going down to see his friends and said we could pop down with him and see it if we liked. We should have refrained but we went along to see and it was there. I knew as soon as I saw it that I wanted to give it a home, no doubt even more so because it was so like Jesse, especially it's beautiful eyes. Mark's wife Samantha did one of her expert "he or she" examinations and exclaimed "it's a she" AND, we all agreed "HAVING KITTENS". Oh dear! That seemed to put the blocks on things. "Come on" said Peter "Let's get going".

My heart dropped. What would happen to her now? She was even more in need of a loving home now if she was having kittens. But Peter, more sensible than me, weighed it all up and didn't think it at all practical and urged me to forget it. No one was prepared to give her a permanent home so all I could ask or hope for was that the lad and his friends and anyone else who had fed the cat would continue to look out for and feed her and perhaps take her and her kittens in. As a last desperate measure I said that if she was still around after having had her kittens and not homed that we would come up and get her. Leaving wasn't being made any easier either, as she meowed up at me and wound herself seductively all around my legs.

Suddenly, I heard some unbelievably magic words.

"We'll take her with us."

I couldn't believe my ears, but the truth of the matter was that Peter was as soft, or softer than I, and had weakened. Mark scuttled about and obtained two cardboard boxes from the corner shop and we soon had puss in it, along with a tin of cat food someone had provided us with.

"Jessica" as it had to be, forced her way out of the box so I had to hold her tightly in my arms while she loudly meowed continuously. Back at my daughter's home she wandered around all over the place exploring and not seeming unduly concerned. Just after midnight that Thursday night we set off home and made good time without rushing.

Jessica was boxed up securely but she cried pitifully a lot of the way. I poked my fingers through the holes in the box and stroked her when I managed to locate her. Then about two thirds of the way into the journey home, she had to go to the toilet and unavoidably got some of it onto herself and was very pongy, poor thing. Getting towards dawn at 5 am, we arrived at the boat which was slippery with a film of ice on its steel upper structure and wooden deck boards. To our great relief the cats were fine in their fur coats. I lit the gas fire while Peter scrambled down the forepeak for wood to get the stove going. Jessica was then released and wiped all over with a warm cloth. She was soon purring and strolling around as if she had always lived on a boat. By 7 am. we were all asleep snoring and purring together.

During the following morning Blobs slipped on the narrow icy gunwale into the water which was freezing. Luckily I heard a noise and thought it was up on the roof, but on investigating saw Blobs struggling to swim round the boat to the bank. But I don't think he would have managed on his own as the part of the bank we'd moored along was reinforced with steep metal which he would not have been able to get a grip on with his claws. I soon had him out and Peter dried him as best he could with a towel and the gas fire did the rest. Blobs had the first of his colourful winter singes to his fur coat, making him ginger, white and singe brown. Jessica, such a beautiful, graceful, gentle natured cat, purred and meowed loudly and seemed content enough to stay on the bed, under the bed in the boxes or in the kitchen when she was peckish and on the scrounge, but very frightened when I took her up on deck to see if she wanted a run ashore on a harness and lead, so she obviously wasn't ready for that adventure yet. She went up to Yetti and sniffed noses with him then spat at him and walked off. Yetti was a bundle of fun and loved to retrieve silver balls of rolled up tin foil which we would throw for him to chase. He usually intercepted them and caught some in his paws. Very early one morning he came noseying in at me in my sleeping bag. He trod clumsily on my face a few times, before crawling in and out of the sleeping bag. It was all a ploy to get me up and into the galley to dish up the cat food.

A week after returning with Jessica, she decided one evening after dark to venture out, followed by Yetti all full of fun and mischief. An hour later there was no sign of her and we trudged around, through the hedge, up the hedgerow and towpath calling her but she just sauntered back when she was ready, much later on. It had been a worry settling both her and Yetti down but soon we'd be able to relax more with them and get rid of the two litter trays. With all living in such close proximity to one another it was impossible to escape the many 'PONGS' which always seemed to happen just as we were settling down in bed or just after I'd emptied the trays and put fresh litter in. Or even worse, just as we'd sat down for a meal.

Jessica quickly proved that she was another 'hunter' when she jumped aboard with a dead mouse dangling from her jaws. Yetti managed to get hold of it and spent about 45 minutes throwing it up in the air, leaping around and playing with it till he wore himself out.

During these long winter months we looked forward to occasional visits from Gerald and Freda and my friend Shirley and her husband Fred. We always had lots to talk about and often walked up into Fenny Stratford, perhaps for lunch at one of the pubs or a social game of darts. We got to hear all the local gossip, including all about the latest spate of thefts going on. A chap moored by the bridge warned us to make sure our generator was secured as they were always a target for thieves. He said that the previous year in the area between Milton Keynes and London around 200 of them had been stolen off boats.

On a happier note, I cycled into Bletchley mid December and ordered a 7lb turkey at 99p a lb before we travelled a few miles into an area of Milton Keynes where I was able to cycle up into the main shopping centre to look round the shops and market to find a Tiny Tears' doll for my grand daughter Danielle. Good job I hadn't cycled there the previous day as there had been a bomb scare and the centre had been shut off.

I was spending more and more time awake during the nights and having to get up just to ease the pain in my knees, hips and back, walk around a bit, drink tea and try to be quiet so as not to disturb Peter. But he never worried about being woken up and he too was suffering discomfort with stiff and aching joints. We were a right pair of old crocks but whatever the time of night we were always ready for a cup of tea together and a talk about anything and everything and lots of therapeutic laughs. Under the circumstances a less healthy climate and UK lifestyle surely would have been hard to find in the winter.

It didn't help matters when we unavoidably had to travel, rain, snow or what. After my shopping trip into Milton Keynes we aimed to move on some miles to Cosgrove where the moorings were good and pleasant with other boats moored. But this was easier said than done, as the downpours became more frequent and we came to a halt at bridge 69 which was closed for repairs until the 18th Dec (two days time). One compensation, however was to find that BW had been clearing and thinning trees near the bridge and had left a lot of branches, so, already soaked to the skin we spent a couple of hours retrieving as much wood as we could, piling it up on top the boat before turning the boat around and returning south of Wolverton to find a suitable spot to moor up. 'Muddy and wet' sure was the 'rig of the day'. After settling down and getting dry and warm and ready to have some hot soup we couldn't find Blobs or remember having seen him for quite some time, which was out of character for warmth loving Blobs. We looked everywhere and decided he must have got ashore when we were wooding and that we'd left without him, somewhere up near bridge 69. Our hearts sank but inevitably with no sign of him anywhere we decided we would have go back and look for him, which would be difficult in the dark, and as Peter's bike brakes were not working and one of his tyres were flat we'd have to walk. We walked and called for what must have been in total a round trip of three or four miles to the bridge and back but no Blobs. Completely worn out we fell into the warmth of the fore-cabin and thought we were hallucinating. Blobs was stretched out up on the window shelf fast asleep! "Roll on Christmas!"

Two days before Christmas temperatures dropped below freezing, ice formed on the insides of the windows and icicles hung down from the stern doors.

Problems with the car not starting altered our Christmas day plans but Freda's son kindly came to the rescue and gave us a lift over to mum's. Having travelled a quarter of the journey there we realized we had left the cooked turkey in the oven, the safest place to leave it from the cats, so we had to do a U turn and return to the boat.

After the present opening ritual which took up most of what remained of the morning, mainly due to the fact that my Mum took such painstaking care removing the paper on each present, without tearing it because it was "so nice and a shame to spoil it". We found this very amusing and Peter said "Next year we'll just give you nice wrapping paper instead of presents".

Phone calls to and from family and friends, lots of cards and letters to open then I prepared the dinner ready for 1.30pm and a buffet tea later followed by various card games and big time relaxing. It was so easy to live in bricks and mortar and so warm and comfortable. We appreciated what most people took for granted but did not want to change places. On Boxing Day evening a neighbour took us back to Fenny for £10 and, with our brief Xmas respite over, it was back to foraging about for wood for the fire, and fishing bits out of the canal and hedges. Once all these bits were cut up it was surprising how much it amounted to, enough for three or four days.

During the freezing conditions we almost had a tragedy on our hand when Yetti was walking down the waterside gunwale, stopped midships and stared out at the large floating sections of broken ice and suddenly just took a great flying leap and promptly landed on one just momentarily before skidding off it into the icy water and disappearing. As fast as he'd gone into the water he was scrambling out and up onto another sheet of ice, then back in the water and swimming to another one where he momentarily stopped as if assessing the situation before taking a further leap into the water and frantically continued his perilous journey through and over the broken ice till he reached the side of the boat and made it to a tyre fender which he clawed his way up. Peter by this time had stripped off down to his vest and trousers ready to go into the water if Yetti hadn't been able to save himself. Just as well that when it happened I was away from the boat shopping and missed what surely could have been a tragic incident. Within half an hour of Yetti being dried by the fire he was trying to get out again. A pair of large ducks were struggling and sliding about on the ice looking extremely comical and they eventually came ashore for a wander round the bank. Yetti's eyes were like saucers as he watched them.

As New Years Eve came upon us we burned the last of our wood. The washing was hung up over the hip bath until it became non dripping and could be re-hung around the fore cabin. Our first New Years Day task was definitely going to be foraging for wood.

We made our way up towards Stoke Hammond, collecting wood here and there but nothing very much until we found a derelict area of ground across the canal, where there was a lot of wood and fence posts scattered around which had obviously lain there a long time as much of it was tangled up and partly concealed in the undergrowth. Peter nipped across the bridge and floated a good supply across the canal to me on the opposite bank where I pulled them up and out of the water and stacked on top of the boat ready for logging.

Chapter Eleven

Another Mouth to Feed

Life wasn't all a bed of roses, especially at this time of year when living on a boat was not very comfortable. We had our ups and downs, let off steam at each other and maybe it did us good but whatever fallings out we had they never lasted long.

There was a spate of thefts from boats moored near to the Fenny stop lock, most of which at this time were unlived in so more vulnerable to intruders. A TV was taken from 'Daffodil' and 'Fu-urther' and 'Proteus' were also broken into.

We were moored further down past the Bridge Inn on our own mostly, our nearest boat neighbours usually at least a hundred yards to a quarter of a mile away. Like us, they didn't want to be on top of each other.

Winter hibernation routine set in and we settled down to a lot of reading, writing and painting. Sitting quietly one evening there was a tap at the door and it was Dave off a boat wintering along the same few miles as us. Before we opened the door to him he announced.

"I've come to see if you want a blood test Pete?"

Our minds boggled at the thought of what this offer might involve and conjured up visions of Dave with a giant sized syringe needle.

He came in and explained that he'd got some tests involving sticks of litmus paper and small needles. His test had turned dark green on the sticks denoting a high sugar content and he wanted to see what ours would show up.

"It's only a pin prick" he said, wielding a small syringe and waiting for a volunteer. Peter and I thought it was hilarious. Who needed friends!!!?

Well, cats did it seemed, especially those who pampered them.

A little ravenously hungry black tom cat found his way onto our stern deck one afternoon and peeked inquisitively into the doorway. He had large bright eyes set in a comical Siamese cat shaped face with a pointy nose. His head looked almost too small for his body, but he had the appetite of a tiger and polished off everything we fed him, meat, munches, milk and scraps. He then became quite bold and began to saunter in and around the boat examining every nook and cranny. He and Yetti appeared to be of similar ages and started to run around, chasing and playing together.

Over the weeks, he became a regular visitor and before long we met up with his owner, a pleasant young man nicknamed "Muppet". He told us that the cat was called "Maurice" and that he had rescued him when he was a few weeks old from a box with about five other kittens in, all of whom were destined to be drowned. As Maurice was really too young to have left his mother he'd had to be fed by spoon for a while but this didn't prove to be very successful and Maurice ended up suckling off the bitch they had, along with it's puppy. Now the puppy was bigger Maurice maybe didn't get as much food as he wanted.

"He thinks he's a dog" said Muppet. "And he plays rough with the puppy too. If you throw him a loo roll he leaps around with it and shreds it to pieces in minutes."

We told him that Maurice was beginning to spend a lot of time on our boat and asked if he would consider us adopting him. He thought for awhile and said that he was very fond of him but would let Maurice decide where he wanted to live.

When Maurice came bounding aboard our boat in his boisterous dog like mode, the cats scattered in all directions. We noticed that he was often around when his boat was not and realized that, unlike us Muppet did not always make sure Maurice was aboard when he had to go off somewhere. Maurice would stay in and around the place his boat had been moored, take refuge in the hedges if need be and just wait till his boat returned. On these occasions he visited us more often.

Muppet was out working on the bank one day, renewing all his deck boards and gas piping so we stopped to have a chat and he asked us if we still wanted to adopt Maurice. We said "yes" providing our cats didn't abandon ship.

We all realized that while our boats were moored near each other Maurice would continue to treat them as communal homes for him.

"You can take him with you and see how he gets on" said Muppet adding that he thought he would be better off with us and the other cats than with his dogs and the little toddler they had.

So with ship's complement now six plus one mouse stowaway caught in the morning by Yetti and which when I attempted to rescue it ran off squeaking in terror from Yetis claws and Jessica leaped off the bed to join in the fun. I managed to shut them both into the kitchen as the mouse hid under the curtain by the porta potti and as I moved the curtain it ran out and shot under the bath, out of reach of cats and humans alike where it became a prisoner on "death row." There were so many inaccessible places for a mouse to hide on a boat but the cats would be able to hear it move around and eventually catch it if we couldn't first. Seems the more cats we had onboard the more mice we ended up with, but they didn't last long and we preferred them to be alive and running around outside rather than on our boat or in our cat's bellies.

We made sure Maurice was on board when Muppet left on his boat to moor up some miles away near Simpson bridge.

Di, Dave's wife came walking past with their placid old Heinz 57 English sheepdog type dog Toby on a lead. When she came back she was very upset as when they had reached the paper shop in the main street of Fenny she had tied Toby to a large square litter bin while she'd gone into the shop. A car passing by had back fired, and put the fear of God into Toby who took off like a bat out of hell, bin and all, clattering about in all directions in and out of the traffic. All Viv could hear was the screeching of car brakes and the clattering of the bin as Toby ran amuck. He then disappeared and Viv finally found him sitting forlornly at the bottom of the canal bridge steps with the by now empty bin on his head. A tale with a happy ending and both Pete and Ray thought it was extremely funny at the expense of poor Viv and Toby.

As we stood chatting we watched some kids up near the bridge throwing milk bottles out of crates left outside the work unit offices, into the canal. Di shouted to them and they all ran off leaving dozens of half submerged bottles bobbing about neck up, all down the canal.

We all agreed that maybe it was time to wander off and find pastures new even though at Fenny everything was handy to the canal.

A lady came along early one morning and complained about a boat engine running late the previous night, so we told her that it was ours and apologised. As it had been cold we had run it to make sure the batteries wouldn't be flat in the morning. She asked why we needed to run it like that so Peter explained about the batteries providing all of our lights etc and I think she was happier about it when she understood the reason.

As ever, wood stocks dictated whether we moved or not regardless of whether we wanted to. So we headed off towards Peartree Bridge and noticed piles of freshly cut young trees all around 6 or 7ft long, trimmed and stacked. Our eyes almost left their sockets before we saw two people down behind the bank with a chainsaw and saw bench, who at first we thought must be workmen but then noticed a cable running from a boat. The two loggers turned out to be Ray and Josie off "Dorothy Louise" and they told us that the Council workers had told them to help themselves along with any other boaters who should turn up and want any. Well it was akin to winning the lottery for "smokey stovers". Before long we had transported some 15 of the logged tree trunks and stowed them on the boat roof. We had visions of endless warm blazing fires.

Moving on towards Great Linford Peter spotted a blue sports bags deep in the water and fished it out with the boat hook. It was heavy with water and also had a slab of stone inside it. At this time of the year, with few boats moving, the water was very settled and clear enabling us to see the submerged bag. Apart from a few small Canadian coins, a small silver broach, another maple leaf broach, a pin with two small hearts on, some empty ring and broach boxes, a child's water wings, and a number of cigarette ends in a side compartment that was all it contained.

Mooring at Gt Linford Dave and Viv were also there and the following morning Dave came along in his rowing boat on his way to the shop and called out to us to see if we wanted anything getting. On his return, not to be outdone by our previous find, he too fished out a blue sports bag from the water. I told him that there was also a large white carrier bag floating a few yards further on so he fished that out as well and it was full of clothes. The sports bag looked as though it had been packed with gear by someone going away on holiday, with underwear, paperback book (Rumpole of the Bailey), jeans and top, a selection of jewellery, track suit, toiletries, hair brush etc. Both bags contained sizes 18 and the clothes in the carrier were bone dry but the sports bag was waterlogged. Obviously there was no link between the bag we had fished out the day before. Dave contacted the police and handed the stuff in and we wondered if we'd ever get to know why and how it had got into the water. I wrote a brief note to the address we'd found in the bag we'd fished out in case the person concerned was interested but never heard anymore about it.

As a cold crisp and sunny first of February arrived, the first snowdrops and winter aconite appeared along with splashes of blue periwindkle and a smattering of early primroses. We wound our way along to Grafton Regis stopping along the stretch of canal where we'd buried Jessie and placed a stone in his memory with a few words, date and black cat painted on it. It remained undisturbed on the bank by the fence of a farmer's field and was reassuring to find it intact as the weeks passed by.

We called at Baxter's boat yard for fuel and wandered up to the Post office shop in Yardley Gobion, a pretty village with many chocolate box thatched cottages. Little did we know what a big part of our lives this village was to play in the future.

Cosily moored up at Isworth Farm we watched six swans in a farmer's field of sprouting kale. In just a couple of days the number of swans had increased to 29, all cropping away on the young shoots. The farmer must have been furious with them especially as they weren't a bit fazed by his explosive bird scarers.

My nightly routine continued to be one of frequently waking up after a few hours sleep then having to get up and walk around to ease back and joint pain for awhile, sometimes light the fire and potter about doing things before making cups of tea and going back to bed and talking with Peter. After managing to doze off, Yetti would often wake me up again by walking all over my face and then deliberately, very gently pat my nose and eyelids with one of his soft paws to tell me it was surely his feeding time. Sometimes I'd pull the covers right over my head to deter him but then he would tug at a vulnerable gap in the bedding defences until I mostly gave in to his constant demands.

The most kingfishers that we ever saw were along this stretch of canal. Their bright colours were outstandingly beautiful at this time of the year. There was also a resident Barn Owl which we occasionally used to see perched on the ruins of the farm. Both Jessica and Yetti loved going over there, across the bridge, once it was safe in the cover of darkness.

One such dark evening we were surprised when a large coal boat and butty called 'Caldy' passed by. Not many boats were on the move at this time of year but earlier in the day two more boats, "Squirrel" and "Proper Job" had passed us, going in the opposite direction to the coal boat.

We were invited to spend an evening with a couple called Patricia and Allen, a retired headmaster and teacher, who we had met on our travels. Their boat was like the Queen Mary in comparison to ours. A nice evening and they gave us a bottle of their home made elderflower wine which we had already sampled and given full marks to. We decided to save it for a special occasion of which many came and went and yet the wine remained unopened and still is some 20 years later. Perhaps I'll launch it when I launch my book and make a toast to "our happy days on the boat".

One evening with nothing better to do we started to discuss and redesign the interior of the boat, all 30ft or so of it. With my womanly home making instincts, I felt sure I was more capable of designing the space and utilizing it to the best advantage but Peter disagreed emphatically, saying that I wouldn't be able to do all the work required and that he knew how to do it best.

Well, as the writer of the diary, who recorded the conversation, I at least had the privilege and satisfaction of writing, in so many words, that he could "get stuffed", without actually verbally telling him so.

Revenge could have been sweet the next day when Peter needed a beard and moustache trim as I nearly cut his top lip off. That would have stopped him being lippy and if I had lopped off his ear at the same time he would have looked like Van Gogh. I'd accidentally sat on my glasses and broken an arm off them so I was having great difficulty in keeping them on to see what I was doing. Peter thought he should get danger money for allowing me near him.

Blobs became a very unhappy cat when he was cold and would often sit in front of the unlit fire yowling in protest as if he was suffering from frost bite. One day, obviously cold and in a bad mood he chased Maurice and cornered him under the bed then gave Jessica a bat round the ear as he passed her in the gangway.

Toby was in the news again. Di informed us that "he's been courting and looks as though he's going to be a dad to puppies sometime in June." It had only been the other day that Di had been telling me that Toby had never been interested in females and hadn't a clue how to go about being a dog. Well he seemed to have proved them wrong on that issue.

I discovered one of Peter's jumpers had a 50p sized freshly eaten hole in it and hoped the mouse wasn't as fond of plastic water pipes.

At around 2.30 a.m one morning we saw the mouse that had managed to evade us and the cats for a number of days. He ran out by the wood stove and through the for'd cabin into the bedroom. I quickly tried to catch it but lost it before I finally managed to grab it. It was so small that I had a job to contain it in my hands and it was frantically biting me in a desperate bid to defend itself and stay alive, so I wasted no time in getting out of the boat with it and releasing it into the hedgerow, hoping it wouldn't get caught by one of the cats after managing to survive trapped aboard for so long with them.

On our way towards Stoke Hammond we came across an elderly lady with two long haired little terrier type dogs on leads and wearing coats. She was pushing a pram which contained another dog all wrapped up and who suffered from arthritis.

I wondered if Blobs might benefit from a little warm coat, but it wouldn't have been practical for a cat. Blobs was now about 17 years old and not in the best of health. He was wheezing and bringing up catarrh and we were attempting to give him tablets prescribed by the vet. We never knew if he was getting sufficient medication from them as when we tried to put a tablet into his mouth he would struggle and panic and the stress made him wheeze and gasp for breath. So we crushed them up into his food or a little evaporated milk but often he left some of it so it was all a bit unsatisfactory. One thing he did need was some warm sunshine like the rest of us.

Maurice was young, strong, and very wiry. He'd jump up on the bed and attack Yetti, so Yetti stopped sleeping up there and took to curling up in the front cabin. Yeti didn't seem to be putting much weight on at all, so I would make a particular fuss of him and nurse him and hope that he would grow enormous and be able to assert himself a bit more. He was so small in comparison to the others and not a bit aggressive towards them. A noisy kafuffle and clatter astern about 10p.m one night had me dashing to investigate. Jessica and Maurice shot in and as I went up on deck I could hear a gentle lapping of water and spotted Yetti in the drink, swimming frantically and trying to get out. But the bank was steep and shored up with metal which he couldn't get a grip on with his claws. I made a couple of unsuccessful grabs at him and he disappeared then reappeared. I was worried he would drown as his long fur would be heavy and waterlogged. However on my third attempt I managed to grab him by his collar and haul him to safety, drenched and frightened.

We were near Leighton Buzzard on the day that Peter wanted to watch a big fight between Eubank and some other boxer but we were unable to get a TV picture so had to settle to reading, snoozing or talking. Earlier in the day we had walked up towards Heath and Reach woods and seen early celandines with their shiny yellow petals looking as though they had been covered in silicone wax.

One of our winter pastimes as we travelled was to collect many fishing floats that fishermen had lost to hostile bushes and trees along the canal. They hung in all shapes and sizes, tangled up on branches, so we just nosed our way into them and retrieved what we could and Peter always had a good supply to fish with. During one such manoeuvre our nearside brass coach lamp which was one of two we had displayed on the front of each side of the boat, became dislodged and entangled in a hawthorn bush and the top of it came off and fell into the canal water. The main part of the lamp stayed put in its brass holder. We fished around with the landing net trying to locate the brass top but it was like trying to find a needle in a haystack, especially once the water had been churned up and turned mud brown. We had to give up and continue on our way but decided we might get chance to look on our return journey when the water might be settled and clearer. Rather a million to one chance but worth a go.

There was no privacy on the towpath which much of the time was the only place we had to sort out jobs much to the curiosity of walkers who wanted to chat or offer advice, good or bad. Some we loved to talk to, others we quickly disappeared from before they had chance.

With bike repairs done it was time to get some logs sawn up so Peter started the 'jenny' up and also the engine to charge the batteries. Chain saw out, extension plugged in, fuses checked, but 'no go'. We turned the engine off to listen to the jenny, but all was quiet, no jenny running so no wonder nothing was working. There was no oil in the jenny so it was a good job we had just bought 5 litres. We'd also bought a 60ft extension lead with safety cut out which was very useful. Once the jenny was topped up with oil and running all was well with the world but not for long when smoke started billowing around and into the boat. Peter with his back to it seemed oblivious until I kicked into my panic stations act and started to run in all directions at once. I didn't know whether to run astern and grab fire extinguishers or rush for'd and turn off the gas supply. Peter seemed to be in just as much of a dilemma, didn't know if the fire was fore or aft or if he had the shits or heartburn. His mind filled with visions of petrol doused bilges, engines and generator fires and explosions.

Meanwhile I shot for'd, grabbed the rotary line complete with washing hanging on it and threw it up onto the roof out of the way so that I could get access to the gas locker and turn the gas off, whatever good that was going to do. Peter grabbed the petrol can and safely deposited it ashore out of harms way and was then at the ready with a choice of fire extinguishers.

God help us if there had been a real fire, we'd have killed everyone in the stampede to safety. It might have been advisable if we'd had an occasional fire drill. The cause of all the smoke was from the oil burning off where Peter had over filled the jenny and spilled some onto the housing. The adrenalin rush from the incident was akin to being thrown into shark infested waters.

It crossed our minds that perhaps we should abandon logging wood and convert to coal, but using the new extension lead, we managed to log up the wood without further ado.

We continued to travel through Marsworth and the locks to Bulbourne junction, carrying on to Tring Summit with its steep wooded embankments. Then on to Cowroast boatyard to buy 19k propane and 15k butane gas bottles and top up with water. But we had filled up a day or so ago so water was soon overflowing into the bilge while we were ashore sorting the gas bottles out. There was never a dull moment, one minute fire drill, the next flooding.

The whole stretch of towpath from Marsworth top lock to Cowroast (about 3 or four miles) seemed to have been taken over with newly erected 'visitors mooring' posts. The new mooring regulations implemented by BW stated fees as **£5** per day for 15-28 days, or part day; **£10** per day for 29-56 days and **£18** per day for 57 days or longer. As a result all the lovely old boats that used to be moored along this part of the canal had been moved on. To where, was anyone's guess, but there had obviously been a purge Protests would of course have fallen on deaf bureaucratic ears. Daubed on some of the notices, in red paint were words like "visiting what?" and "visitors to what" and "illegal notice" and on the bridge was written "£100 a week for bugger all." This, no doubt must have referred to the permanent mooring fees. Last year on approaching Cowroast the bank was full of narrow boats moored up, a little community full of characters living harmoniously and harmlessly together. Their demise left a bland empty void and in time was a policy that permeated throughout the system with discriminating, almost dirty tricks department rulings to force many boaters off the canal. Bringing in the Boat Safety Certificate of Compliance some years later comprising of a somewhat mega paged manual of a trillion billion must do's and must not do's in order to qualify for a pass certificate, leaving you broke and on the verge of a nervous breakdown, on a boat you had lived safely on for years but was now considered an all round floating hazard. At least the recently established **NABO** (National Association of Boat Owners) was making a good stand for boater's rights and pressing for a review and amendment of these draconian rules.

Peter was hiding at the top of the embankment (not from the BW warden) but from potential roosting pheasants. Not much luck apart from coming across some old burnable fence posts lying in the undergrowth. While he was out stalking, I ventured down into Tring to the shop and got caught in a short lived blizzard. Peter blamed the lack of 'pheasants for the pot', on the rifle sights saying that they must be grossly out of line because if he couldn't hit one at that range he had better give it up. The two pheasants that normally roosted in the nearby trees suddenly went elsewhere, and who could blame them.

March the 1st and everywhere was covered in snow. We met a chap out shooting pigeons and he said he shot hundreds of them and sold them to the market. We walked to his house with him and he gave us four for £1. They were so small, I felt quite sad to see them like that with no feathers on, just bare little things, hardly a mouthful. I decided I wouldn't be partaking of any pigeon pie.

Maurice disappeared around 8p.m one night. He was last seen just before that when he was on the bed with Yetti. He hadn't been in all night, so in the morning we got up, dressed and went out calling him up and down the towpath, up to the road and up along the bank to the field. We felt very despondent and worried and hoped it wasn't going to be another case of disaster as we had experienced with Jesse and Ibley Dibley. We made frequent trips out during the day, looking for and calling Maurice, all down the towpaths, fields, hedges and everywhere. We saw a man in the field with a shotgun and panicked till on a closer look we realized it was a metal detector and not a gun. We found a large fox-like hole only 30 or 40 yards along the top of the bank and some fresh-ish droppings. A lady out walking her dogs said that she kept her cats in at night because there were a lot of foxes in the vicinity and that a fox had got one of her cats and others of people she knew. Well that didn't do much to cheer us and at about 7.30p.m we went into the pub for a drink before continuing our search. We felt at a very low ebb to be sure and by 11p.m had almost given up that we would ever see cheeky little Maurice again. 11.30p.m and a distinct pitter patter of feet on the roof, and seconds later a little black nose appeared. Maurice was back and it was like winning the pools to see him safe and sound. He came running in to us and did little rolly-overs, all pleased with himself.

We were reminded when we saw the man metal detecting that we had a cheap old specimen somewhere, so we fished it out and went off to the field we had seen him in. We didn't expect to find anything much and weren't surprised during our hour of searching to find just silver paper, pieces of iron, bottle tops, two circular pieces off binoculars plus the best find of a metal comb with "Tim & Bev" scratched on it. As we dug a hole while detecting Peter said "it's a worm detector", as loads were wriggling around as we dug. He kept getting a strong buzz so I dug and the buzz kept disappearing. Before I was completely exhausted with digging and orders to "come on Mag dig deeper", I realized the detector was honing in to the metal on Peter's 'toe-protector' boots. We'd never be rich but who cared as long as we could laugh at life.

Hurry up and get a container Mag, I'll have these worms for fishing.

It's a UFO

Who invited them for dinner?

RIGHTS FOR MOLES

We'll never find any treasure at this rate.

7th March. I decide to do a mega wash of sheets; blanket; pillow cases;

Long Johns; two padded shirts; towel; jogging bottoms; shirt; undies and socks, all by hand with lots of water in the sink and some whites boiling up in the big metal cauldron on the stove.

Some I scrubbed on the draining board and washed sheets and bedding in two separate loads in the hip bath, each of which had to be emptied by bucket as the pump still wasn't working.

I hung it all outside, hoping it would at least drip dry enough to bring inside and finish off drying there.

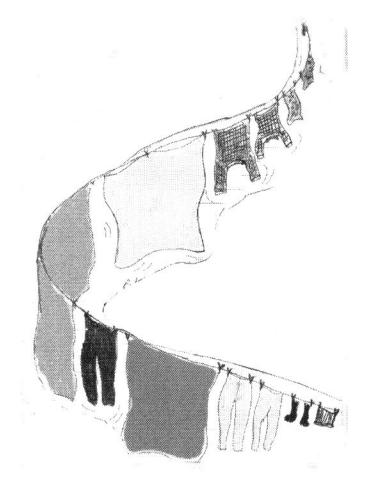

Our 14 days free mooring was almost over at Tring Summit when Peter developed a bad chest cold or maybe it was flu and flu jabs weren't available then like they routinely are now. He was also prone to bronchitis. To move now in any direction would involve many locks, some with quite hefty gates. To head towards Berkhamstead was out of the question as it was endless locks. It wasn't an ideal time to be on the move if you were well but with Pete unwell I decided to go and see the warden. He was sympathetic to our problem and said he would turn a blind eye to our mooring over 14 days till we were able to travel on. Peter went below to get warm while I turned the boat round and headed back to our last mooring just past the bridge near Tring railway station. It was dark and difficult to see going along the cutting and we had no light on in order to save our batteries. Another boat loomed up out of the trees, just a black shadow as I went through a bridge hole He also had no light on but stopped midstream and showed his light to make sure I'd seen him or to see what was approaching him. I also flicked on my light.

Peter was rough all night and stayed in bed dosed up on flu powders. At 2pm the following day I cycled into Tring for more groceries and came back loaded down with bags, one in the front basket, one on the rear carrier, a bag on my handle bars and a rucksack on my back. Parts of the towpath were too muddy and narrow so I walked part of the way until I reached the road. Peter had had another bad night so it was important he stay warm in bed and rest.

During the days when Pete had told me all about his life and I started writing his biography, he told me about his escapades as a young Able Seaman in the Royal Navy during the war and at the D-Day landings. I asked him if he had any medals and he laughed and pooh poohed the idea. I said I would write and find out, which I did and as a result Peter was sent five medals and a clasp. They were interesting but Peter said "give them to the poor buggers who died". I suppose that is how many men felt.

Peter was shivering badly the following night and then the fever broke and he felt a bit better. I suggested getting a doctor so that he could get examined and treatment if required but he said he would be alright. I decided that come next September I'd get him down for a flu jab. After a few more days when we thought Peter was improving he became worse and had chest pain, difficulty with his breathing and was coughing a lot. He could not lie down. I made him a steam inhaler with Vic vapour rub which seemed to ease it a bit but then it flared up again and he looked like the Ghost of Christmas past from Scrooge. When he got up to go to the toilet he had a terrific vice-like pain in his left lung, struggled to breathe and I thought his lung was collapsing again. I now, in hindsight, realized I should have got him to the doctors' at the first signs of the cold or flu symptoms. I decided however, that if he was going to develop another collapsed lung that I better get some medical assistance, so at 2 a.m I got up, dressed, started the engine, pulled the offside plank up out of the water and the fender tyres, turned on the lamp for'd, pulled up the mooring pins, undid the ropes and set off down the canal to turn the boat which I managed to do in the dark without so much as a bump this time. There was quite a hard frost and against the starlit sky two pheasants were silhouetted up in the branches over the canal. I moored the boat up by Tring bridge and hastily made my way along the lonely and deserted road to the Railway Station to phone the number I had for a doctor. When I got through to him, he was very unenthusiastic and abrupt. He put the phone down after three or four condescending grunts, begrudging ones at that at my request for a call out. It was quite frightening knowing Peter's past medical history and under the circumstances I did not feel it was an unreasonable request even at such an unearthly early hour of the morning. Some twenty minutes later I met the doctor on the bridge and we went down to the boat where he examined Peter but said he couldn't really say what the lung condition was and that it might be a good idea for him to have an x-ray and examination at the hospital. In less than half an hour the ambulance arrived. One paramedic put Peter on some oxygen which immediately brought some colour to his face and eased his breathing. They bundled him into a chair and struggled precariously along the unmade, muddy towpath, stopping frequently to re-direct the wheels which seemed to be on a determined course into the canal. To make things worse, the path edge was too close to the canal for comfort and the chair wheels kept sticking in the mud and tipping forwards and sideways with a jolt. Peter was in a sweat from it all and being strapped in had visions of going in the cut and sinking like a stone, chair and all. They had a job getting him up the flight of some dozen or so steps and had to keep stopping to get their breath. Peter was about 14 stone. Once in the ambulance they put him on a heart graph monitor which showed up his irregular heartbeat. He was feeling very sick so they took him off the oxygen.

The journey to Hemel Hempstead hospital seemed to take ages. I had a long worrying wait while they examined and X-rayed Peter and while the x-ray showed some bronchial inflammation in the left lung, there was no collapse which was a big relief. After some discussion it was decided that Peter could return to the boat, go to bed and keep warm and make an appointment to go for another x-ray when he was well enough. He was to get some antibiotics too which I cycled into Tring to the surgery for. But it was the wrong surgery and the other one "Rothschild House" was on the other side of Tring. So off I went and it was like a 4 star hotel rather than a surgery. The doctor who had seen Peter wasn't there and I was told I could have an interview with another doctor. So I waited until I was told to go into the interview room, which when I did I expected to see a doctor but instead there was a chair and a telephone on a shelf which the receptionist said to answer when it rang and to speak to the doctor. This I did and he prescribed Peter a course of antibiotics which were computerized and ready at the surgery dispensary two doors away before I arrived there to collect them. On the way back I stopped to buy some grapes, oranges, bananas and a nice piece of cod, some chocolate and some throat lozenges. It was dusk when I arrived back at the boat.

Mid March and signs of Spring and Spring cleaning urges. Peter was on the mend again, not surprising with all the groceries I'd been stuffing down him. On the latest grocery run I'd bought him steak, new potatoes, mushrooms and some mixed veg. Plus bananas, grapes, grapefruit and half a bottle of whiskey (purely medicinal of course). At that rate he was going to be strong as an ox, hopefully, as there was a long list of jobs waiting for him to get stuck into.

While I was having a bit of a clean up on the stern deck I turned the bilge pump on and lifted a deck board to see how much water we had collected and realized that the pump wasn't working. There was only about 2 inches of water to shift, most of which had accumulated via the stern gland on the prop shaft by dripping in around it. I grabbed the pump cable and gave it a shake as the pump itself was not easily accessible from up on deck and I had no intentions of clambering down into the mucky wet bilge. Peter came out to have a look and we decided we'd have to get the pump up and examine it to see if it was blocked or jammed. Otherwise the fault may have been an electrical one. So I sat on the engine, the top of which was just below the deck boards and dangled my legs down between various pipes and casings. I was volunteered simply for my gnome size ability to fit into smaller places. I aimed my legs down towards the pump and used my feet to lift the stiff plastic water hose attached to it, over a metal sill, enabling me to pull the pump up high enough on its cable for Peter to get hold of, loosen the jubilee clip and take off. So much for being a 'bilge rat'! I'd been everything else lately, so why not? The pump was only jammed so was easily sorted out and put back working. We decided we must invest in a new length of flexible hose so we could manipulate the pump more easily. We checked the gear oil, engine oil and batteries and topped two up with water. Peter showed me where the oil was changed, and a more awkward place you couldn't imagine. I played 'the dumb blonde' just in case he decided to volunteer me for that job too.

Gerald came to visit while we were up on the Summit and helped us out with wood and logging but he himself was suffering repercussions from a bad back. He bought lots of mail that had been forwarded on to my mum for us which was a treat.

We had our first sightings of butterflies, – Small tortoiseshells and brimstones flitting about and some noisy Spring ritual going on up the bank with four jays making a racket. There were lots of white and mauve sweet violets growing all along the banks, their smell reminding me of freesias.

Maurice did another carbon copy disappearing act of his previous one and was missing two days and one night. As usual we searched high and low for him but once it was dark there was not much we could do apart from wait, worry and wonder:-

Was he stuck up a tree?	Possibly
Killed on the road?	No
Lost?	Unlikely
Gone for a walk about?	Perhaps but we didn't think so
Gone down a fox or badger hole?	No
Shot?	No, we had heard no gunshots
Fallen into the water, drowned?	No, he could swim and get out.
The fox or 'thing' had got him?	Yes and no.
Poisoned?	What a dreadful thought.

Come home Maurice, all is forgiven, we love you!

At 8.15p.m Peter went up on deck and Jessica was standing up meercat fashion on her back legs looking across the canal. Pete could hear a loud guttural distressed meowing, so I fetched the torch and shone it across the canal while Pete moved the boat slowly across to the opposite bank which was inaccessible with lots of overhanging bushes, trees and undergrowth, made worse by the pitch darkness. It took us some time to manipulate the bow of the boat into an accessible cat rescue position and once aboard Maurice scampered into the boat and rolled around on the seat by the fire, purring happily. We wondered if he had fallen into the water and swam across to the opposite bank and with bridges few and far between our mooring site he would not have been able to get himself back. We learned in time that if they did end up on the far bank they often became disorientated as to how to get back on the other side where the boat was.

We really had overstayed our welcome at the Summit now and with Peter well enough to travel we headed back towards Leighton Buzzard. As we passed the spot where we had lost the top of the brass coach lamp I suggested we had another attempt to find it. Peter thought it was rather a futile exercise but we had nothing to lose by trying and Gerald who was with us agreed to help. He scrambled ashore over the barbed wire fence with the boathook while I followed through a gap in the barbarous blackthorn bushes and equally threatening barbed wire, with the landing net at the ready. Gerald prodded around in the depths while I scooped up nets full of thick oozey grey silt and large fresh water mussels about 6 inches by two and a half inches. Gerald made contact with yet another object and we were hopeful it might be the lamp top, but it was yet another mussel and a small live fish in the net. Another scoop and as the mud slid out of the net a shape slowly revealed itself, much to our amazement a now tarnished (after weeks in the water) copper coloured brass lamp top lay in the net. Very pleased with ourselves we continued on to Leighton Buzzard to fill up with water.

The following morning after mooring up for the night near The Globe pub we found our batteries were flat and couldn't understand why after the journey we'd done. But obviously for some reason they hadn't been charging up, so we weren't going anywhere in a hurry. On further inspection Peter found that the 'drive belt' had gone so Gerald volunteered to cycle to Bletchley and get a new belt. On his way he spoke to a lad on a boat called 'Fiona' who had a spare belt which he brought along to us with his friendly young whippet bitch. She enjoyed some biscuits and came into the boat but fortunately didn't bother any of the cats. Unluckily the fan belt didn't fit so when Gerald came back, after a brew and a bacon butty with Peter and John he went into Leighton Buzzard for one. A chap called Phil off Lark Princess came to our assistance with jump leads to the battery and before long we were sorted.

A strange coincidence happened one night, a Monday, when I dreamed that my 'travelling the world' son Matthew had returned home. I told Peter about it Tuesday morning and that afternoon my mum informed me on the phone that "Matthew was home and on his way to see us". I did a trolley dash around the supermarket to stock up with food and made a nice meal. Peter was happy, as Matthew ate mostly vegetarian food like me. Peter commented that "My best friends are all vegetarians", as he lustily tucked in to all the bacon, pork chops and sausages.

We now had three clapped out batteries so while we were buying diesel (red) at the boatyard, 13 gallons for £10, we bought two more 6 cell batteries for £106 plus VAT £126.

Little Yetti had a lot of mossy lumps and pooh all stuck in his fur so we got the scissors to attempt to cut them off and trim some long fur from around his stern quarters. I held him tight while Peter wielded the scissors, taking care of Yetti's tiddley bits. But Yetti, we discovered, had no tiddley bits and was a HER! What a surprise that was, no wonder he/she was only small. We would have to rename her 'Yettica'. On second thoughts 'Yetti' was quite a unisex type of name so we stuck with it. We had always thought she was rather delicate for a tom. So we would have to get Mister Maurice neutered pronto, else we'd be having a litter or two. We'd have to get Yetti spayed too.

Peter nipped ashore and came back carrying a ginormous plank on his shoulder. I nearly fainted as it must have been 12 or 14ft long and 3inches thick. He said it was lying discarded on the towpath and too good to leave. Not till it was aboard did I realize just how heavy it was, too heavy by far to lift up onto the roof so we had to heave and shove it down into the galley and through into the mid ships gangway alongside the bed. It must have weighed about 160lbs. I was a bit annoyed at Peter as, after his latest lung collapse the doctor had told him not to lift anything too heavy. We wondered if it had been left on the towpath by BW workmen. It was far too heavy and thick to be used as a gang plank by a boater.

Half of our front cabin

In order to get it out we had to manipulate it half in the forward cabin, half mid ships, propped on two stools and cut it into 4 sections with the chain saw, then Peter split each section with the axe and cut them log size with the chain saw. Lots of lovely dry logs!.

Our saw mill duties done we commenced to wash out and sterilize a pressure barrel and ferment bin, into which Peter then racked the two forty pints of beer from two more pressure barrels we'd made a few weeks back and added some finings to speed up the process. We were trying out a brew called "Mighty Mo" which was only £2.45 for a 40 pint tin. We were now almost a floating brewery with 120 pints brewing.

Late afternoon and we sat out to the sounds of bleating lambs, birds and the drone of an occasional aeroplane, creaking of the rotary line for'd; rumbling of a distant train; lapping of water around the boat hull and watched a mink scurrying around on the far bank where golden kingcups spilled over into the water. Peter whittled away making a walking stick while I sat and day dreamed,

After getting Maurice neutered at Bletchley we went on to Great Linford where Muppet's boat was moored. He came along to see Maurice with the little bitch who had suckled Maurice She remembered him and went up to him where he sat on a low wall and put her paw on him as if to say 'hello'. Maurice knew her too and was not afraid, just the opposite when he realized who it was and gave her nose a rub with his.

We cycled to the house where the owners of the sports bag that we had fished out of the canal lived in order to return the bag and the few remaining bits found in it. No one was in so we left it with a neighbour who told us that the lady had lost everything in a burglary, including all of her mother's jewellery.

Chapter Twelve

'Bottle Kicking' Custom

Earlier in the day two men and a women dressed in old country style waistcoats, floppy hats, knee length trousers and boots, the woman in long skirt, apron, and a shawl came past on a charity walk for 'Save the Children'. They had walked from Manchester and were heading for London. We gave them a donation, chatted and showed them Peter's walking sticks. They liked the thumb sticks so we gave them each one to help them on their hike and they were very pleased. They now looked like 'The Wurzels' to be sure. Maurice nearly left home he thought they were out of the Dick Whittington pantomime.

There were some odd, and comical boat names but I think the one we saw near Linford took the biscuit as on it's bow it had "SHEILA MAY" and on it's stern it had "OR MAY NOT".

Maurice seemed no worse for his little snip op and must have been the fastest feline feeder on the planet. We decided to call him 'Moggo' which seemed to suit his character far more and was less of a mouthful to say. I was stroking him after his morning feed and when he had had enough he nipped me so I said "Hey don't bite the hand that feeds you" and as though he knew what I'd said he gave Peter's hand a bite on the knuckles. He did seem a little less aggressive of late and liked to be stroked and tickled on his tum when he was laying on his back stretched out to his limit, a 'real yard of cat'. As soon as I got up in the morning the cats all assumed it was 'breakfast' and action stations. Moggo was up on the sink top dashing across to the oven and back across the sink, following the tin opener and tin as I attempted to open it without catching his nose in it. Yetti was getting under my feet, tripping me up, while Jessica graciously padded about up on the worktop, filling the only available space for dishing up. She was all cajoling and anticipating while Blobs, hovered on the top step of the stern door. ' It was like feeding time at the zoo.

Yetti had actually been in season recently and had flaunted herself around proudly, rolling around the towpath with "come and get me" airs and graces. Moggo tried his best to oblige but fate had dwelt him a cruel blow to his manhood with his recent neutering. Yetti even sang most seductively to him. That was the night Blobs fell in the water and he was far too over the hill to even think about being out on the tiles.

Easter brought surprise visits from family in the shape of my daughter Maggie, with her partner Bradley and Joelle my 6 year old grand daughter all dressed in pink and growing tall. Maggie and Brad had given us the good news of another little grandchild due around the end of September. We had a short boat trip to Stoke Hammond and back and later on left Peter on 'cat watch' while we went to visit great granny at Kensworth. There were four generations of us chatting away. Joelle stayed the night on the boat with us and I made her up a cosy bed on the front cabin couch and read her a story about the Little Mermaid who wanted to be human.

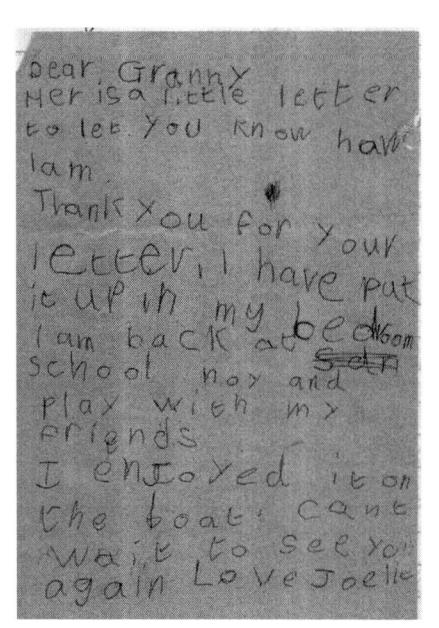

In the morning Joelle amused herself pottering about feeding the swans and mopping the deck. She said that all three cats had slept on her bed. Shortly after Maggie and Brad arrived, my friend Shirley and her husband called in so we took the boat for a trip up Milton Keynes way and Shirley and I had a few sherries and played card games with Joelle while Maggie and Brad sat out on top of the boat enjoying the scenery and warm April sunshine.

A week later Matthew, called in on us with partner Jakee and son Joshua. We took Josh to see his great granny and stayed the night so that we could all spend a day at Whipsnade zoo the following day, My mum now almost 80 and Josh just 2 were both amazing walking all around the zoo which covered large distances to the many open enclosures set on the downland. Nowadays I had mixed feelings about zoos though. I didn't mind the large fields with grazing animals but wasn't happy to see caged lions, tigers, bears and such animals confined in captivity. For Josh it was all just another day on his enormous voyage of discovery. He called the sea lions in the underwater viewing tanks 'big fish'. He was a lovely child with fair hair and big blue eyes. When it was time for them to leave mum's I reached for Josh's hand at the door and he reached back and gave me such a magic look, almost soul searching. My mum saw it too and was as deeply touched as I was.

I stayed on for a week at Mum's to do some decorating jobs for her. After a week I set off back to Fenny but missed the bus into Dunstable and as there wasn't another one for two and a half hours I returned to wait at mums. I then caught the 5p.m bus into Dunstable and had an hour to wait there for the 6.10 Buffalo bus to Fenny. A cold wind added to the discomfort of this long wait. A Buffalo bus on the opposite side of the road stopped and the driver beckoned to those of us waiting across the road. He shouted across to say that he was the bus we were waiting for but was running late due to a breakdown and that it would be another hour before he got to Luton and back to pick us up in which case we might as well get on the bus and travel with him to Luton and back where at least we would be warm and comfortable. So most of us did just that and an hour later arrived back in Dunstable ready to start heading at last in the direction of our destinations. We were still out of luck as the bus would not get going so an engineer was sent out from Flitwick. The young and cheerful driver informed us that the bus was out of order from having a burst water hose. That was all we needed. Some passengers went off to get taxis while the remaining half dozen of us waited 25 minutes until a mechanic arrived to see what he could do. We began to wonder if we would ever get home that night. Then one of the passenger's husband arrived and he and his wife asked if anyone would like a lift to Milton Keynes, so three of us gratefully accepted and I finally arrived at Fenny about 8.30p.m It had taken me some three hours to travel about fifteen miles.

Moggo was becoming a horror. He never stopped galloping about and running around the roof dislodging things up there and it was very unnerving at night with him clattering around when we were sitting quiet or in bed. After each crash, we anticipated a loud splash. He also would suddenly hurl himself at and into the sliding door which divided the bedroom and front cabin and make a thunderous din and also elevate himself up onto his back legs and frantically scratch with his claws on the flat surface of the door as if he was trying to escape certain death. We'd heard of mad March hares but not mad March Moggo.

We moored ahead of a boat called "Aspley" a sixty odd footer with a smart looking cat sitting alongside it. It made a nice change to have cats for neighbours. Peter walked along towards the boat followed by Moggo and Yetti when another little cat, a tortoiseshell came bounding off the boat and chased them back to our boat. A nice couple called Rob and Ann lived on the boat with the cats and a parrot. They were devoted cat lovers and told us how one of their previous cats had been mown down by a cyclist and killed on the towpath. They had rescued a tiny kitten who had been on the brink of death and it's mother had been brutally kicked and ill treated and left badly injured with broken ribs. The vet had been of the opinion that the kitten would not survive but gave it an injection and Rob and Ann had fed it with a special food at regular intervals throughout the day and night for two weeks and it had recovered and was now thriving.

The following morning Moggo went ashore and invited himself aboard their boat and was very interested in the parrot. I felt sure he would like to know what he tasted like. About 4 a.m he came in with a dead baby rabbit, growled at Peter and ran off out of the boat. We found the remains of his rabbit meal, just a tiny white tail, two front legs and the gall bladder. Rob and Ann said their cats were just the same, catching and bringing in their victims, alive or dead. Rob said that he got out of bed one night and put his foot down onto a dead rat that his cat had brought in. Even worse I think was to get out of bed in the dark and tread on the bloody remains of a mouse.

There was a big splash at 11p.m. We both jumped up and Peter shot out for'd while I dashed for the torch. Peter went along the outer sill of the boat (waterside), hung onto the hand rail and leaned down into the water and grabbed Yetti off the safety plank that we lowered down for the very purpose of providing a platform for any of the cats to get onto should they fall in on the water side of the boat. Yetti had swum to the plank, she was shivering with fright. We wrapped her in a towel and nursed her. I think Moggo the Menace may have been chasing her.

Moggo was getting worse, running amuck all over the boat with the wind in his sails, up on the roof, in and out, charging and pouncing on everything. He scattered the other cats and pounced onto Yetti with his jaws on her neck. She was too timid to retaliate so he seemed to pick on her all the time. Jessica tried to keep out of his way but when their paths crossed she spat and growled at him and would lash out if forced to do so. She would flattened her ears like a 'matadors hat' and give him a slightly cross eyed black look.

One morning Moggo was clattering around the boat so much. He was in and out on the stern deck, then laying across the doorway blocking access for Yetti and generally terrorizing the ship's cat compliment. Peter was trying hard not to be distracted by him, from cooking breakfast. But by mistake he inadvertently picked up the bottle of washing up liquid which was standing right next to the bottle of cooking oil and squirted it into the frying pan onto the fried bread. Trying to get into the Guiness book of Nutters – ooops – Records maybe!! He cleaned out the pan, got the bread and tomatoes frying again, added some oil and realized he'd added more washing up liquid AGAIN. Ah well it made a change from burnt toast. I think it was a ploy to get excused from galley duties.

This peaceful and relaxing boat life was becoming more stressful by the day. The previous night the weight on the pressure cooker lid had flown off in an explosive jet of steam. As Peter dashed into the galley to investigate, he unknowingly caught the tap on the beer barrel, turning it full on. Too busy sorting out the pressure cooker he didn't realize what the sound of running liquid was, till he turned round and saw the beer cascading out onto the deck, about 2 pints of it. We must have been the only boaters on the canal who washed their decks in beer.

Now that we were into the merry month of May there were lots of boats passing by and a couple on one boat gave us the news that Di and Dave's dog Toby was now the proud doggie dad of six puppies.

With only damp green kindling wood to get the fire going Peter put some on top of a petrol soaked cloth he'd used for painting the new boat pole and put it in the fire. It went up with a real W-OO-F but the fire still went out so Peter got it going with the blow lamp.

The duck we saw yesterday with eleven chicks only had ten today and one of them didn't seem to belong to her. By the following day she only had seven chicks left. The lone orphan was still surviving on its own. The moorhen who had been sitting on eggs a long time finally hatched them out, a small brood of just three fluffy black chicks. She and the male fussed around and looked after them devotedly, both parent birds equally attentive. Sometimes the hen would sit on the chicks on the nest while the male went off to forage and returned with food in his beak. He'd scramble up to the hen and pass the food over to her and she then fed it to the chicks. While I was watching them a large heron swooped down and stood in the water a few yards away from the nest. The hen puffed herself up to twice her size and sat protectively on her young in the nest. The heron looked suspiciously interested in the nest so I went on deck and scared him off.

Yetti kept going off to the willow tree by the hedge and a blackbird was giving off alarm calls, so we brought Yetti in and Peter found a nest with two tiny chicks in and one cold unhatched egg. It was possible that Yetti or one of the other cats had already had a chick as Peter thought there would have been about three or four so we decided to take the boat and cats elsewhere to give the birds a chance. It was a bad time when all the birds were nesting and the young such easy prey for cats and other predators. A young bird, a pied wagtail, flew into the front cabin by mistake. Peter caught it and put it out and it flew off up into the trees.

Peter fell into the water when mooring the boat after going for water. Now that the undergrowth was taller it was difficult to know where the bank was and wasn't. In this case it wasn't where he anticipated it to be, so he slid down into the water with his feet going under the boat. He quickly grabbed the side and clambered up the bank. I didn't know as I was doing some washing, until I went astern and there he was with the 'wet look', from the waist down and no dry trousers to put on. So he put his swimming trunks on and went off with the long handled axe to split the huge sections of tree trunk lopped off a large willow over on some waste ground. I followed with the large plastic laundry bag and red holdall and we filled them up with the logs and made three journeys with six full bags. The wood hold was full with more spare wood on deck.

The duck with the remaining six chicks now seemed to have adopted us as their 'mother ship'. Mother and chicks parked themselves on our cat rescue plank, floating alongside us and had a rest. We fed the swan (cob) out on his nest patrol duty, asserting his territorial rights. He would swim as far as the bad tempered Canada goose who resided on the bank at the bottom of some gardens and was not afraid of anything including the dog that every now and then bounded around it barking. Everything seemed to be chasing everything else and we watched two magpies chase a rook which in turn chased a tern, trying to make it drop a small fish that it was holding in its beak.

Most days we continued to take an interest in the progress of the mother duck and chicks of which there were still six. They came for food followed by five marauding drakes, followed by the duck with four chicks but today she had five, so perhaps the lone chick was hers. These were all followed by the Canada goose, making quite a gathering at the breakfast table. Two more Canada geese flew in on the scene and chased all and sundry.

Yetti and Moggo were both hiding on the bank where the ducks sometimes slept. They were watching the duck and her chicks approaching the spot. Much to my relief they swam across to the other side of the canal.

We tried to keep the cats in more during these months when so many young creatures were being born, especially early in the morning. However, Moggo was like a caged lion and was belting around one morning about 4 a.m, so we gave in to him and opened the doors. Before long there were loud chirping sounds from the galley. "Oh! No!" My heart sank thinking it was a bird. I volunteered Peter, who was better at bird rescues than I was. I was the 'mouse rescue' department. He went into the galley, still half asleep and announced that it was a baby rabbit. "What doing bird imitations?" "Oh no!" he added as he scrambled out after Moggo "it's a duckling". Moggo had taken off up the towpath with it by its neck. At first he had brought it into the boat and dropped it in the galley and was teasing it until Peter appeared on the scene, then he made off with it. He dropped it on the towpath and it ran towards the bank to get back into the water but Moggo was too quick and grabbed it again, by which time Peter had caught up with him and shouted at him in no uncertain manner. Moggo froze, dropped the chick and sought refuge in the undergrowth along the path edge as Peter dashed to the scene looking like an over enthusiastic marathon runner, bare footed and naked apart from his boxer shorts. Peter grabbed the chick and put it into the water where it just floated around lifelessly and its mother and four other chicks headed up the canal away from it. So Peter threw bread to attract her attention, and she swam back towards it with the chicks. Meanwhile, Maurice was acting like a black panther trying to get out of the mid ships cabin where I'd shut him and he succeeded in squeezing himself through a gap that he had forced open and through the sliding door and was back up the path in a flash. Twice he escaped before we finally secured him. Another duck with four smaller chicks came along and the other duck with five chicks chased her. We thought the little chick would be sure to die of shock after all it had been through, but miraculously it recovered and swam off with its family. While all this was happening the moorhen opposite sat tight keeping her three little soot-like balls of fluff safe.

Where else could anyone run amuck barefooted and scantily clad at 4 am without being locked up?

It was about 5 a.m before we got back to bed and had to be up again at 7a.m as we had an appointment at the vet's to get Yetti spayed. She made no protest when we put her into Peter's fishing basket which over the years had served more as a cat basket than a fishing basket. Yetti was very frightened in the vet's surgery when I took her out of the basket to have her pre-med injection and she looked at me pleadingly as she was taken off.

Later in the day we cycled back to the vets in the rain and brought Yetti back. She was all over the boat when we got back, up on the shelf, on the bed, off the bed, under the bed, and finally settling on the bed to sleep.

We were saddened a few days later to discover that the moorhens had lost one of their three little chicks. There was also another brood, recently hatched out by another pair, comprising about six chicks, two of whom didn't look too healthy and another one floating and struggling along on its back. We picked it out of the water and I dried it on tissue paper and put it back in the water but it floundered onto its back again and looked so helpless and newborn, opening its beak and crying out with little chirpings. It was heartbreaking. Such was nature, and the law of survival of the fittest could be and was so very cruel. And everything was eating everything else including us humans. Moggo seemed to have had more than his quota of ducklings and seemed very partial to them. We found a half eaten one in the hedge gap plus the remains of a large mole. It wasn't often that they caught a mole but when they did they usually left it uneaten.

Moggo, ever seeking attention found a new way to get it by pouncing out onto the towpath in front of anyone and everyone who should walk past. Then he'd roll over in front of them and run around their legs hoping they would make a fuss of him.

I had a trip over to Luton to visit Shirley and stayed the night so we could watch some home movies and enjoy an evening together. We had been close friends since starting school together (about 1946) and although I had left home at 17 to join the WRNS and never gone back home to live, we had stayed close friends over the years. On our way back to the boat the following day we stopped at a derelict garden centre in Manor Rd so that Shirley's husband Fred could feed the three feral cats which he did on a daily basis. They came running when they heard his car, two lovely black fluffy ones and a big black and white one, a mum and her two offspring and now all as big as each other.

As our supplies of food were getting very low we decided it was time to stock up and set off with rucksack and bags to the market and Kwiksave. I think we might have broken all records for 'on bike' biggest shopping expedition. Peter had the huge nylon red bag on his back plus front basket full and carrier bag on handle bars while I had front and rear baskets full, rucksack on my back, plus carrier bags on my handlebars. One thing was for sure we'd be having a three course meal that evening.

There was good news! The little moorhen family that we had feared had lost one of their chicks was seen one evening, all safe and sound.

It was lovely at the end of a hectic day to climb into bed, rest our weary bones and read and doze. Peter was reading a good yarn and said he would read it to me which he did but as I usually fell asleep after a few sentences. Peter often carried on reading not knowing I was asleep. When it came to the following evening and he continued reading the story to me, he didn't know where we were up to so usually went back a few pages. At this rate he said that we'd never get to the end of the story because he was mostly reading it backwards. I told him he would have to change his hypnotic voice and not send me to sleep so quickly.

We were getting fed up with too many uncontrolled dogs along the towpath. Some were harmless enough but others were a real threat. One day Peter shouted and I ran astern to see three dogs chase Moggo along the path and then trap him between themselves and the water, in which case he had no choice but to leap into the canal and struggle to get back up and out further down. However, the concrete edged bank was steep and he had difficulty scrambling out. The woman with the dogs dragged him out and plonked him back onto the bank where the three dogs promptly continued to set about him and he shot along the towpath towards the boat. Peter managed to intercept the dogs as they ran in pursuit of Moggo and caught one with his foot on its front leg, temporarily bringing it to a halt. Not long after this fiasco, all three cats rushed in like scalded cats, spitting and hissing at one another in their dash to safety, their fur all hackled up. Three dogs, greyhound, lurcher types raced past on their own, their owner way behind out of sight. I decided to paint two little signs and put them ten or twenty yards fore and aft off the boat, to make people aware of the cats and ask them politely to please put their dogs on a lead. It was becoming very unnerving at times and we were constantly on the alert. We were of the opinion that two or more unleashed dogs was not being at all considerate to others. As well as the dogs, wherever we moored our first job was to get the hand shovel and trowel and remove any offending whoopsies. If we hadn't have done so we'd have inevitably trodden much all through the boat onto floors and mats and squashed it into shoe treads. It wasn't always practical to remove one's footwear every time we had to go in and out. We had to be extra careful when mooring up in the dark when we couldn't see what was on the bank. Nowadays many people are more thoughtful and pick up their dog waste and deposit it in waste boxes provided but these are only measures that have come about in more recent years.

It was perhaps easier just to move and find quieter moorings, which we did, out in the sticks. Peter went through a hedge and down a farm track alongside a field of oilseed rape, to explore. He stopped to look at the view across the fields and out of the corner of his eye saw a boiler suit clad body lying at the edge of the field just a few yards from him. He froze and a thousand things flashed through his mind as his heart turned somersaults. As he focussed on the body, headless at that, he realized with relief that it was just a redundant scarecrow.

It was nearly the end of May and we decided it was time to get travelling and find pastures new.

As we set off early one morning we stopped near Grafton Regis to locate Jesse's grave stone and moved it over the fence out of the farmer's field so as not to damage his fence. I cleaned the stone and cleared a patch of nettles, grass and cow parsley, dug a flat patch of earth and planted a clump of oxeye daisies that I had in a pot on top of the boat. I scattered some nasturtium seeds and Virginia stock and left a bunch of artificial silk daffodils and maybe a little bit of my heart.

We were reminded even more of Jesse when we reached Bugbrooke and took a walk through the beautiful area known as 'God's Acre'. There was a sheep grazing area as picturesque as a scene from a Thomas Hardy novel, where tall majestic horse chestnut trees with breath-takingly lovely pink candelabra-like blossoms, dominated all the other trees. A small stream meandered peacefully along its way, making a perfect setting. The sandstone church and churchyard were a real credit to the parishioners, many of whom voluntarily tended to the grounds in what appeared a very enthusiastic manner. In one wilder corner of the graveyard a lady was tackling the tall weeds and proudly announced "This is my section, the wildlife area". It was a quiet corner for conservation of flora and fauna but was being managed so as not to get completely overgrown. Every part of the yard was maintained and so many graves had fresh flowers on them. We found it all very praiseworthy. The village was lovely too, lots of nooks and crannies, lanes and pathways and pretty cottages tucked away. We climbed a stile to take a short cut across a field of calves. Peter, never keen on herd animals in fields, was so busy keeping his distance from a large black one that he didn't see the big fresh cow pat in front of him and put his foot right into it with a resoundingly squelching slurp.. His trainers had just been washed and dried, clean on – typical Peter. I hoped it was a sign of 'muck for luck' but doubted it, going on previous experiences.

We moored up near Brockhall Park. The cats loved it in a little clearing that I made for them, cutting the nettles, cow parsley and other undergrowth down with the scythe and allowing access to a little copse area with a low Y shaped divided tree trunk. It was ideal for them to climb and sit up in and play. Yetti and Moggo were like a couple of kids in an adventure playground, chasing along the branches. Jessica was up the tree too but Blobs was only interested in his food dish. Yetti still didn't like it when we were travelling and would run around meowing nervously.

Peter and I strolled up and over a small bridge to the gates of Brockhall estate and over the bridge the other way past fields full of cattle beans and fields full of peas. The smell from the bean flowers was like being in a beautiful perfumery, a mixture of bluebell scent and lily of the valley. The countryside was all carved up by the noisy M1 motorway, railway line and the canal and not far away the A5 Watling St of Roman origin. We wondered what the Romans would have made of that lot all running parallel with one another.

The old steam powered fly boat 'President' came chugging past with butty boat Kildare in tow and was an impressive sight and a unique example of the steam powered working narrow boats that operated at the end of the 19th and early 20th centuries. A crew of four or five men were on it all dressed in old fashioned boating attire, caps, white shirts, waistcoats and neckerchiefs. This particular old working boat was built by Fellows Morton and Clayton in 1909. It was now owned by the Black Country Living Museum.

Our travels took us on up Buckby locks where at 6 pm there were no boats going up but hoards of them coming down in twos and queuing, so there were plenty of locks ready for us and lots of helpers. From there we moored just a couple of bridges up the Leicester arm of the Grand Union which was a new stretch of canal for us. It looked nice and we were lucky to find a bank we could get close enough alongside to be safe for the cats as most of the banks comprised of the high metal structures or natural banks that were too shallow for us to get close enough in to.

We planned to do the Watford staircase and Crick tunnel the next day and didn't anticipate it taking us very long. However, we were wrong as it took us about three hours to cover three miles, two hours to do the locks due to a queue of boats and a 'one up, one down' system through the narrow 7ft beam locks. But the sun came out, hot, and we enjoyed talking to other boaters and helping here and there through the locks. We helped a couple operating the locks down, on a boat called 'Merlin' with a falcon painted on it. They had three cats aboard, a Siamese and two Burmese which unlike our motley crew of alley cats weren't allowed to go out or leave their boat. We shared some locks with a nice retired couple on a little (water bug) boat called 'Harvey'. Another boat in front of us had a nasty collision while negotiating the first staircase lock at an angle and going too fast. A girl on the front put her foot over the bow to fend it off the stone wall at the entrance and could have had it crushed as the momentum and weight of the boat would have squashed it like a fly if caught between bow and wall. The previous boat had hit the same spot which showed signs of having recently been rebuilt.

Our eyes were met by breathtakingly wonderful sights. Fields full of bright yellow oilseed rape and every conceivable shade of green imaginable in all directions stretching as far as the eye could see. Gentle rolling hills and scattered woods, sheep and cattle, some with calves, grazing. A pair of swans, mallard and moorhen chicks and the cuckoo's of course who had been ever present almost every day for the past month or more.

We thought we'd have a break from the boat one day and enjoyed cycling about three miles to Stanford Hall via Kilworth. The Hall stood on the banks of the River Avon. It had been rebuilt in the 1690's after the original medieval manor had been pulled down. We anticipated a leisurely look around the house and gardens including seeing the life sized replica of 'The Hawk' an experimental flying machine which was built in 1898 and invented by Lt. Percy Pilcher who was killed while flying it at Stanford in 1899. But, unfortunately, we had chosen to visit on the day the hall was closed to the public, so we stood by the gates munching our apples and admiring the pastoral scene, through the closed gates. For a minute we thought we were getting a free glimpse of the flying machine as the strange shape of a hang glider came into view over the tree tops. No such luck but we'd enjoyed our ride out and felt all the better for it when we returned to the boat.

With renewed energy after a good night's sleep we made our way through Husband Bosworth tunnel (1071m long).

Lots of people and boats, sightseers and boaters were gathered at Foxton Locks which were built in 1810 and comprised of two 'staircases' of five locks which on average would take a boat about 45 minutes to work either up or down the 75ft rise. These locks were the largest flight of such locks on the English canal system.

The canal arm up to Market Harborough was very river like in parts, quietly meandering along, and was added to our favorites list. We moored in a remote spot bordering a field full of cows who came up to the fence and stared at us curiously. Yetti was just as curious of them and climbed the branches of an overhanging tree to get a closer look at them. One or two of the cows came even closer to investigate her and one nosed its face onto the branch that Yetti was on and she moved forward and they actually sniffed noses. I even caught it on film on my camcorder.

A heat-wave set in, so we sat out and baked in the sun. Peter drew my attention to an air balloon floating very low above us and carrying two people who waved to us. It rapidly descended lower and lower and finally landed two or three fields away, scattering a herd of cows as it did so.

We saw very few people and were surprised when a cyclist came along as the towpath was very lumpy, bumpy and badly defined. As he passed the boat he looked up, said "hello" and proceeded to fly up over the handle bars landing in a heap on the towpath. The front wheel of his bike had hit a pot hole, come to a halt as the back wheel flew up in the air and threw him off.

I wished I had had my camera at the ready. It looked so funny. He was none the worse for wear, thankfully, although a little embarrassed.

This arm of the canal was very narrow and after having been up to the terminal basin at Market Harborough and turning to come back to our quiet mooring there was no easy way we could go back to the town on the boat. To do so would involve having to travel twenty minutes in the opposite direction of the town to find a wide enough turning point and then twenty minutes back to where we had started from in order to make the half an hour trip up into the town's basin. Although the towpath was not ideal for cycling it was a quicker option. On our first trip up into the basin our throttle cable snapped. Peter managed to wedge it in and we limped up to the boatyard. When the chap at the yard undid the holding screws and bracket retaining the cable it sprang up and whizzed the lot off into outer space. £45 and one and a half hours later we had a new cable and were informed that the 'morse control unit' was on its last legs, something we'd known about a year ago when we were at Preston Brook. A new one would cost us about £80.

As we travelled through different counties we came across some strange customs but I think 'Bottle kicking' took the biscuit. It was and still is, an old Leicestershire custom which takes place on Easter Mondays and is said to date back to the late 18th century or some say earlier before the Christian era. I didn't know how it all started but I was amused by the tale that the rector of one of the villages involved was opposed to the tradition because of its pagan origins and he tried to ban the event in 1790. He soon relented though after the words "No pie, no parson" appeared scrawled on the wall of the vicarage overnight. Part of the custom involved the vicar providing a hare pie, twelve penny loaves and two barrels of beer to the poor of the village. The villagers would fight each other for the food and drink and on one occasion the neighbouring villagers joined in the fight and the rivalry between them continued yearly. The event began with a march through the villages and residents carrying a large hare pie and three bottles which were small kegs or barrels. Two of the barrels were filled with beer and the 'dummy' barrel painted red and white. Before the pie was cut in pieces and some of it thrown to the crowds it was blessed by the vicar. The rest was put into a sack and carried up Hare Pie Hill. There were hardly any rules applied to the 'bottle kicking' game except "no eye-gouging, no strangling, and no use of weapons". The bottles/barrels had to be manipulated by village teams, across two streams and obstacles such as ditches, hedges and barbed wire. I think the aim was for teams to get the casks into other team's territories. Broken bones and other injuries were not unheard of. Rewards at the end of the game were celebrated by participants and spectators alike retiring to the pub. Yet another example of 'Mad dogs and Englishmen'!

The weather during our trips along the Market Harborough arm turned very wet and windy, hot and humid with torrential rain and thunder storms. We couldn't contemplate travelling up onto the river Soar in such weather and it was a good job we didn't set off some days earlier as the river Soar was un-navigable when in flood and boaters were restricted by warning signs and 'no go' lights warning people of the dangers. We didn't fancy ending up stranded in a water meadow or worse, becoming a sunken wreck again.

It was becoming difficult to find shops to buy walking stick ferrules and Peter had completely run out of them and had a good number of newly made sticks waiting for them to be fitted. While I was out on my bike exploring the town I came across a rubber factory, so I parked my bike up on the kerb and went in and asked the receptionist if they made ferrules for sticks. She kindly rang through and spoke to somebody and a few minutes later a business type man came in with a plastic bag containing ferrules. "What sizes to you require, etc etc" he asked. I asked him how many I would have to order in one go before they could supply me with them and he grinned and said "Oh about 2,000 at least". I laughed, picturing Peter working like the clappers and desecrating the hedgerows for sticks. I explained that I only needed regular small supplies and he was very pleasant and understanding. "Take these" he said handing the bagful to me "and try them, see what your husband requires and if you ever want to order a lot you know where we are." I asked him how much he wanted for them and he just dismissed my enquiry and said "Oh that's all right they are only cluttering up my desk at the moment." I was over the moon and couldn't wait to give them to Peter and see his face. There were a selection of thirty-two ferrules in the bag and I was very grateful to the man in the factory who could easily have just chased me away, unimportant water gipsy that I was. Un-snobbish people like this always reassured my faith in the human race

As much as I loved little Yetti and was 'her mum' she was very intrusive at night. During a terrific storm about 1.30 a.m I woke abruptly as a flash filled the cabin and I thought our number was up and had visions of headlines in the paper saying "canal boat hit by thunderbolt – no survivors." The flash of light was only Peter turning the light on. Yetti might have been un nerved by the storm as she started walking all over my head. I put my hands over my face protectively, but she nuzzled her nose under and around them, pawing as well, all very determined. If I happened to raise my voice or shout, she would lick my face as if to say 'calm down'. She'd lay, right across my face and to avoid suffocation I'd turn over and hide under the covers but she'd keep on trying to dig me out. In this instance Peter got up and gave her a bit of the last half of a tin of cat food and some dry biscuits but she still wanted to get me up so he shut her in the for'd cabin but not for long as she got out, so he shut her in again, then Moggo started scratching at the door to get in to where she was. Peter was beginning to think he was a reincarnation of an elastic band. Sleep that night was very little and due to the fact that we were moored up in the boatyard for the night waiting for it to open in the morning, we had kept the cats in.

When I got up at 8a.m it was all stations go, like being in a Geriatric or rather a **Gericatric** ward, emptying litter trays, preparing food with Blobs hovering on the sink; Jessica on the other side, Moggo and Yetti around my feet. It was like feeding time at the zoo. I managed to put cat food onto a dish while dancing around the cats and caught the edge of the dish on the cooker, sending it flying onto the floor, while at the same time my elbow caught a cup of water on the side and that spilled down my leg into my shoe. Enough was enough! I wasn't amused although I could hear Peter in bed laughing at me. I bawled out at Blobs who was now perched on the other side of the sink by the cooker with his tail on fire (again). "Your food's down there on the floor you silly old bastard, and don't go shitting on the mat again when you have had it." Poor old Blobs! Good job he hadn't a clue what I was ranting about, as he was only being a cat and it wasn't his fault if the litter trays had been all used up when he'd wanted to 'go'. I saw the funny side of it all and we laughed at the thought that if anyone had been passing the boat hearing what I'd been shouting at Blobs they might have thought I was shouting at Peter. How cruel I would have sounded, making him eat his food off the floor and accusing him of being incontinent and having dirty toilet habits.

Peter thought the bottom had dropped out of his world when as he was peacefully dozing in his old reclining chair, it suddenly collapsed and unexpectedly flung him back into 'flat out recline' position that the chair wasn't programmed for. It was so funny I almost went hysterical. He managed to prop it up against the bulkhead and carefully sit in it, half expecting to end up on the floor any minute. He only had that to sit in as on the other side of the cabin between the woodstove and bulkhead was the 3 or 4ft long box top seat I sat on. We could perch on it together no doubt if the chair was un-repairable. It was, and in time we managed to find a pair of old fashioned fold flat deck chairs in a second hand shop for a few quid. Peter was happy to replace his chair with one of them for the time being.

The longest day, June 21st saw us within a few yards of the River Soar. There were 7 locks spread out all through Leicester and the first one at Meadow lock was by the lovely wide weir linking the canal to the river. In this lock we nearly lost the big 'moustache' shaped bow fender which had come adrift one side when a retaining bolt sheered off the chain. Peter soon secured it again and we continued on through Leicester, not feeling inclined to stop on our way, especially when a couple of teenagers lobbed half a brick at our stern as we went under a bridge. We were always vulnerable to missiles being lobbed from bridges while we stood unprotected astern. One part of the river approached a very long wide weir and put the wind up me as we seemed to be heading straight for it with no alternative route, till with relief we saw the narrow turn of the river which was the course we had to take. Six locks on to Barrow on Soar and we barely had time to moor up when we saw a bloody great Doberman dog bearing up on Moggo who had wasted no time in getting ashore. Moggo shot up the trunk of a tree and clung on while the Doberman barked and jumped up after him. Its owner, who was some sixty yards away shouted and bawled while the dog totally ignored him until he was near enough to grab the dog and hurry off with it. Moggo meanwhile was stuck 18-20ft or so up on the first branches of this huge tree. He was very agitated, running along branches looking for a way down and meowing. No amount of encouragement or calling and tapping the food plate would bring him down so we had to leave him eventually and go to find the Post Office, which was shut as it was early closing day. Moggo was back down the tree when we got back.

Surprise! Surprise! Late Wednesday the following day, Gerald and Freda arrived. We really hadn't expected to see them before the weekend as it was a long way for them to cycle all the way from Dunstable. I joked with Freda and said I bet she had had to pull Gerald up the hills on a towing rope. Freda had a rather posh natty hat so we nicknamed her Lady Loughborough. They had only set off Tuesday and had been cycling for 11 hours non stop. They were bedded down early in their sleeping bags out in the open field alongside the towpath, hidden by the hedge, so hopefully wouldn't get disturbed. The cats sat on the fence singing lullabies to them.

Mid summer day, 24th June, my birthday and Gerald and Freda treated us to a meal out in the town followed by a nice relaxing evening. As it was pitch dark when we returned it was easier for Gerald and Freda to sleep aboard, rather than try climbing over barbed wire fences and other potential obstacles.

We continued our journey with Gerald and Freda in tow, down the Deep lock onto the river Soar and decided we would all have a day out the next day and ride into Loughborough on our bikes. It was a perfect day, hot and sunny and the highlight of the day was a trip on the steam train 'Boscastle' All very nostalgic, especially the marvellous smell of the trains. If that smell could have been bottled there would have been a lot of oldies buying and sniffing it.. It was just like stepping back into the 50's for us. There were porters and station workers (all volunteers), well kept waiting rooms and even a 'ladies waiting room' all clean, no graffiti. As we chugged along, the train stopped at little stations along the way, some of which we got out on and had a walkabout. On returning to Loughborough we looked around the engine shed and as we walked back towards the station a lovely old loco came down the track and stopped for water near us so I took the opportunity of filming it on my camcorder. The chap in the cab with the engine driver, noticed my enthusiasm and called out to me, saying, "Give yer camera to 'im (Peter) and come on up here." I didn't need telling twice, bunged the camera across to Peter and clambered over the fence and up onto the footplate of the train which was quite a haul, up into the engine. I was so thrilled I was lost for words. Up in that loco engine cab I was shown how everything worked and marvelled at the enormous furnace of a fire. It was the highlight of a perfect day.

I just loved steam trains, they had been such a fun part of my childhood when Gerald and I along with other children had cycled to various stations or railway tracks and spent hours train spotting. One of our favourite spots had been down by the Vauxhall factory on the outskirts of Luton, out in the country along a steep embankment cutting. I remember how excited we would get when we saw or heard a train approaching and how mischievously naughty we sometimes were when we placed pennies on the line to see what they would look like after they had been mangled by the train wheels. Some of the boys thought it was very clever to put their ears to the line to detect if a distant train was approaching. If only our mothers had known what we were getting up to. But we certainly hadn't wanted to pose any danger to the trains, though I suppose unwittingly our very trespassing along the line did cause some concern. Lots of children took part in the train spotting hobby though, it was harmless enough and kids have to learn lessons in life and can't do that in my opinion if they stay wrapped up in cotton wool. I am very thankful that my mum and dad allowed me to be a child, to roam the fields, play out, scrump apples and climb trees, jump off haystacks, fall over and off roller skates and have a wonderfully happy and magical childhood. The only part that had spoiled it for me was having to go to school.

Chapter Thirteen

'Run In' by the Police

There were more cabin cruisers than narrow boats on the river Soar. We were being eaten alive by insects and whatever they were they seemed to particularly like feasting on my blood. Tall stands of sweet smelling meadowsweet with fluffy white plumes looking like sticks of creamy candyfloss had taken over most of the banks. In Anglo Saxon times it was called 'mede-sweete' because it was used to flavour mead. It was also used to cover floors to make rooms smell fresh and sweet and was used medicinally for many ailments as it contained salicylic acid which is one of the properties used in asprin.

We navigated about 9 miles on the Soar enjoying scenery around Normanton but it wasn't so scenic around Kegworth when the Castle Donnington power station came into sight and dominated the skyline for miles.

Reaching the River Trent, a wide expanse of water where the Erewash canal runs up to Nottingham and the Trent takes off up the Cranfield Cut one way and to Shardlow the other, we were a bit puzzled at the automated dual locks we located and it took us a little while to fathom out the sequence of buttons to press. It made a nice change though, to just press a button and the gates shut or the sluices closed. Sawley Cut was one mass of boats, the most we had ever seen. By the time we had negotiated ten locks we decided enough was enough for one day and moored up just short of Shardlow.

The atmosphere at Shardlow was very flat to what we had expected to find. The whole place seemed dominated by a couple of pubs along the canal displaying bright umbrellas and lots of people eating and drinking. Other than that and lots of boats in the boatyard it had little to offer us.

We will never forget Shardlow lock, especially me. As I took the boat into the lock, a small fibre glass cabin cruiser followed in after me, so I took our bow up close to the top gates to allow room behind as it was too wide to fit alongside of us. Really I could have done with a rope just to hold our boat steady and safely away from the cabin cruiser. Had it not come into the lock with us there would have been no problem but once the sluices and gate paddles were opened there was a surge which pushed anything in the lock backwards and then forwards. Peter usually opened them slowly to minimise these effects but sometimes surges were unpredictable so to be on the safe side I moved up close to the gates, keeping a good eye on the position of our bow fender on the lock sill below the gates. At the same time I caught Peter's eye and in sign language pointed to my nose, indicating our bow close to the lock gates He looked and signalled me to back off but realized I had to keep pretty far forward of the crushable cabin cruiser's bow. It was difficult to communicate under the circumstances of not being able to hear what anyone was saying or shouting about. Suddenly I felt as though the fore part of the boat was being sucked down, pointed to my nose and yelled at Peter to look and act on it but could not convey the seriousness of the situation and what was actually happening. It was a horrifying moment as I realized that I was going full astern but nothing was happening except that the stern of the boat was rising with the propeller up in the air out of the water and the bow was being trapped under the gate beam above the sill tipping up further and further as more water flooded into the lock. I knew that something had to be done immediately and yelled to Peter to "drop the paddles". The chap on the cabin cruiser saw the predicament and impending disaster and leaped off his boat and up the lock side ladder, ran along towards Peter who had by this time dropped the paddles to stop anymore water going into the lock. I shouted to the man off the cabin cruiser to open the bottom gate paddles to allow the water out, so with the top ones shut and bottom ones open the water level dropped just in time to avoid us capsizing. As the water level started to go down the bow of the boat sprang out like a Jack in the Box from the gate beam with an almighty boomerang of a bounce. The water had only been about 18" from the bow top and I dreaded to think what would have happened had it gone over it into the boat and if the cats would have been drowned. We wouldn't forget Shardlow in a hurry or feel happy sharing locks with fibre glass boats.

In the next few days Peter developed a fever, hot and cold shivers, so he dosed himself up on powders. We delayed our travelling plans so he could rest up and recover from whatever lurgy had invaded him and the best place was in bed warm with lots to drink. We thought we had found the ideal spot opposite a sewage treatment plant where there was no smell at all till the morning when the wind changed direction and the boat was filled with the smell of rotten eggs and which no amount of joss sticks could camouflage. That left us with little choice but to move on to some less smelly spot. We found a place near Weston, and while I went to phone Mum, Peter heard such a commotion from two moorhens fighting over territory. They could be extremely vicious and both birds were so exhausted that Peter was able to scoop one up out of the water and lay it on the bank. The other one, he thought had had it, and looked half drowned. However, it slowly recovered enough to swim off. Peter put the one he had scooped out, back into the water and it too swam off but unbelievably about half an hour later they were fighting again and one flapped and splashed its way out of the water while the other one chased it along the field edge.

It was always good to chat to locals and learn a thing or two about the place we were in. One chap we met seemed to know just about everything, even where the lovely 'blewit mushrooms' grew. He had shooting permission with the local land owner and had seven guns and mainly concentrated on wood pigeons. The Donnington race course was just over the hill and on the hill was a tall monument to the Duchess of Hastings who, it is said, had her hand cut off on her death and buried there so that she could 'still have a hand in managing the estate'.

He also told us that during the war a nearby airfield served as a base for Wellington bombers and that Eyebrook Resevoir was used for practice by the Dambusters before their raids on the Ruhr Dams took place in 1943.

Temperature soared up into the 80's and Peter was still ill with what looked like a bout of bronchitis. Not the sort of thing you would expect to get in the summer. He sat out on the towpath sniffing and coughing, stretched his legs out and fell asleep, then woke with a howl of pain as a little girl out on a bike with her family ran over his foot. It could only happen to Peter.

We didn't feel in a hurry to move on but had no choice when the gas ran out. A 19k bottle usually lasted us a couple of weeks but this time had only served us 9 days. We had a loose fitting which caused a bit to leak out of the locker so we had it tightened up at the Marina when we replaced the gas bottle. There was quite an explosion (no not of gas) between Peter and I having a heated argument which started early in the morning when Peter suddenly said we would have to move the boat just up past a lock because we were too near the railway line which was worrying with the cats. I'd just dried the dishes up and was just about to have my wash and get dressed, when Captain's orders came thick and fast. "Call the cats in; turn the engine on; pass me this; pass me that" all in a tone of great urgency. I hurriedly got dressed and was doing my best to get the cats all in but of course Maurice was absent without leave as always. I took some cat food on a plate out onto the bank and called him while Peter was ready to set off and said something that just tipped the scales of my patience level and before I knew it I'd hurled the plate of cat food at Peter on the stern. Lucky for him my aim was rubbish and the plate shot past him into the canal, the fork followed and missed him but I felt better for it all the same. It was good to let off steam now and them and it gave us a good laugh later. Peter chuckled and said "I could have got that fork up my nose". "Up your arse would have been better", I replied. I was glad that another boat hadn't been passing us at the time as they might have ended up wearing a dish of cat food. The way things were going it would be 'Murder on the Rainbow II' never mind on the Orient Express.

A large black and white cat sat at the bottom of our gang plank one night, preventing all shore leave for our moggies. Yetti was growling, Jessica was sitting unperturbed on one of the stern seats and Moggo was peering down at it from the roof. I put some food on the towpath for it in case it was hungry. It looked a real battle scarred tom and as there weren't any houses or farms in view we couldn't begin to guess where it had come from. No sign of the cat or the food the next morning.

I had an interesting hour or two exploring the plants along the bank. It was always nice to see the quite common floating rafts of arrowhead with leaves as their name suggested shaped like arrow heads. Water plantain, a stately looking plant with much branched pyramidal inflorescences of tiny pinky purple flowers, bowed graciously as passing boats drew the water sharply away from it.

Little strikingly violet blue flowers of trumpet shaped skullcap, growing out of lock gates, walls or banks. The plant contained 'scutellarin' a very strong oil said to be effective against nervous disorders and to have calming effects, but that too much or the wrong dosage could induce the very ailment trying to be treated. One species of skullcap used to be nicknamed 'mad dog weed' as it was believed it could treat and cure rabies.

In contrast to beautiful plants, Burton-on-Trent was a terrible 'blot on the landscape', absolutely carved up at random by what must have been a blind assortment of architects. There were DIY and supermarket blocks thrown down anywhere at random. If it hadn't have been necessary to stock up on stores we would have given it a miss and it was quite an awkward ride back with £25 of groceries. Glad to move on we found a nice spot to stop just past Alrewas, a picturesque village where the river Trent crossed the canal.

The following day I cycled to the village and found a doctor and made an appointment for Peter at noon so I had just over an hour to get back to the boat and get him back in time to keep it. The doctor said that Peter had left the infection too long before seeking treatment and that at his age (Methuselah?) he should see a doctor and get treatment at the first signs of illness especially with his record of chest problems. We always made the same mistakes though whenever he was ill it was a case of –

Me	–	How are you feeling today Peter?
Peter	–	I'm okay, its not on my chest
Me	–	Are you sure – perhaps you should see a doctor for antibiotics?
Peter	–	No I'll be alright. I'll tell you when I need them.
Me	–	I'm not so sure. Don't want you getting a collapsed lung or pneumonia (both of which he had already had twice in his life.)
Peter	–	No my lungs are alright – I'll be fine. Just give me a co-codamol.

And that's the way it usually was. The doctor prescribed antibiotics and said next time he was ill to get to the surgery sooner.

Co-codamol eased his aches and pains and the recurring fever abated after about six or seven more days and we began to think the worst was over but in his weakened condition his recovery was slow. He took it all in his stride, laughed a lot at himself instead of moaning although I knew he felt far from good. I knew that if it became really necessary to move the boat three or four miles on to Fradley junction, up three locks, I would manage if need be. But we hoped the fuel and water would eke out till Peter felt fitter.

The weather didn't help and turned wet and squally and our mooring pins and ropes had worked loose, the bow rope so loose that it allowed our bow to swing out across the canal in the wind. I managed to heave the boat back alongside and Peter came out to help secure it. The bank was very soft so the pegs came out easily especially after a few boats had passed.

The small fridge we had acquired and connected up on the fore deck conked out and I had to throw all the spare ribs, liver and bacon and a small block of ice cream out. It had happened once before and I had ended up giving Peter the meat eater's meal of a lifetime with about two weeks assortment of meat rations piled high on his plate. We managed to salvage some chicken before that failed the 'sniff test' – we didn't need sell by dates.

Mid July and we finally did run out of water so had to move up the locks to Fradley junction, rather a nice place but a very slow water tap. I hadn't really wanted Peter to travel on yet as he had no energy and was washed out, but he wrapped up warm and took the boat into the locks while I opened the sluices and gates.

That job done we were able to find a quiet mooring by the river Trent. A boater informed us that just along the river bank opposite our mooring, under an over hanging bank there was a mink with three kittens. So I got all the cats in before we went to bed as I felt sure that Moriarty Moggo would fancy baby mink for his supper for a change. Moggo was obsessed with catching anything that moved. We caught him leaping around on the bank one day after something in the grass, a mouse I thought, but when I went to investigate the movement I could see a black shape bigger than the usual brown mouse shape or the smaller shape of a shrew and when I pulled the grass away the shape moved on burrowing down in the grass roots ahead of it. It was a little mole as I caught sight of a pink quivering nose and little flat feet and a half inch or so beaver like tail. It continued to frantically scuffle and root around and at last signs of soil and excavation took place. I silently willed it on, to hurry up and get burrowed out of cat's claws way. I had a battle keeping Yetti away especially each time she saw the soil move, and became very excited as to what it was moving around under the grass. At one point she managed to get past me and leap on the mound. There was a pitiful little squeak and movement of the mound of soil ceased. 'Oh! no!' I thought and hoped it was still alright. I kept Yetti well away and there was a bit more movement but not a lot so I put a large wooden box over the mound to make it cat proof. I'd never had such contact with a live mole before, nice little thing and very strong. A quotation from Mahatma Gandhi came to mind 'I hold that the more helpless a creature, the more entitled it is to protection by man from the cruelty of man'. In this case maybe 'from the cruelty of cats' would have been more appropriate.

July turned into a chilly month of monsoon weather and muddy towpaths. The rain didn't deter Moggo from his hunting jaunts and he came running onboard with a live mole which we rescued and put into the field and watched it burrow deep down out of harm's way. Later he bounded down the towpath with a large rat so I quickly shut the door, deciding that it was one meal he could have and eat outside. It wouldn't have been a very welcome passenger if he had brought it into the boat and let it escape.

We had travelled about eight miles on from the Wedgwood pottery through industrial Stoke which we had imagined would perhaps be a bit troublesome to navigate. However, it wasn't and it had a pleasant atmosphere most of they way and no brick throwing kids. However, just moored up near Milton later in the day Peter went storming off up the towpath and I heard him shouting so went after him. He was apprehending two youths with an air rifle. As he came back I went up to the youths and asked them what they were doing. "Only shooting rats" they said. A likely story I thought, we'd only seen a rat or two in months and we lived on the canal. I said I hoped they weren't shooting at birds and one lad piped up "Oh you're allowed to shoot blackbirds." God! I thought, there was no hope with morons like that on the loose.

Reaching Etruria we turned off up the Caldon canal, where a large statue of James Brindley the canal engineer stood prominently at the entrance. A good number of bottle kilns announced for sure that we were now in the Potteries and the air was clean these days compared to how it used to be some fifty or sixty years ago when Stoke 'stoked' its fires and blotted out the sun with a blanket of smoke and soot across its towns.

The eighteen mile long Caldon Canal was built between

Etruria and Froghall in 1776 and was intended to transport limestone extracted from the quarries. Coal from the Cheadle coalfield and ironstone from local iron ore mines was also carried on the canal. Later in 1801 a branch was constructed to Leek

We found many of the bridges to be very low and had to move a lot of stuff including Peter's bike off the roof and take care to duck our heads low to avoid getting fractured skulls. As we approached what looked like a bridge even a submarine would have difficulty to get under, we slowed down wondering how on earth we were going to negotiate it. Something about it didn't seem to make sense. Then the penny dropped, it was a lift bridge. An automatic electrically operated one, which we operated with our

BWB key, after we first lowered the two barriers to stop the traffic. All the other lift bridges were manually operated using the windlass.

There were notices warning people about blue green algae on Rhudyard lake. A boater we met told us that they had lost their 11 year old bitch who had died as a result of being poisoned from it.

We reached Leek terminus but felt a bit penned in and disappointed so turned and headed back to the three locks. An hours run down to join the Froghall branch of canal took us to Cheddleton where two very well preserved flint grinding mills stood with their two impressive working water wheels. It was here that the famous "Toby Jug" originated.

At the mill, flint used to be brought from France to Runcorn down the Trent and Mersey and also from the South of England. The flints were put onto the flint kilns and calcined to make them easier to grind then, once sufficiently ground, they were sent to the potteries. One of the mills used to be a corn mill dating back to the 13th century. The mill cottage was 250 years old and well preserved inside to retain the character of the last occupants who had lived there (the parents of the lady who now resided in the other cottage). The large hearth with its cooking range, was the focal point, displaying large black pots, kettles, flat irons and other utensils of the day. A portrait picture of the miller and his wife stood on show along with the piano and violin that they had played. There was a small washroom and store room and just one bedroom upstairs as was normal in those days.

I became a 'cowgirl' for about fifteen minutes of the day. When we were getting ready to go down a lock we saw a cow on the towpath. "Put it back in the field Peter", I suggested. But Peter went very deaf and continued to open the lock paddles and ignore the cow that looked up and gave a snort of disapproval. Well, deciding that someone should round it up and that that someone must be me as no one else was around or volunteering, I grabbed a stick and went down the path, struggled to open a heavy gate and shoved it aside far enough for a cow to squeeze through. I then noticed there were two more cows on the towpath, so after successfully maneuvering one into the field I approached the other two and yelled at them to "come on". Nothing would persuade them to do so until I hid behind the hedge and then they plodded along and into the field and I promptly shut the gate behind them. I felt quite pleased with myself then a horrible thought crossed my mind. "What if they didn't belong in that field?" There were more cows across the bridge in another field. I might have ended up getting done for cattle rustling! Oh well, at least they were safer in the field than on the towpath.

Finally we made our way along to Froghall tunnel which led to the New Wharf. But the tunnel was too low for our boat to get through as it was for most boats. It was a bit frustrating as just past it was the Wharf where we had hoped we were going to fill up with water. We'd just have to ration ourselves.

Apart from the unsightly Copper Works, the valley here was like something out of paradise and definitely top of our favourites list up until now. We moored in an idyllic spot across from the towpath side of the canal, wonderful for the cats, no threat of dogs being walked and millions of trees.

This valley was a haven for wildlife and very isolated, so much so that it was quite an expedition to get to a shop. So ideally we should have been well stocked up on essentials. We weren't, so before long we had to cycle to Froghall wharf and cycle up one heck of a long steep hill, which was impossible on our clapped out old bikes. So we walked, pushing the bikes and frequently stopping to gasp for breath and rest aching legs. From the wharf it was one long two mile-ish walk uphill to the one and only shop at the top, at a place called Foxt. Coming back was a real breeze and took us just minutes. One of Peter's brakes went on him so it was a good job the other one worked. After that I slowed down considerably as I only had one brake working and went cold to think how fast I had been descending the hill and picturing what would have happened to me had that brake gone.

Later in the afternoon we sat and enjoyed the surroundings and watched some green woodpeckers coming down into a small field full of rabbit warrens. We couldn't make out what they were doing but a local farmer called Reg told us that the field was full of ant hills and the birds were after feeding on the ant eggs. We climbed over a style into the field one day to watch them and some of the farmer's cows wandered back into the field with their calves. They weren't bothered about us, although Peter was uneasy about them as he never felt comfortable being one of a herd in a field. He kept a good distance between them and himself. Suddenly Jessica appeared, calling out to us so we gave up on our bird watching and made our way back to the farm bridge across the canal. As we reached it, one of the cows with large horns stopped to stare at us but was obviously not staring at us but at Jessica. We strolled over the bridge and I just glanced round to see the cow, head down moving intently towards us. I yelled out "it's coming for us, run" and pushed Peter aside as I took off towards the style. I didn't have to tell Peter twice, and we both seemed to reach the style at the same time and attempt to climb over it together in one big heap. When we told Reg, he laughed but said that the cow 'Daisy' was a bit of a one and could be quite fearsome when with a calf and would have attacked a cat, dog or anything while she had her calf with her. The calves, raised for beef, would stay with the cow for two years.

Reg had lived in the valley all his life, and was born in a cottage next to the farm his grand parents had there. Eventually his parents took the farm over when Reg was about 22 and he worked on it rearing beef with his father until he passed away well into his 90's in 1992, after which Reg continued to run it. During the war, the last place you would have imagined to have been bombed would have been this peaceful valley, but one night three bombs fell, probably destined to fall on the copper works or maybe the railway, but had fallen off target, with two coming down in the proximity of where we now had our boat moored and the third had fallen near the farm house. Reg's grandfather refused to leave his bed that night but the rest of the family left to spend the night at a farm further up the valley until the next day.

Reg and his wife Ruth often walked along the canal with their collie dogs Zak and Lady and stopped to chat with us. They lived down at Froghall now and their daughter ran the farm. Ruth met Reg when she was sixteen and on holiday with a friend in Blackpool. She grew up in the Potteries and worked on a pot bank as a flower maker, making flowers out of clay by hand. If they were anything like the lovely bread she made and sometimes brought along to us, they must have been very nice.

We couldn't get enough of living in this wonderful valley and decided that when we had to go back towards Cheddleton to find a water point, we'd come back and spend more days here. Before that happened we had another grocery run, but this time cycled as far as the wharf at Froghall and then waited for a bus into Cheadle which was all up hill and down dale. After finding a Kwiksave and doing our shopping we had two hours to wait for a bus back so found a café to have a cup of tea in. On our return, we got off the bus and onto our bikes and were drenched in a cloud burst. Peter had had the huge red travel bag on his back and when we arrived back at the boat and I went to unload it I found it was half full of washing up liquid. I usually supervised the packing of groceries into the bags to prevent things like this happening, as Peter would just bung everything in, upside down, bread at the bottom, tins on the top, whatever and however. Luckily most of the groceries were alright, as most of it was tinned stuff and although the Go Cat biscuit box was soggy with liquid, the biscuits inside were salvageable. "Some mothers do 'ave them," I thought. I made a nice fruit pie and we were looking forward to it with lashings of custard but found out that we had left the box of six cartons of milk in the shop.

There was a considerable colony of feral cats living down near the factory and we came across about ten all trying to get at some food from out of a carrier bag which had been left there. A black one scuttled away when it saw us and two black and white ones moved in, then three ginger ones and three kittens. There was evidence, from numerous scattered containers and bags left in the bushes that people were feeding them.

We enjoyed walking and exploring the area and one day walked along to Froghall to find out where the river went from there. It wound very secretively and inaccessible down towards Oakmoor, and was so beautiful in places that we visualized building a little house there with vegetable and flower gardens, some fruit trees, chickens and a few animals. We disturbed a family of wrens in an elderberry tree who were all of a flutter, before we found a nice spot to sit on the river bank looking for signs of trout. Though Peter thought there would only be the odd one coming down from the reservoir which was stocked by anglers. We walked along the disused railway line and came across hundreds of spotted orchids growing, most now finished flowering but a few still displaying blooms. A few harebells, St Johnswort, self heal and woundwort were also still flowering. On our way back we came across a lone rather flown out' racing pigeon. Peter tempted it with some bread and managed to pick it up. He showed me the owners address stamped across its wing feathers and we saw that it was from Leicester. There was a phone number. It was a lovely bird, a 'blue check/chequered Mick' and it soon flew off only to land on the bridge as we walked past,. Then off it went again and we hoped it would get home safely. It was only a young bird born this year.

We saw 'private fishing' notices along the river but we never saw a soul fishing or a bailiff checking it out. Peter discussed it with a few locals one day and all seemed of the opinion that no one would be that concerned if

Peter went down and had a little walk and fish along the river. So Peter lived dangerously and did just that, it was so tempting for him, the walk along the bank as much as anything else, clad in his waders and fishing jacket, looking for likely pools and fish on the feed. He caught two small grayling and a brown trout, some roach and a chub another day, all of which he returned to the river. Some parts of the bank were very overgrown and high and, while lowering him self down into a shallow part of the river to fish it, he put his hand down onto a thick branch which snapped like a twig and sent him whizzing down into the water. However, as he fell he had the presence of mind to fling his rod aside to avoid the risk of breaking it. He survived with just one wader filled with water and the tops of his trousers wet but that didn't deter him. Bet it frightened the fish off.

Reluctant to leave the valley just yet, we went back as far as Consul Forge to fill up with water, and returned back to our favorite mooring overlooking the river one side and steep wooded hillside the other. I'd managed to paint another butterfly or two on the boat plus a castle scene, so we were looking nice and bright. Many people stopped to admire them and take photos of the boat.

Now we had water again we could have a nice hot bath, or half a bath. We used to take for granted full length baths, to stretch out and relax in. Now we had to sit crouched up like squatting frogs, knees up under our chins, but it was still nice to soak in the hot water. The shower we had hoped to use after I had rigged up a shower curtain was unsuccessful as it was only connected to the hot water and 'hot' was often 'scalding hot'. The bath pump had not been working for about 2 years now so we were used to baling the water out by the bucket full, or leaving the water in the hip bath and using it to soak washing in overnight.

Yetti caught the most beautiful little mouse I'd ever seen. It was a reddish brown colour with big round ears. I yelled out and she dropped it onto the path where it sat up on its little back legs, with whiskers twitching. I leaped on it before Yetti had chance to pounce, grabbed it up in my hand, yelled and dropped it as it viciously sank its teeth into the end of my finger, but quickly grabbed it up again by its tail. Moggo came running up to see what was going on so I shooed him and Yetti off and deposited the little mouse down the bank where it ran off. That night Yetti didn't move off the bottom of the bed all night which was unusual for her. We discovered that her back left foot was very painful when touched and later she was limping around on it. We looked at her foot with a magnifying glass and she growled and spat at us. We could see nothing intrusive there but thought a thorn might have gone in between the pads of her paws somewhere. We soaked the paw in warm salt water and she didn't object to that so we soaked it again later. Whatever it was must have resolved itself as she was soon running around again.

A local man who we spoke to one day happened to be involved in helping to keep watch on the many badger setts in the area. He told us that a constant watch had to be kept on some setts to provide protection from gangs who would swoop in, usually very early in the mornings. How anyone could be so wicked to even contemplate badger baiting and digging them out and subject them to horrendous atrocities we could not comprehend.

Reg kindly informed us that he had put two bulls in the field with his cows. We wouldn't be going in there anymore for sure. A few days before he'd put the bulls into the field he told Peter we could go down into his fields and get some wood and saw up parts of a dead tree which he pointed out to Peter. Interestingly he told us that the valley used to be full of glow worms up until the time when the canal had been restored and opened up. I'd only ever seen them before on the cliff tops near Perranporth. The kids would gather them up into paper bags and hold them up in the dark where they shone like lanterns.

A couple called Jean and John on a boat moored astern of us named 'Lleuwen' invited us to join them for a coffee. They had recently retired and had built their own boat in their back garden in the 80's. Neighbours had been quite suspicious of this activity and whispered their suspicions to one another, convinced at one stage that John was building a nuclear shelter. They must have thought he was equally crazy when the so called shelter took on the shape of a boat. A combined shelter and ark maybe!

We planned to walk up to the animal sanctuary which was situated at the top of one side of the valley, but rain had set in so we would have to wait for a nice day. Blobs came in out of the rain and sat plonk on my diary, rendering 2 pages almost unreadable. Jessica was missing and still not in when I woke just after 5 am which was unusual for her as she was usually curled up on her little part of the bed. Feeling uneasy about her I called her and rapped on the metal hatch cover with a fork which all the cats, apart from Blobs, responded to. Torrents of rain poured down making quite a din but I must managed to hear a mournful and distressing yowling and looking to where it was coming from I saw the bushes across the canal move and reveal one very hangdog or in this case hangcat cat. I quickly donned my cagoule, unhitched the rope from the mooring peg and shoved the stern out over and across the canal to Jessica who was now on the bank. She wasted no time in leaping aboard, bone dry. The woods were extremely thick with plenty of cover to shelter beneath but how she had got over there will remain an unanswered question Either she had strayed quite a way down the path and crossed the farm bridge and wandered too far back along on the other side, or fallen in and swam across and climbed out, and dried herself in the hours she was stranded before I discovered she was missing. Whatever had happened, she made such a fuss and after a feed settled on Peter's lap and purred ecstatically for ages.

Finally, we managed to take to the slopes and make our way up the muddy and slippery hillside to the Wildlife Sanctuary but just missed the last of the two daily 90 minute tours around it. So after chatting to one of the voluntary workers we carried on walking up to the top of the valley, across fields and into Kingsley and back via the main road and country lane to the sanctuary before descending the steep climb back to the canal. We must have been gluttons for punishment as the following day we re-trod the route back to the park and waited with eight or so other people to go on a tour. It was difficult to hear what the tour guide was saying as we were at the back of the group being taken around. However we saw various owls and birds of prey and a variety of animals, some which had been rescued from zoos or parks or such as the little monkey which had been confiscated from its owner who had kept it in a flat. Among other animals and birds that had been injured and rehabilitated at the park there was also an arctic fox which had been rescued from a fur farm. Many of these animals would never be able to fend for themselves again in the wild. There were also able bodied ones that had been taken into captivity as private pets including two lynx and two foxes, one blind in one eye and a 9 year old one who would never be returned to the wild. Down in the small hospital buildings things looked busy but of course we couldn't intrude there as the animals were being treated and hospitalized. The guide brought out a small hedgehog and told us some tales about various incidents including one call they had from a women saying she had found a live 'lobster' in her garden which turned out to be a crayfish. In all we found it not a very pleasant place to visit really as the birds and animals, although fortunate to some degree, were unfortunate in their incapacities and or captivity

At least the cow in the field with its calf looked happy and the two bulls that were having a gentle 'head to head'. Reg was concerned about one of his cows that was suffering from 'August bag' (summer mastitis) which is caused by a fly that infects the cow's udder which swells up and causes the teats to retract upwards and if not treated daily the cow would probably die.

As soon as there was a relatively dry day or two, I made the most of it and washed the candlewick bedspread, 2 blankets and sheets in the bath. Also turned and aired the mattress as damp pervaded everything. While hanging things out to dry on the fence a couple came by walking their three Alsatians, including one they had rescued after it had been deliberately turfed out of a car and left. The car was seen pulling up and dumping the dog which then ran amuck. I think their other two dogs were also acquired from the nearby dog rescue home. All dogs were well trained and obedient. Their owners turned out to be the couple who ran the tug drawn trip boat at Froghall but I didn't recognize them out of the traditional boater's dress which they wore when doing the trips.

One evening discussing the lack of space in the boat we spent about three hours redesigning it all and by the end of that time we had had so many different ideas, some absolutely hilarious, that we decided it would be easier to leave it as it was. The main idea was to try and create a bit more space by getting rid of the permanent double bed in the mid ships compartment and put a suitable bed settee in the for'd cabin so that the midships space could be used in the day, or ideally made into a galley. The total space inside the boat comprised of approximately 24ft. The front cabin 8ft or so long, bedroom 7ft, WC area 3ft 9" and rear end galley 6ft long. All cabins were of course 7ft wide or, after taking into consideration the space between the actual steel hull and gap filled with insulation materials between it and the tongue and groove panels, it must have been more like six and a half feet wide. Some of our ideas made a lot of sense, especially the open plan lounge/galley design doing away with the midship double bed room. However the cost was the biggest obstacle and having a suitable place and the time to spend doing it and importantly someone to help with the work.

Peter had been attacked voraciously by some kind of 'Vampire' midges when he was down at the river and his nose and eyes were very swollen as a result of the bites. He looked like a prize fighter. We were running short of stores again so off we went on our bikes and locked them up at the pub near the bus stop and waited for the bus. We were waiting for the 1.10 to Cheadle but by 1.45 there was still no sign of a bus. We put our thinking caps on and decided that as it was Saturday there would be a different time. So the best bet seemed to be for one of us to stay one side of the road and the other to cross and wait on the other side and see in which direction a bus turned up first and get on it regardless, as we didn't mind whether we went to Cheadle or Leek as long as there was a handy shop. So I sat one side of the road and Peter on the other side. As we waited we saw two police cars by the canal and they came past heading for Cheadle. Another one pulled out at the junction, the policeman driving looked at Peter (no doubt thinking he was a likely looking rogue) and Peter signalled with his hand that he wanted to speak to him, so he pulled over. Peter asked him about the buses but he didn't know how they ran at weekend but was good enough to call up his station and ask them to look up the times for us which they did and we learned that the next bus was due at 4pm. Seeing our plight the policeman very kindly said "I'll run you in." We all saw the funny side of this statement and had a laugh. It was a lucky break and we were very appreciative. We made sure we knew the times of buses running back.

With our water now down to the emergency supply kept in a spare beer barrel on the stern deck, we very reluctantly had to leave the lovely valley. Ruth and Reg seemed sorry to see us go and we agreed to write to each other and hoped we would be back someday soon. We said our goodbyes and Ruth handed us a bag containing 6 free range eggs and one of her nice freshly baked loaves of bread.

Moggo became quite addicted to the dried Go Cat biscuits and being a bright little spark discovered that if he knocked the box off the shelf or table, onto the floor he could manoeuvre and get his paw into the opening or just scoff what happened to fall out. If we were around he would just knock the box off the shelf then roll over on top of it meowing as if to say "Oh I do like these".

Chapter 14

Blobs Missing

We were on a new leg of our journey now and I reckoned that we had, since commencing our journey, traveled some 1,500 miles and navigated through over 1,000 locks.

Now with Autumn not far away on the heels of a somewhat cheating summer, which had mostly deserted us this year we continued to head North through Stoke. Back to operating heavy locks, and lots of them, our muscles and joints ached painfully I collected a large bunch of comfrey leaves, boiled them up in the washing cauldron, sieved the water into the bath, added a few drops of lavender oil and had a wonderful hot soak in the bath. Peter had second soak when I was finished. We saved the water to soak all the dark coloured washing in, then I washed and scrubbed it in the sink, rinsed it and emptied the bath water out with buckets.

On reaching Middlewich we put Blobs into Peter's fishing basket, strapped it onto my bike and took him to see a vet. The vet diagnosed a small growth in his mouth so we left him overnight to have an anesthetic and the growth removed.. We picked him up the next day along with a hefty bill and some medication. All he wanted to do when we returned to the boat was eat, but we'd been advised not to feed him for twelve hours.

We made good progress as far as Preston Brook and called at the Marina hoping to see Gary and Heather but they were out so we left a note plus a bottle of home brew, a painted cauldron and a small glass window sun catcher. We were sorry to miss them as it had been a long time since we'd seen them but we didn't want to lose time and had to journey on. Just back from shopping at Stockton Heath a narrow boat pulled in behind us and we heard a shout, turned and saw Gary and Heather waving to us. It was great to see them both looking so well and on their new (no name as yet) steel narrow boat plus two new crew members in the shape of 'Beauty' a great dane and 'Ethel' a tiny terrier. We had so much to talk about and catch up on.

Before we arrived at Lymm we stopped alongside a field full of corn on the cob. Peter had a notion to try a few and disappeared completely into this field of tall fully grown corn cobs. I searched with difficulty to see where he was and at last could just see his green hat bobbing along level with the plants. In order for him to see where he was going he would have to jump up and down to get a view of his surroundings. I nearly died laughing and thought to myself that he wouldn't last five minutes out in Africa.

After leaving Worseley I became concerned about Maggie and the soon to be born baby. I needed a news update and a chat. We were on the lookout for a place where there might be a phone box but the stretch of canal we were on was very bleak and unaccommodating. We were tired and a bit at sixes and sevens by the time we reached Poolstock locks, late in the day about 6 or 7 p.m, and not a very nice area to have to stop. The canal banks were built up and high so we decided that the cats would have to be kept in.

Blobs was improving a lot on the tablets and had a good appetite. I put his food out astern on the deck and shut the doors quickly to keep the other cats from dashing out and made sure they were in the galley before I opened the front cabin doors so that Blobs could come back in. It had just started to drizzle. Blobs always toddled a few yards off the boat to do his toilet after a meal but came straight back to the boat. Peter called out that he'd found out where there was a phone box and said "Come on, we'll go now, I've got the bikes off". So I dashed off and forgot Blobs was not in. As we had had no intention of letting the cats out we had not put the rescue plank into the water or the tyre fenders, both of which might enable any cats that fell into the water to get onto and out. Out of habit, Peter had put the board up forward to block off access along the narrow gunwale and was on his way astern to put the folding chair up to block off the other end but got talking to a chap off another boat and forgot. So off we went and when we returned there was no sign of Blobs. With it drizzling, Blobs would only have been interested in getting back in the boat and he would no doubt have gone along the offside gunwale to get to the bow but would have come to a grinding halt when he found his way blocked by the board. All he would be able to do under these circumstances was either back all the way along the gunwale back to the stern, or turn and make his way back. These two options were both pretty impossible on such a narrow strip and we were gutted to think he might have fallen into the water and drowned. Had the banks been low he would have had some chance of scrambling out, but they weren't. Also he may have been short of breath after too much exertion. Needless to say, we searched the area, high and low and felt absolutely demoralized when we didn't find him. We blamed ourselves and I kept picturing him in the water with no one to help him. Every time I related the incident to anyone, I tortured myself repeatedly and became so emotionally upset that Pete suggested it would be best to say Blobs had just sadly passed away during the night Unless, of course, we were putting out information hoping that someone had seen him and that miraculously he would turn up safe and sound. I couldn't bear the thought of telling my daughter Maggie what had happened, especially in her present 'mum to be' condition. She had been with me when just a young girl when we had gone to see the litter of kittens that Blobs was one of and we had chosen him together. She had always been the one out of all the family who had been Blobs' best friend.

I felt I had let Blobs down but Peter said it was fate and we had done our best for him and the others but no one was perfect and accidents did and would always happen. We continued each day to search and call and ask people if they had seen him. A young woman passing with a child said she walked the canal path once a week and that her father frequented it often. She took my Mum's phone number and a photo of Blobs and promised to call if she saw him.

Reluctantly we knew after a few days we had to move on and start the long haul up the big Wigan flight of 23 locks. Each lock gate and each paddle (six in all) had anti vandal locks on so were even more time consuming to operate. Pete did all 23 locks while I handled the boat in and out of them. A pleasant young lock keeper helped us who helped us on a previous trip and down the flight three years ago kindly prepared eight or nine locks for us which was a great help. He also took details of Blobs and said he would inform us if he came across any information about him or a sighting. At the latter half of the locks a lad on a bike assisted us. We loaned him a windlass and anti vandal key and he emptied locks, opened gates and opened and shut paddles right to the top of the flight. At the top lock there were loads of youths jumping into the lock, some had had quite a bit to drink by the looks of them. We gave our helper a glass of beer and a few quid for his help. He said that if poor old Blobs had drowned and should turn up in the water, as casualties of drowning sometimes did, that he would make a point of burying him for us. It had taken us about five hours to navigate up the locks so we were ready physically and emotionally for a rest.

The following day it was a heat wave and we cycled down the flight looking out for any signs of Blobs and carried on into Wigan for some stores.

That evening we sat out watching a bright orange sunset. I saw a shooting star fall and thought 'Ahh that is Blobs going off into the sunset'. How he would have loved the hot weather we were now having. What little epitaph could I give him? I was too sad for words. He had been with me eighteen years and I think that the three he had spent on the boat were his best, nice and warm most of the time and Peter's lap to sit on and be made a lot of fuss of. Wigan would now have sad memories of him as Bugbrooke had for Jesse and 'Ye Olde No 3' near Bollington and Preston Brook of Ibley Dibley who was the most tragic of all, being such a young cat.

Our continuing journey heading towards Burnley was jaded by our recent loss but there was the birth of a new grand child to look forward to. Apart from that our spirits were not very high and we were looking forward to the end of this journey north. Before long we would have to be back at our strenuous wooding tasks. Often we came across decent sized pieces of wood and branches floating in the canal and fished them out if possible. There was quite a forest floating along one section of canal, large sections of tree trunks which it was impossible for us to pass by. Peter hauled what he could out with the help of a rope and one piece was about eighteen inches diameter and 3 foot long so was quite a struggle pulling aboard but he managed. We reckoned we would have enough to fill the fore peak hold once added to an old lock gate post we'd salvaged the day before.

We won't be cold tonight Maggie

Moggo seemed to be possessed of the devil most days and would fly around in a crazy playful mood, leaping and darting around. Nothing was safe when he was this way inclined with the wind in his sails and in a just few minutes he could leave a trail of mayhem as he knocked things around.

The radio went onto the floor followed by a box of my pens and pencils and paint brushes on one such occasion. We sure had taken on 'trouble' when we adopted him.

Our huge metal dhobi pan full of an assortment of towels must have fallen off the stern seat into the cut as the towels were all floating around. We fished what we could out of the water but there was no sign of the container so Peter tried poking around with the boat hook, then a more determined effort to locate it with the grappling iron but all he recovered was branches, plastic bags and smelly mud. I would really miss the pan for boiling up washing.

As we at long last approached the outskirts of Burnley and the area Maggie and family were living in Peter shouted "There's Maggie, waving.' She had seen the boat on her way to the doctor's and parked up by the canal. It was a lovely surprise and I went to the doctors with her after picking up Joelle from school and Joelle and I were able to listen to the baby's heartbeat which was all very exciting. Later on my eldest daughter Marina called in to see us and also Maggie, Bradley and Joelle, so it was a cheerful evening, quite a tonic after the events of the past few weeks. It was good to see the family as I had missed them all. Daughter Michelle popped in and sons Michael and Mark with lots of news to catch up on and as always lots of laughs. Especially from Michael who at the time was crippled up with a very bad back and having a job to walk or even move. He had gone to see the doctor but his usual doctor wasn't on duty and was replaced by a temporary one who looked about ninety years of age, and possibly a veteran from the Crimean war.. He was somewhat eccentric to say the least and over enthusiastically ranted on to Michael insisting that, "Your posture is all wrong." While at the same time promptly leaped up onto the couch demonstrating leg and other therapeutic exercises as he did so. He seemed to be on a planet all of his own and as suddenly as he embarked on this posture routine he stopped and said out of the blue "I'm thinking of changing my car for a newer model, what do you think of the Zephyr and where could I get one?"

"Try the museum" thought Michael, and that he might have been better trying it himself instead of visiting this doctors.

During our get togethers the subject of boat redesign cropped up and took over much of the conversation between the men who made plans to transform the insides of the boat, while 'baby' talk was more of an option between us women members of the family

Blitzkrieg on the boat was soon under way. We ripped out the double bed and much of the tongue and groove where it would be necessary to fit kitchen units and worktops. Cooker, sink unit and corner worktop all to fit in a six foot space. That evening with the galley space cleared and empty I put the double mattress down on the floor and made us up a bed. The three cats were most appreciative.

Work came to a grinding halt as gales and deluges of rain blew in and waterproofs definitely became the fashion.

We'd taken the boat to the BWB yard where they had given us permission to moor while working on the boat alterations. Soon the yard was almost taken over with family vehicles loading and unloading gear and tools for work on our boat to hopefully begin in earnest.

With work to fit the kitchen sink unit under way we had to get rid of the double mattress. I then had to sleep on the rather short and uncomfortable locker seat in the front cabin while Peter tried to kip down on a camp bed but after numerous attempts it either collapsed or tipped him backwards, and all I could hear was much shuffling around accompanied by muttered 'bloody hells' and sounds of frustration as yet another attempt to hit the hay fell through. Out of curiosity I went to see what was going on and Peter was all tipped up at one end of the bed, legs in the air and looked extremely funny, to me anyway. As if that wasn't enough to cope with at 12.30 am Peter woke me up saying "We're adrift and being stoned." He had had to get up to go to the toilet and had seen shadows pass by the boat. He also heard and felt movement of someone moving on the boat. Every now and then some large objects were landing with a splash in the water and a few of these missiles were hitting the boat. It was very worrying as the yard was pretty isolated and deserted at night and we felt vulnerable to whoever was intruding upon us out there. Peter saw some dark shapes on the bank across the canal and we decided it was safer to stay in the middle of the canal where we had drifted after being set adrift. At least there we were safe from unwanted boarders though not from the missiles being lobbed at us. After awhile we thought we would be sensible to move out and down towards the town. So we turned the boat and found a mooring along the embankment, behind another boat. There was safety in numbers. We found a phone box and contacted the police and two plain clothed officers came to see us before going off to take a look round the boatyard.

The next day we were back in the yard and work on the boat resumed with Michael sorting out the gas and water pipes, immersion heater and ending up having to take the bath out to sort out the various pipes from the kitchen and where what went, renewing and re routing them then connecting them to various gadgets. It was becoming a plumber's nightmare. He said that all the pipes and wiring resembled 'Spaghetti Junction'. Nothing seemed to be straight forward. He had to dismantle the immersion heater from the stern cabin and re-site it in the galley then cut a fresh vent for it in the roof. Once all this work was done he was going to make a start on a complete rewiring of the boat.

Bradley arrived with the new sink unit and put it all together and fitted it and the work top with cupboard beneath it. It was exciting to see it all taking shape after looking like the wreck of the Hesperus. During this upheaval it was necessary in the interests of their own safety for the cats to be taken ashore and looked after for a few days during the worst of the upheaval aboard. All the family popped in at different stages of the work, Marina bringing fresh cream cakes and biscuits of which we needed a continuous supply to go with endless cups of tea. Michelle took measurements to make us some new curtains and covers for the new single locker bunk foam mattresses which were planned for the stern cabin which had been the previous galley. It was all systems go and all hands on deck and everyone was doing what they could to help.

Feeling peckish one evening we decided fish and chips would be nice so Peter went to the chip shop which was some 250 yards away out of the yard and down a busy street. First he called at the off licence another 50 yards on from the chippy then returned to the chippy. While he was inside he noticed a black cat on the step and stopped to stroke him on his way out. In amazement he realized it was Moggo who certainly was quite fearless.

The galley continued to be fitted and the little cooker re-sited. Once that was in place, fitted up onto a raised base to make it level with the sink unit and work top, Brad was able to continue work on the bed lockers astern.

The one on my side had to be made shorter so as to allow access round the bottom of it into the galley and also in the opposite direction to access the stern door. So he fitted an extra foot or so length on a hinge at the bottom of the locker so that the bed could be extended at night, otherwise I would have had to sleep with my feet hanging over the end into space.

The cats had not settled at all well as land lubbers and Yetti was quite traumatised. As soon as possible we brought them back to the boat but it was very unfamiliar to them at first and they were very unsettled for awhile. Brad had fitted a cat flap into the for'd steel doors which we were sure would make life a lot easier and a lot safer. Up until now, for much of the time night and day, we had been leaving the stern doors open regardless of whether it was winter or summer. Moggo was first to learn how to use the cap flap and was soon batting about in and out of it.

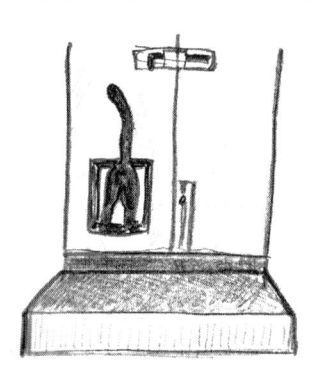

The state of the surrounding yard alongside our mooring area was such a muddy and slimy green mess from goose droppings, which were so slippery it was lethal and unpleasant. I filled buckets of water and sluiced about 20 or 30 yards of it around the boat area then using a stiff brush, shifted as much as I could till we had a nice clean washed approach. It was a never ending job, cleaning, sorting and shunting debris and stuff around onboard. We had no gas or electric at times while the pipes and wires were being renewed and no loo as the porta potti was constantly moved around to make room, here and there, even at one stage out on deck. Good job there was a loo in the yard to use. So little space and so much work going on and clutter and chaos everywhere, it made Steptoe's yard look tidy. But everyday things were taking shape and we could see good progress was being made. Michael came down to start rewiring the electrics throughout the boat, not an easy job in such cramped and awkward spaces.

Then, work had to be delayed for a while so we decided to move out of the boatyard, travel through the town and into a quieter area off Barden Lane, but before we left, I had nipped ashore for some supplies and Peter had gone to visit nearby relatives. He told me to prepare myself for some news which I would find upsetting. I held my breath as he went on to tell me that, during the conversation with the relatives it had been somewhat casually mentioned that our cat had been found! "What cat?" Peter had asked. He was so shocked to discover that apparently someone had phoned them up months ago to tell them that they had seen a black cat around their place for a long time but had never managed to get near to it, until gradually they coaxed it into the house and read the name Jesse with address of 'Rainbow II' and phone number of the relatives on its collar. They said that the farmer near them had often seen it in his field and during the winter months had put food out for it. I was speechless, poor Jesse, alive? Was I dreaming? But why had it taken so long for the relatives to let us know, why had they not tried to contact us at the time of the phone call? It was hard to understand. Jesse must have had a terrible time as it had been October when we lost him, believed killed on the road. All winter he'd managed to survive on his own, left to eke out food and shelter for himself among the fields and hedgerows. No doubt hunger had forced him towards the nearby farm and their neighbours who lived alongside the canal. What must these kind people who had cared about him have thought of us when we had not returned their call or even asked after Jesse or thanked them for looking after him? Frustratingly, the contact number for the people who had phoned all those months ago could not be found. In desperation I went to the library and looked at survey maps for the area and could only find one farm in the area we had moored. I searched the Yellow Pages for 'farmers' but there were none on a farm of that name. So on the off chance, even with remote odds of it being the farm we were looking for, I decided to write. I couldn't sleep for worrying about Jesse and the feelings of guilt haunted me endlessly.

As we left the boat yard and made our way through the town we passed the aqueduct bridge and saw three police trying to get a man down off of it. He was sitting astride it, waving a bottle of vodka about and shouting and cursing at the police as well as threatening to jump off. At a distance I saw him a few minutes later down on the towpath.

Thankfully there was always some incident that made us laugh, which was just as well at times like these. Peter had placed his deaf aid into its posh little box and inadvertently (a nicer word than stupidly) put it on top of the wood stove. A short while afterwards he lit the fire and the stove became hot and started to melt the hearing aid which was then rendered obsolete. I shouldn't have laughed as a few days later Peter went off to the bank cash point to get £20 out. He returned with two £10 notes safely folded into the piece of paper I'd written the card number on and handed it to me. Thinking the note was nothing more than that I screwed it up and threw it into the blazing fire. "The money's in with the note" called out Peter from the galley. I jumped up hoping I might recover the notes before they turned to ashes but no such luck they had gone up in smoke. God, we not only washed out floors in beer we also literally had money to burn. My excuse was that I could not think straight for thinking of Jesse's predicament and waiting for my new grandchild who was having none of this 'being born' lark. I was on edge and impatient hoping to get a reply to my letter. If it had been possible I would have jumped into a car and shot down to Bugbrook to find him, but that was not a sensible or viable option at the time. It would also not have been in Jesse's best interests to be snatched up, shut in a cat box and taken on a long unpleasant car journey. Even worse, then at the end of the journey to be introduced to a strange boat and three alien moggies. No, we would have to plan his recovery in his best interests and choose the right time to do it, however badly we wanted to be reunited with him.

It was a breath of fresh air to be out of the confines of the boatyard and in the countryside, especially for the cats. The only downside was that within just half an hour of mooring up Peter counted twenty-three dogs with seventeen dog owners, which wasn't good news for the cats but we had no other option.

The days passed and there was still no letter and no baby. I was constantly tired from worrying and also unable to get much sleep on the four foot long locker seat for'd in a sleeping bag. Peter wasn't faring much better on the camp bed and we both looked forward to getting the thick foam for the new stern locker bunks and additional front cabin locker seat which was to replace Peter's temporary deck chair. There was still some work to be done in the stern cabin, the upper tongue and groove wall panelling had to be sanded down and re-varnished especially where the cooker and sink had been. Peter had borrowed a sanding tool so it would not take him long to do, then I'd be able to varnish it all along with the locker on his side. Once both frames for the two locker seats were made we used them as a base to make a bed up on by laying boards and the old door across them. We had at last managed to get all the thick foam we required for seating and mattresses so although it was not a very stable sleeping arrangement it was comfortable enough and warm compared to the freezing temperature in the stern cabin. We found it necessary to buy a small portable calor gas fire which we could put in there to warm it up on cold nights and it just fitted between the two locker beds. All this shunting around at night in order to get to bed was becoming tiresome but we knew it would not be long now before it would all be completed. We were extremely thankful and appreciative of all the work being done for us and it would make our life on the boat more comfortable and enjoyable we were sure.

Michelle and Darren came down one day and brought us some wood off cuts to burn. Michelle gave us some very nice fancy cushion covers with frills and tassels that she had made for us in the same material as she had made the seat covers. She also made us a nice big lined curtain to hang across the middle of what would now be our open plan lounge/galley area. We were able to draw it across on a rail Peter fixed up running across the gap between the galley and fore cabin to cut down on drafts.

At last on the 5th October a lovely healthy baby girl was born to Maggie and Brad, so it was a very happy day. It was a great relief that everything had gone well. 'Rainbow granny' (me) now had four lovely little sunbeams in her rainbow.

My mum had phoned Bugbrook post office to enquire about Lower Farm and the post mistress knew about Jesse who she said was at Lower Down Farm and that the people were called Roberts. So I wrote again explaining all and enclosing an SAE for a reply and thanked them for caring for Jesse. Gerald and Freda said they might cycle up to Bugbrooke at the weekend and see what they could find out. However, before that came about we had a letter from the farm explaining everything and which read as follows:

"Dear Margaret and Peter

Thank you for your letter, it was passed on to us by our neighbour. We were very pleased to hear from you and how much you cared for Jesse. He took a long time for us to get friendly with him but each morning I sent some food down with my husband and Jesse would listen out for the sound of the Diahatsu and come out of the hay bales to meet him at once. Eventually my husband (Doug) could stroke him and he purrs and rolls over and loves all the fuss. Our farm buildings are between the canal and the main railway line crossing at Banbury Lane; the fields you described where you moored are ours and only a little way from the buildings. Mrs Reid lives in the house near the canal and she has taken over the feeding of Jesse, as Doug went into hospital in June for a major operation. He is making good progress with his recovery now and fusses Jesse every day as Jesse lives in the buildings and wont go inside Mrs Reid's house although he is loved by all the family. We should be pleased for you to call if you come along the canal in the Spring. I know Jesse won't wander away.

Yours sincerely. Mary and Doug

It was wonderful and such a relief to get this letter. I phoned them up and spoke to them about our situation and the pros and cons of picking Jesse up. We all agreed that in his best interests it would be best for us to travel down in the Spring and see if we could gradually re introduce him to the boat, however long it took, and of course if he would want to with three unknown cats and a changed around boat. The choice would be Jesse's and it wouldn't be fair to force him back to the boat if he preferred his new life and surroundings. We would see. How I wished I could just see him again and make a fuss of him, or just explain to him what had happened and that we hadn't deliberately abandoned him. But the main thing was he was fine where he was for the time being.

The nights were now cold and frosty. All work was now complete on the boat, nice and shipshape so we decided we had better find a decent winter mooring. We stopped near B & Q to get a few things that we needed for the boat and then the boat wouldn't start, nothing Peter tried would get it to go. So we decided to manually pull it back to our previous mooring and get to grips with the problem the next morning. Well, easier said than done and we spent the next two hours tugging it along by the stern and for'd ropes for about a mile. Manipulating ourselves and the ropes past and around numerous small trees and bushes was the most tedious part and keeping the boat moving along where the water was particularly shallow at the edge of the canal. We found a phone box and called Leo who said he would come down the next day and see if he could resolve the problem. He did just that and temporarily fixed a break in the connection leading to the solenoid and said he would come back now he knew what the problem was.

It was now the end of October and definitely the weather for 'long Johns'. We were still looking for a suitable winter mooring, somewhere where we wouldn't be too blocked in by BWB winter stoppages and restrictions due to closure of certain locks or dewatered stretches of canal where they had work to carry out. What with one thing and another we were running behind schedule to get settled somewhere suitable. Moggo didn't help with his anti social behaviour. Trying to get him to come in was at times a nightmare, and he would just run off down the bank. We had tried for ages to coax him aboard one day but he was having none of it so I went down the bank and through the barbed wire fence, calling and stalking him and finally managed to grab him and pass him over the fence to Peter but Peter stumbled and had to let him go to avoid falling on him. Off shot Moggo again, little pest. He seemed to know when we were setting sail and didn't want to come in. I managed to get him in once, all locked up and the next thing he was out on the towpath again! I'd forgotten to put the cat flap shutter stop in. I gave up calling down the bank to him where I could see him sitting all nonchalantly in the field taking no notice of me at all. I had an idea and attempted to do an impression of what we now knew was the 'cat in distress' call, or more like howl. So I made this horrible yowling noise and was amazed when he turned and looked at me, so I did a few more yowls and suddenly he called back and started to head up the bank towards me until it was 'GOTCHA' time. Well that was a new tactic which would come in handy no doubt. I was glad no one was around to witness my feline distress impression.

We travelled up through the seven locks to Barrowford and had a three quarters of an hour wait at Foulridge tunnel for the lights to change to green. The scenery now started to get very nice and the banks were good ones for the cats. We were happy to moor and get settled for a nice supper and peaceful evening. Peter's knee had been swollen up with arthritis and was at times very painful, so he needed a good rest. It had been troubling him for weeks now and although he had seen a doctor and been given anti inflammatory drugs, but it wasn't improving much. He was getting quite down with it and we even discussed the prospects of abandoning ship and becoming land lubbers – heaven forbid. Peter worried that if it continued to deteriorate he would not be able to log wood, open the locks and do the many jobs that I couldn't do. Good job we both enjoyed reading and nothing better than getting warm and cosy with a good book. However, we both agreed that pain was better than the agonising thought of leaving the boat.

There was a very handy boat yard at Barnoldswick, so hopefully we had found the ideal area for winter mooring. We were weary and more than ready for hibernation. It had been a hectic time since we had left the Churnet valley.

The weather became colder as November weeks passed by and we became frozen in unable to move the boat at all which in one way was good as we had to stay put and not do a lot. But the water and gas wouldn't last forever. We'd sensibly managed to cycle to the boatyard before the ice and snow set in and bought a 56lb bag of coal to help tied us over if we couldn't find wood. It was I think the first coal we had ever bought since we embarked on our journey. We also bought a 7k bottle of gas which we strapped to the rear carrier of my bike and Pete carried the coal on his handlebars. The gas bottle was a spare for the little gas fire.

We had a few boat neighbours now which in a way was reassuring and nice to see smoke curling up from their chimney flues. There was a small boat of about 25ft long moored about 150 yards from us and the chap of about 35-40 had only been on it four or five months. I'd spoken to him briefly and he seemed a loner. He wasn't very happy as he had just lost his dog. It had just disappeared so I said we'd keep an eye open for it. His boat was in a bad way inside, almost gutted. He was working on it one day and invited Peter in to have a look at what he was doing to it. Peter nearly passed out with the stench and dirty state inside, all a terrible mess. Rather a shame to get like that and we wondered what sort of life he had led. He seemed inoffensive enough. We saw him get a bowl full of water out of the canal, (before it froze up) squirt some washing up liquid in it and wash his dishes up then throw the water back. He came out once and filled his kettle up out of the canal so we hoped he wasn't going to drink it. He had no toilet, porta potti or anything. We were amused, as every now and then he would nip off his boat with a bow saw and disappear over the wall into the narrow hedgerow where he was sawing up the last of a fallen holly, or was it hawthorn, tree? Peter too made excursions into the undergrowth to forage around for wood but there was very little to be had and dry stone walls made up a large part of the landscape around these parts instead of hedges. Luckily for us the family were still bringing us any wood they could get hold of and that supplemented our stock and if we really ran out of anything to burn they would bring us bags of coal, but we hoped we would manage to provide enough for ourselves by looking daily for anything we could lay our hands on to burn. We touched out very lucky finding one or two old railway sleepers buried under foliage alongside the nearby disused railway line. We had to be very careful and burn a bit of them at a time as they were soaked in tar and burned up ferociously with large globules of sooty tar flying out of our chimney flue and any boats moored near us depending on which way the wind was blowing would be covered in them, as we ourselves were. But as long as we were warm we didn't mind. Another of our neighbours just down past the bridge had a small fibre glass cabin cruiser and a small rowing boat tied astern of it. He was pleasant enough and we didn't see much of him as I think he worked during the day. There were two narrow boats of a similar size to ours, one with two lads on who had two big motorbikes. The other boater, just a young lad also had a motor bike and five dogs which he was always out walking with in the fields. All these 'smokey stovvers' would give us a friendly wave when passing by. Further down there were two or three funny looking, very makeshift cabin cruisers, with hardly any home comforts in then by the looks of it. Many were not well off compared to us, by a long chalk, had no proper wood or coal fires or electrics, just candle for lighting and one had a paraffin heater. We thought we were hard done by when we couldn't get a TV picture, which we were having a job to do along this part of the canal. We noticed that one or two boaters had aerials extended on long high poles so that was a clue as to why we couldn't get a picture. So Peter temporarily rigged up a long piece of wood, lashed to the lamp bracket outside and fixed the aerial to that. It wasn't very successful and with the doors constantly being opened the boat was as cold as the freezing conditions outside. Even when the picture was good for a few minutes, if the aerial slipped or moved a fraction the pictures started to roll and flicker or disappear. It was easier and warmer to just forget TV and read or write or snooze. Peter said he'd get it rigged up more securely once he could get hold of a decent extension pole.

We shut the cats all in at nights while the canal was frozen over as we didn't want to risk them going through any thin patches and under the ice unable to get out. We knew they had at times ventured out over the ice as we had seen their footprints. The little rascals would have to stay shut in with us. We were cosy enough in our new stern sleeping quarters, apart from a lot of condensation on windows, and the roof in particular. There was a lot collecting where the water heater had previously been situated, through a vent, so I blocked it up on the outside with a plastic tub which stopped any rain or draughts getting in. Occasional drips of water built up over a long period of time during the night and were dripping down onto Peter's bedding over his feet so we put a plastic table cloth over that area to stop the bedding getting wet. "All the more reason for me to have breakfast in bed now," laughed Peter.

As soon as morning arrived, Moggo was going demented to get out, so as I was up I let him out. No sooner was he out than he was down the bank, onto the ice, through the ice, panic stricken, and frantically clawing to get back onto the ice. He repeatedly clawed at and broke the ice then swam a bit, clawed and broke more ice, like a little ice breaker. He at least had the presence of mind to turn towards the boat and once he reached it clawed at the sides. The bike, chair, petrol container, drums of diesel all cluttered astern prevented me from being able to get to the edge of the stern quick enough to reach over and grab him and he swam away from the boat in a panic. He then swam where the ice was broken back towards the stern and bank. I thought it was going to be curtains for him but he managed to reach the bank and scramble out and ran off into the undergrowth. I was surprised that he had survived so long and sure he had had his nine lives plus many more. I hoped that would deter him from ice skating antics in the future.

That evening the ice froze solid bank to bank. It was on record as the first snow in November since 1969. It was well below freezing and stayed freezing all the next day. Michelle called in to see us and brought her dog Chevez with her and we nearly had heart attacks when it went leaping out over the ice into the middle of the canal. Thank goodness it was too thick now to break. Chevez was in the dog house and locked in the boat. That night and a few following nights we swapped our sleeping quarters for warmer ones up in the front cabin. It was more of a palaver shunting stuff around to make up a bed but worth it for the extra comfort of warmth and dryer conditions.

We were trapped good and proper in the ice now and were expecting the water to run out soon. The chap on the small cabin cruiser told us that there was a tap in the field by bridge 149 which the farmers used, and a slim chance it might not be frozen up, but we thought that most unlikely. However we nipped along to have a look and found the water, no tap as such just a bath/trough with a ball cock that once the water level in the bath dropped water came out of a pipe to top it up. Peter broke the ice on top of the trough to see if the water pipe was frozen but to his surprise it flowed quite freely, so at least if we became desperate this water would help us out, first and foremost for cooking and brews.

Pete was always in the habit of taking out his hearing aid and putting it down somewhere then not knowing where he had put it, so we played lots of games of 'hunt the thimble' but in this case 'hunt the hearing aid' When we had gone to the hospital to get a replacement hearing aid, the receptionist said, "Don't worry, it is commonplace to lose them". She said that the most common losses occurred when people's dogs chewed them up or they accidentally fell off people's ears into cups of tea, or got dropped down the loo or got put into denture glasses of water with teeth. So Peter didn't feel so daft after all.

Continuing to hunt for his new replacement aid we turned the place upside down and found numerous other bits and pieces we had lost, but not the hearing aid. If nothing else, at least it was one way of sorting out lockers and gear and making it all a bit tidier. Annoyingly there were signs of a mouse resident in one of the lockers where Pete kept some of his bulky clothes. Two big jumpers had neatly chewed holes in them. We weren't so worried about the clothes, more so about plastic pipes and wires. We wished the cats would not bring mice in and instead dispose of them out on the bank. It really was a nuisance. Good job I wasn't scared of them like a lot of women were.

As we gave up on the hearing aid hunt for the time being, Peter started laughing and said it would be funny when the ice melted if a fisherman hooked a huge carp wearing a deaf aid. It turned up a week later, all un-lost and obvious on the bookshelf.

I sometimes thought Peter or maybe both of us had 'lost the plot' but if we had then it was a good recipe for happiness anyway. One day the fire would just not get started and I sat freezing staring into it for a glimmer of a spark. Peter appeared with a de-icer spray, kneeled down and aimed it at the fire. I thought he was off his trolley.

"Never mind the fire Peter, squirt some on my feet." I said. "Well" he said "It says it's inflammable and I'll try anything once Mag." "It might be the last thing you try," I muttered disapprovingly. It was warmer to go to bed early which I did.

After over a week of being stranded in the ice and desperate for water, signs of a thaw set in and Peter was able to break up the ice around the boat quite easily with the boat pole. We thought we should be able to break a way through it a few miles to the water point, so while Peter continued to break ice for'd I started the engine and slowly moved the boat to and fro till we had turned in the right direction and could head towards Salterforth. It was slow going and we slowed to almost not moving when we passed the moored boats at the boat club. Fibre glass boats could be very easily damaged and only recently a boat breaking through the ice had been in such a rush, going far too fast that the forceful pressure of moving ice had trapped and crushed a boat between another one and the pressure from the ice had made a hole in its hull and sunk her. It could have been a fruitless journey to the water point as a boater told us the water tap there had been frozen up most days and they had even used blow lamps on it to try thawing it out. So we not only filled our water tank but every other spare container including empty beer barrels that we had available.

Back at the Wharf a chap nicknamed "Mad Mac" who lived on a cabin cruiser, loaned us three books to read and I gave him a couple of books we had finished with. He was quite a character and we often stopped for a chat about this and that. Peter was approaching his boat one day, on his bike when a full packet of bacon whizzed out of the boat onto the towpath much to the joy of two or three dogs who were in the line of fire and soon furiously attacking it. With it had come a few loud expletives and words to the effect, "'Ere ave this lot, I don't feel like cooking it anyway." Peter nearly jumped off his bike and joined in the fight for it. One dog had one end and another the other in a veritable tug of war till the packet split and it was a free for all and the bacon was devoured in a trice. We later learned from Mac that he was getting in such a sweat trying to open the damned plastic heat sealed packet that he lost his patience with it and threw it in a rage off the boat. We knew how he had felt as often felt the same trying to open various packets of food.

We struck lucky and found a couple more old portions of railway sleepers in the undergrowth and Peter soon had them logged up into suitable burnable sizes. Some perhaps a bit too big as they did go off dramatically once alight and flare up. We were lovely and warm and Peter was singing, "Chestnuts roasting on an open fire" as the fire blazed away one evening. Flames were leaping out of the chimney into the night, creating a bright orange glow. A hole burned in the rotary washing line cover which was lying alongside the chimney flue, it just melted. Sparks were flying a bit too much so we decided to burn just one sleeper log instead of three at a time. Suddenly I leaped up in a panic as my nose caught a whiff of something burning in the kitchen (not unusual for me). Phew what a relief, it was only Jessica's tail which she had put too near the gas fire.

We were in dire need of some more suitable fuel to burn on the fire; what little we managed to find and saw up only lasted a day or two. Well, we touched out very lucky when Michael rolled up in his new van and said he would take us to a chair making factory which was advertising 'free wood'. We went to investigate and found the factory where a dozen or so men were working. I went in and a chap told me to help myself to any scraps I could find on the floor or in the bins. So I filled a sack and went out to tell Michael. He said he had found some old lengths of wood which had been lying around a considerable time by the looks of them, so had bunged some in the van. They were so long the doors wouldn't shut properly but he managed to secure them and off we went. Happy customers. Peter's face lit up when we returned. There would be no problems now for a few weeks. Michael said that he and Mark would get us some more.

We developed coughs and colds during December which didn't really amount to anything too bad and by Christmas time we were able to spend a nice Xmas day and Boxing Day with Michelle and Darren at their house. What a treat, home comforts and mod cons galore. Michelle cooked a lovely Xmas dinner and we all opened our presents together. We had so many from friends and family. Matthew had even left a card and some money for me to get myself a pair of Doc Martin boots which he knew I wanted. Life was wonderful.

Chapter Fifteen

Blizzards and Hooligans

With the weather not fit for man or beast, apart from hippo's who would have loved all the muddy conditions, we more or less just had to sit tight and wait, which no doubt much of the rest of UK inhabitants were doing at this time of year.

We'd been under the weather with one thing and another, sniffles and various cold symptoms, for weeks and on top of that I developed a nasty swelling under my arm which the doctor diagnosed to be glandular and prescribed a course of antibiotics. However, after a week I still had the swelling, which was very sore so he referred me to see a specialist at the hospital. My appetite was poor and I felt extremely run down.

At least on a boat there was always something happening to take your mind off aches and pains. A fisherman had somehow hooked a long tailed tit as it was flying and managed to get it into his net. But he was handling it rather roughly so Peter went along and offered to help him and the chap let him bring the bird back to the boat. We put it into a warm dark box and left it where it would be quiet and undisturbed astern and would hopefully recover from the shock of its ordeal. Only time would tell. Later on we released it and it flew off chirping away across the canal.

Jessica had a vendetta against Moggo, she would not tolerate him at all and started to sit on the step by the cat flap to prevent him coming in or going out. It was a constant battle between them. I began to doubt if we would ever be able to re introduce Jesse to live aboard with us again.

One morning, Peter got up and started the engine to charge the batteries. He opened the stern doors just in time to see a fisherman who was sitting right on our tail (to put it politely) engulfed in black smoke as the engine burst into life. Peter apologised and said he didn't see him there and the chap laughed and just moved down a bit. He said the sudden burst had woken him up out of his trance and for a moment he'd thought we'd blown up.

Talking to some of the boating community it was agreed that if enough of us were interested we could buy half a ton of coal between us and share the cost. It made sense and we soon had enough peope wanting to chip in for some. We had 3cwt for £15 which if we had bought from the boatyard would have cost us £42. Of course the more we ordered, the cheaper it became. 'Panic' was a boater who we had nicknamed due to his obsessive aversion to letter boxes. Any mention of mail, post or letter boxes sent him into a frenzied panic. He absolutely hated anything to do with them. On this occasion he loaded most of the coal into a tiny plastic rowing boat which was tied up to a BW work boat down at the wharf. He untied it and got the chap off Megan with the outboard motor to tow him up the cut to the other boats wanting coal and helped them load it onto their boats. We didn't like burning coal, for apart from the expense, the smoke played havoc with Peter's chest. Once we were able to get on the move again we would revert back to wood only. We still had a while to go and were confined between locks and nearby stretches of canal which could be closed any time between 1st November and 11th March. Dates varied depending on what work, if any, was scheduled to be carried out. By mid February Barrowford locks would be open so we would be able to start on our long journey down to Bugbrook to be reunited with Jesse.

Maybe Spring wasn't so far away after all. I watched a little fluffed up robin singing away in a small tree and another one chirping a short distance away. Peter saw a beautiful chestnut coloured stoat sitting up on its hind quarters looking at us. We'd never seen so many mole hills as we saw in the fields now and one field had so many in it that it had almost become a ploughed field.

We heard from Shirley and Fred that Fred had finally managed to capture two of the feral cats of which there were three, (a mum and two grown offspring) at the site where the garden centre had been and which I visited with them last year. It was a long weary task until he had finally caged them and made a two hundred miles (round trip) to the sanctuary down in Sussex run by Celia Hammond. Celia would then put them in large pens to settle them down a bit before releasing them in the area. Fred caught the third one and took that also all the way down to the sanctuary to join the others. However, on arriving he discovered that he had caught the wrong cat, a tom stray and not the third one of the family, although it too was similarly black and fluffy. Celia kindly said that it could also stay so Fred returned the hundred or so miles and endeavoured to catch the proper cat which eventually he did and took it down to join the others. All three of the family were in time, to go to a neighbour of Celia's who was devoted to animals and wildlife and had land and outbuildings so that the cats would be fine once they settled down to the new surroundings. I thought Fred deserved a medal for all his endless patience, trouble and care over the months looking after these cats. There was never a day when he didn't go to feed them.

At the water point I got an unscheduled cold shower. Peter was ready to turn the tap on once I had lifted the deck boards, unclipped the lid of the water tank and put the hose in it. But, typical Peter, he switched the water tap on before I'd put the hose in the tank so I had a nice dousing with very cold water. I looked forward to the next time we were at this water point taking on water as I would make sure our roles were reversed and enjoy a little 'action replay'.

Peter was reading the paper in the afternoon and started laughing so much that he couldn't tell me what was so funny about the article he was reading. When he did manage to stop laughing so much, he said that it was about a vicar at a funeral and when the pall bearers had walked into the church carrying the coffin the vicar was slumped over the pews three sheets to the wind. As the service progressed, the verger had to prop the vicar up to stop him from falling over. The vicar was singing at the top of his voice all out of tune and referred to the 'dearly departed sister', when in fact the dearly departed was a 'brother'. Well, enough was enough and the vicar was carried out by the pall bearers and the service carried on without him. It was my turn to laugh hysterically.

Leo (our engineer friend) and wife Mavis came to stay with us for a few days. Peter and I slept astern and Mavis and Leo on the two cabin lockers up for'd. All nice and cosy apart from the fact that we had always somewhat of a starboard list so anyone sleeping on the right side of the boat had to be well tucked in to stop them having a constant battle to stay in their bunk. It was a bit like trying to sleep on the side of a hill. I had adapted to it by now and automatically 'hung on in there' in my sleep even if the bed clothes didn't and ended up in a heap keeping the deck warm. However, Leo wasn't so fortunate, all cocooned in his sleeping bag he suddenly rolled off the locker seat' unable to save himself, with arms and legs being trapped in the sleeping bag. The small stool alongside the seat broke his fall and he became all tangled up half on and half off of it, bit like a fish out of water, all a flounder. Mavis, half asleep wondered whether to just take no notice, roll over and go back to sleep or abandon ship.

What a strange sight we must have been at bedtime, Peter stripped off down to long john pants and long sleeved vest 'Captain Webb' style. He would leap into his bunk, clothes flung to the far end. A wedge of foam placed at his feet protected them from the cold wet steel of the boat, as his feet always ended up sticking out from his opened up sleeping bag. Another piece of foam, a whole seat square this time, one we had salvaged from the water and dried out, acted as a head board or back rest. No curtains were up as yet so we hung a towel up at the towpath side window which was sufficient until Peter could fit the curtain track up at the weekend so that I could hang up the curtains that Michelle had made for us. We had a two foot long fluorescent strip light hanging freely on a length of wire that we moved around as required, hanging it here or there for reading in bed by. All rather haphazard and waiting for Michael to find time to come and wire up properly. We often threw a few coats on our bunks to add warmth and I'd have my usual sexy night attire on, comprising black socks, long Johns, jogging top and jumper plus hot water bottle.

Michael rolled up with five bin bags full of wood and said he'd bring some more later on. He was working in Todmorden for someone who made pine furniture and all this wood was waste which the chap had told Michael to help himself to. Sure enough later on he brought us five more bags full, so there would be no more need of or any worries about where to find wood for awhile. Mark and Darren fitted a piece of steel plate along by the wood stove and in front of it to protect the bulkhead tongue and groove from getting too hot The family were keeping a good eye on us and were always bringing us something nice or useful. Marina kept supplying us with huge bars of chocolate and Maggie always brought cream cakes so there was no chance of me losing any weight.

The swelling under my arm was sore right down my arm to the elbow but apart from that I now felt well. At the hospital, the specialist who examined me didn't know what the lump was so arranged for me to have it removed and a biopsy done on it. I had already had an x-ray and a blood test. I hoped I wouldn't have to wait too long.

Deciding I needed to go into Burnley one day for a few things, I caught the bus and Peter said he would meet me at the bus stop on my return.

Friday 4th Feb.

But I was somewhat delayed and Peter waited and waited at the bus stop and wearily leaned on a wall that ran between the pavement and a field. Suddenly in the dark something grabbed the hood of his coat from behind. He swung round to attack it with his walking stick, and saw two large horns and equally large wild eyes staring at him. He thought the devil had caught up with him until he saw that it was a very big billy goat. It was in a field with some others but being dark Peter didn't know they were in there.

Meanwhile Peter was more interested in the prospects of pheasant for dinner as there were so many appearing around the canal and announcing their presence with their loud calls. I knew Peter meant business when I saw the air rifle was missing. He wouldn't have said anything to me as he knew I wasn't happy about killing anything. He came back with a cock pheasant (free range and quickly dispensed with).

The pub at Foulridge "The Hole in the Wall" as everyone knew was famous along the canal for the tale of Buttercup, the cow that in 1912 fell into the canal at one end of the tunnel and swam the whole mile through it to the other end. She was taken to the pub and revived with a good measure or two of alcohol and none the worse for her swim.

Britain, it said, was set to shiver, and half way through February we certainly did with freezing Siberian winds. We hadn't chosen an ideal time to navigate the seven locks down into Burnley, but we managed all the same and just as it began to get dark we arrived along the familiar but very open and exposed Barden Lane stretch. Ice started to form on the decks making them as slippery as banana skins and the mooring ropes were stiff and awkward to manipulate. We were more than glad to get down below, it was a real 'lash up and stow' night. We just hoped that the canal wouldn't freeze over enough to stop us from moving to a more accommodating mooring which this one wasn't plus the towpath was closed and big wagons and JCBs were working along it, further down from us. It was the coldest weather so far of the winter and the winds gave the boat a real buffeting that night.

The next day conditions were not much better and the gales just as strong and in a direction blowing across the canal directly broadside on to the boat, holding us firmly on the towpath bank. All our efforts to push the bow out and get the boat moving were futile as she just blew straight back onto the bank. We tried pushing the stern out and giving it full throttle astern but no go, and after half an hour we were still struggling against the wind but we kept trying and in a brief lull between gusts of wind we finally made it with Peter giving the bow his best shove off while I opened the throttle full steam ahead. Up to now we had never experienced such gales as these and some of the worst were yet to come as we approached Burnley's straight mile embankment, set high up above the town. Half way along it there was a tremendous gust and Peter's bike which was lying on top of the boat was just lifted up like a feather and thrown off and into the water. I quickly made a mental note of whereabouts along the cut we were, looking for a suitable land mark along the towpath as there was no way we could stop to try and fish it out as we would have just been blown onto the bank and stuck as we'd been earlier. We just had to plod on and head for the relative shelter of the boatyard. Once there and moored up we walked back, doubled up at times against the strong gusts of wind. Peter took the grappling hook and when I recognized the spot where the bike had blown into the water, Peter lobbed the grappling iron in. We didn't expect much luck really as the canal was so full of rubbish we'd probably hook out everything and anything but the bike and spend hours trying to locate it. After about the third try the hook seemed to catch on something, but whatever it caught slipped back off the hook but on the second attempt it definitely caught on the object and Peter gently hauled it in to the bank, expecting to find some old rusty debris or a shopping trolley. But no! It was the bike basket. I thought it was just the basket which was at least encouraging as it told us we were looking in the right place. Then, unbelievably, we saw that the basket was still attached to the bike, so I held the grappling iron with its 'catch' hoping it wouldn't slip off while Peter leaned over the bank and grabbed the wheel of the bike and dragged it out onto the bank, none the worse for its immersion. We were very happy as our bikes were really indispensable and to lose one would have almost been like losing a limb.

Earlier on I had seen a large sheet of corrugated iron fly up in to the air, blow along some ten yards and fall down just short of the museum boat Kennet which was moored up in the yard. These winds sure were causing some havoc and we were better off just staying put till they blew themselves out. Disappointingly there was no water in the yard as there had been a burst and the water turned off at the stopcock. However, I had saved a reserve five gallon in a pressure barrel, so we had some to go on with although sparingly.

The large barge 'Medlock' when travelling on her way down from Barrrowford the previous day, had put a hole in her port side when she'd hit something under the water near bridge 131A. Being about 40 tons she was unable to stop immediately upon impact so the object tore a large fist sized hole into a vulnerable spot in her hull. Gallons of water poured into her but the chap on board managed to contact BW and get the big work boat to come up to him. They were able to tow, or rather drag, Medlock which was very low in the water, up to the boatyard wharf. Once there he was able to loan two pumps and get them going before Medlock took on enough water to take her down to the bottom of the canal which was relatively deep thereabouts. The chap and another were doing their best in the circumstances, bunging a cushion and planks of wood etc in and over the hole as a temporary measure to plug it until they were able to do it properly.

Moggo, ever the comic, had of late been following Peter to the loo and waiting till Peter was sitting comfortably then would jump up onto his knee and proceeded to curl up to go to sleep, or maybe he just liked getting 'gassed'.

After a week there was no let up in the freezing east wind, frozen canal and frozen like sheets of cardboard washing. The windows in the galley and stern cabin had all frozen inside with lovely icy patterns on them.

There had been a phone call to the family from the social services in Dunstable to say that my mum was poorly and needed someone with her at all times. Gerald had been there when he could but was unable to be there day and night. So Michelle and Darren didn't hesitate to whiz me down 200 or so miles to Bedfordshire. I didn't like to leave Peter but the family assured me they would all keep their eye on him and Michael took him a bag of coal.

It was snowing most of the way but the motorways were clear so our journey to mum's was pretty straight forward. She looked very poorly and was very weak and not eating.

The following morning her temperature was up and she was a bit delirious at times. She had just finished some antibiotics and the doctor was prescribing another course plus some tablets to give her system a boost. In a few days she seemed over the crisis and was able to get up without fear of collapsing and eat more, but was still not well enough to be left on her own. Then Michelle phoned to say my hospital appointment had arrived for the next day! I phoned the secretary who said she would see the surgeon and find out if it was possible for me to go in a week later on 4th March and then to have the op on the seventh. Otherwise I would have to wait until the 21st March. Well there was no way I could leave mum and dash back to keep the earlier appointment, and hoped that if I stayed with her another three or four days she would have a better chance to get back on her feet.

In the meantime, Peter had been stuck up on the embankment in blizzard conditions and even had his picture in the paper. He said that one morning he woke up to find himself under a snow drift as the wind had been blowing almost horizontally across the canal all night forcing snow in and over a narrow slightly cracked open window and down onto Peter asleep in bed.

Snow had been drifting along the iced up canal edges, banking up so that the outline of where the canal and the bank were could not be determined, so that made getting on and off the boat a bit of a predicament.

I told Peter to just sit tight, keep as warm as possible and eat lots of hot food and was so glad that he had the family around to pop in and make sure he was alright. They were doing just that, taking him wood, coal, gas, bacon and other goodies and even a nice home made corned beef hash.

News reports came in of awful conditions on roads as they became treacherous and blocked with drifting snow, with extra police having to be drafted in to take hot drinks to stranded motorists.

By the 1st March mum was much improved and almost back to her old self. Gerald and Freda were a great help and visited often, being very supportive and taking mums dog Goldie for lots of walks regardless of the weather. It was nice to be able to spend some quality time with mum once she felt better, but I had to think about getting back to the boat now and keeping my hospital appointment.

I travelled back by coach and Peter was waiting at the coach station when I arrived at 7.30pm. It was nice to see each other as we weren't often apart. I, at least had had a week of nice heating, flush toilet, home comforts and soft bed while he had been more like Scott of the Antarctic. At least the ice on the canal had melted by now as we found out when Peter woke up about 1pm and said he felt uneasy. There was a strong offshore wind blowing and as Peter looked out of the window he saw that we were across the canal. Someone, youths no doubt, had cast us adrift and it wasn't the first time. It was lunacy really and could have caused unforeseen accidents. It was no fun trying to get re-organized in the dark, with our torch out of batteries The wind had blown us across the canal onto the far bank and there was a cat meowing in distress on the bank we'd originally been moored up on. It was Moggo and he was running up and down stopping every now and then and poised to jump. I dreaded him deciding to leap for the boat before it was within reach or of him falling into the water in the dark, or worse that he might get crushed between the boat and the canal side. As soon as I could I got ashore and grabbed him, clambered back onto the bow and then we had to go across the canal again and rescue Yetti who was meowing and running about on the side we'd been stranded on. Then I searched for Jessica, worried about where she was but sensibly Jessica was curled up asleep in the boat and perfectly safe. There were too many pub crawlers and young hooligans along this part of the canal night and day, and up to no good. Two young lads were in the habit of throwing stones across the canal at us and shouting obscenities as they did so. We would be glad when we could get on our way and out into some nice countryside.

I hoped the hospital treatment would soon be over and that nothing drastic would show up as a result. I'd hardly been back on the boat a day or so when I had to go in hospital early one Friday morning and sit in a waiting room for ages. There were no beds in the ward I'd been allocated to so I had to wait for one on another ward. Eventually there was one available and after filling in forms I enquired about going home till I was due to have the op on the Monday. However, the sister said if I did I risked losing my bed and that it would be wise to stay put. So I resigned myself to a long 'prisoner' of a weekend and worried about where Peter was moored up.

The surgeon came to explain the op procedure and also that they couldn't predict the outcome until they had the results of the lymph node biopsy which he said he hoped would be good news but that I must also be prepared in case it wasn't so good. Peter was there when I came round after the op and over the next few days when I had to stay in hospital he spent hours with me and we played crib to pass the time. I had to have an injection before the nurse could remove and repack the dressing which there was a considerable amount of all packed into the space where the node had been removed. At last on the Wednesday after a fresh dressing was done I was told I could go home but still had to wait till 5pm for a prescription. What with the trip down to mum's and the days in hospital I felt as though I had been away from the boat for months. After the heat of the hospital it was very cold on the boat, and I had to get myself re acclimatized. A district nurse used to come to the boat to re dress my wound and after a week I had the stitches removed.

The report from the biopsy showing the result had come in so I went to see the specialist and he said that the test had shown three possible results on the microscopic bacteria. One was '**leprosy**' (my God I nearly passed out). Another was some severe form of **mastitis**, but they had completely ruled out these two options and that left only one which was '**cat scratch disease**', or 'cat scratch fever.' There it was written down on the diagnosis sheet. I had never ever heard of that one. It was a bacterial infection

that could causes swelling of the lymph nodes, usually due to a scratch, lick or bite from a cat. Symptoms apart from the swelling could be of fatigue, loss of appetite, headache, rash, sore throat and an overall ill feeling. The bacteria was usually spread from the scratch or bite of an infected animal usually a cat. But once a person had had the disease they were usually then immune from it for the rest of their lives.

A cheap offer of coal had us loading the boat up. It was too good to miss regardless of our wood burning preferences.

As a reward for all his efforts shovelling coal, I accidentally knocked Peter's one armed glasses off into the murky depths of the canal, never to be seen again. I was taking the rotary line down just as he stepped aboard when an arm of the line swung across and clean knocked them off his face.

March had certainly lived up to its reputation of being a windy month, with endless gales sleet and rain all the way through the month into April. We couldn't have had a more exposed mooring it we had tried, up on the embankment and we had a permanent 'wind blown' sometimes wild looking appearance.

I think that Moggo had by now caught all the mice in the vicinity of our moorings and was getting desperate for something to catch. He started bringing all manner of objects into the boat, sweet packets, lollypop wrappers, bits of polystyrene, crisp bags etc. I think these trophies of his were a substitute for mice. He was such a comic and was also falling into the canal a lot, running in soaking wet. Much of the time he would see something in the canal bobbing about at the water's edge and start reaching down trying to get his claws into it and the next minute he was in the water with it. The edges of the canal sides on the towpath side were quite high but being rough stone he could manage to get a good grip on it with his claws and soon pull himself up and out. We had never known a cat like him for following us, especially Peter, like a little dog. We forgot to check he was in one night Peter went off to the shop in the dark and as he turned to cross back over the busy road he saw him standing in the middle of it, frozen in fright as cars whizzed in both directions each side of him. Peter's heart was in his mouth and he thought Moggo had had his chips. He quickly nipped back across the road, thinking that if Moggo ran back too at least he would then be on the right side of the road to follow Peter back to the boat but Moggo, dicing with death, ran to the opposite side and disappeared, then appeared again and Peter tried to get him but Moggo took off in fright ran into a yard and disappeared again. Peter couldn't find him, he was all hither and thither looking and calling him and in a panic worrying. Luckily he heard him yowling and located him, grabbed him up quickly, hung onto him tight and carried him back to the boat.

We had not forgotten Jesse and I was just glad that we had not gone rushing down to pick him up and bring back to what he would have found very alien surroundings where a cat needed to be very 'street wise' to survive. It would have been far too stressful and unfair to have had him with us over the winter and in the yard with all the alterations going on.

It was so nice to receive a letter from his foster family at Anchor House by bridge 43, next to the farm.

"*Dear Margaret and Peter,*

Just a few lines to say thank you for the money towards Jesse's food etc which Doug and Mary passed on to us as we have been feeding Jesse since Doug went into hospital and have continued to do so. You will be pleased to hear that Captain Jesse is fit, strong and happy and has passed his winter very warmly in the various farm barns. He is fine and healthy now, and very affectionate after his months in the wild, but very territorial, so I don't know how he would take to your cats as he certainly lords it over Doug's farmyard and puts any other animal that appears to flight. I have enclosed a card of Anchor house and one of Doug's barns so that you will know where Jesse spends his time and will recognise it when you come this way again. We do not have him in the house as our elder son is very allergic to cats, but he spends all his time with us when we are in the garden or garage. He is so friendly that he deserves a proper home with someone who is there all day long, as we all work. It would be nice if Jesse recognised you wouldn't it. Just yards from the house is the level crossing and Doug and Mary live in a bungalow on the other side. I am glad to say that Doug looks much better now but it did take him awhile to get back on his feet after his op. I shall continue to look after Jesse and hope to see you as soon as the weather improves. Best wishes. George and Ruth"

We were so grateful to these kind people.

We had less storage space than ever now after the alterations to the interior layout had been made, but we had more space to move around in. Every inch of storage space was guarded possessively and all stuff was down to an absolute minimum with a constant shunting around of gear from one place to another. It would have driven some people mad living in such a small space and having to make up beds morning and night so as to have bed locker space for living space during the day, and with the boat being so narrow we daren't get any fatter. We had utilized the space above the hip bath by putting a broom handle rail across it to hang some clothes up as there was nowhere else we could hang any.

Our son in law had made us some new deck boards and Peter was giving them all a coat of preservative, kneeling on the stern deck surrounded by boards, some propped up drying, others waiting to be done and a large four litre tub of orangey coloured preservative perched on a plank. A boater called 'Lofty' Lord moored near us on his boat 'Piskard' and came along to ask if he could use our generator to do a job with his drill on his chimney flue. He said his uncle was Bob Lord who used to be the manager of Burnley football club. Good enough, Peter moved a board or two in order to get at the jenny, switched it on and connected Lofty's extension lead. When Lofty had finished his job he came along to tell Peter and shoved a large bolt under Peter's nose for him to see. Peter was halfway through coating another deck board and as he moved himself in order to get to the generator, he up ended the plank with the tub of preservative on and the lot cascaded into the canal like tomato soup. Lofty didn't have much luck as his boat was broken into a few days later. He'd stayed a night ashore at his flat and on return found his boat doors open. His electric drill had been stolen but luckily nothing else as he hadn't left anything of value onboard as it was the third time he'd had it broken into and had decided to get steel doors fitted.

During Easter for some reason or other the Mayor complete with chain of office passed us by in a narrow boat, so I was glad that our long Johns weren't out flying at half mast on the line, or worse my tatty bloomers.

All the time we were moored along the embankment we fed a stray tortoiseshell cat who used to come running out of the foliage alongside the steep steps from the car park up to the canal. She got to know our voices when we called her and in time she'd come out from her favourite place under some hawthorn bushes, let me stroke her and strut around with her tail in the air and rub her head on the fence posts, and sometimes she would run playfully up and down the steps. There were no houses nearby, just the culvert and river next to a large car park opposite the bus station, the canal bank plus a few hedges between a large builders' yard and BT's depot and roads, so she was either a stray or a lost cat and had no collar. I didn't like the idea of abandoning her once we set off on the boat but no doubt she would, I hoped, inveigle her way into the affections of someone else and they would feed her. I thought that occasionally someone else was taking her food but didn't know how often.

With all the unsavoury characters and acts of hooliganism we'd experienced over the past weeks, we were seriously thinking of investing in a mobile phone. It would be such an asset being able to contact anyone at the touch of a button whether in an emergency or not.

An incident late one night helped us to decide that we must get a phone. We were in bed astern in our bunks reading when we heard the tiller bar clang. At first we thought it was Moggo charging around on the roof as usual but on realizing it wasn't, Peter jumped up and was about to fling open the stern doors onto the stern deck when he realized he could be an easy target for a whack on the head. Not knowing who or what was lurking around the boat it was better to be a bit more cautious. Peter soon saw through the partly opened doors that his bike was gone. We couldn't get our shoes on quickly enough and clamber out of the boat to pursue the culprit but we weren't fast enough. I ran up the towpath in my long winceyette nightie, like a ghoulish apparition, shouting and bawling in a most unladylike manner at what I thought was the thief making off up the towpath and not till later realized that what I'd seen was more likely just the wind moving bushes and shadows dancing about. As I ran, Peter charged past me on my shopper bike but the thief had no doubt had his escape route all planned. There was a narrow tunnel under the canal which could be accessed somewhere along this part of the canal embankment and anyone familiar with the area would know whereabouts that would be. Peter had tied both wheels of the bike to the metal stern seat supports after lifting the bike over the tiller bar for it to rest across the stern of the boat where it was out of the way but he had forgotten to put the chain lock on and possibly some lout had spotted this during the day and decided he'd come back and nick it after dark.

That made up our minds, we were 'going' and the next day we stocked up with stores, filled up with water, emptied the loo and other jobs necessary, and by 7 pm we were at last on our way South. Earlier I had taken a lot of food down to the stray cat and felt awful deserting her. I'd told a couple of people about her in hopes that they would perhaps take her some scraps when passing that way. If we had not had Moggo I would have taken her aboard as both Yetti and Jessica were placid enough. But Moggo was not and he was giving Jessica a dog's life going out of his way to chase her off the boat and keep her from coming back on. I asked in the pet shop if there was a local cat rescue society and the lady told me that there used to be but was not anymore but gave me the phone number of a lady called Shirley to ring and an address of a chap who was devoted to rescuing cats and who had about thirty in his terraced house. However, I didn't bother with the latter as I couldn't see this lovely cat, who was obviously used to the open spaces along the canal and the undergrowth and bushes, taking too kindly to being incarcerated in a terraced house with so many other moggies. I did phone up the lady called Shirley and had a nice chat to her and she was very understanding and agreed that if the cat was being fed and was happy where she was that she should be left unless a good home could be found somewhere. She said that she would go and have a look at her, take some food and keep an eye on her so at least a number of people were aware of her and maybe one of them would give her a home.

As we chug chugged along with a beautiful rainbow across the sky behind us, there was a loud unhealthy grinding clunk from astern somewhere and we came to a sudden stop. The engine was acting up, starting and stopping, so there was no guarantee we would get anywhere like that and we didn't want to conk out in Gannow tunnel which wasn't so far off. So we started to pull the boat back to the embankment and were lucky to get a tow from another boater. We wondered if we were ever going to see the back of the embankment. Our good friend, Leo, was only too willing to come and 'sort us out' once more, checking the fuel pump and the injectors, and other things, which he did and in a few days we were ready for another attempt at setting off. This time we invited Leo and his wife Mavis to join us for a week of our journey as far as Preston Brook if all went well.

One of the nicest things about this journey was eating the cheese potato cakes Mavis made on a griddle and one of the worst was the endless trail of debris we encountered travelling through Blackburn. It accumulated in and around the locks like mini refuse dumps and consisted of anything and everything from all manner of plastic garbage, containers, shopping trolleys of which we counted nine along a short stretch of canal near all the big DIY stores. There was timber in all shapes and sizes, car tyres, settees and chairs, footballs, old fridges and even a dead lamb and cat and these were things we could see so to think what was beneath the water was mind blowing. At the last of the six big locks we made our way with some relief out towards Withnell Fold and some countryside at last. But we were labouring to get along so we moored up so that Peter could lift the generator out and access the weed box to see what was going on. Well, he cut loads of plastic from around the propeller, blue, white, yellow, black and orange stuff, also string and after that we moved along much easier.

We were on the move early the next day in order to get the next seven locks out of the way but Peter went aground while waiting for the second lock to be made ready. Nothing would shift him and the engine cut out. So we spent the next two hours man handling the boat down the remaining six locks and debating what the next plan on the agenda was going to be. After a brew and further discussion Leo and Peter went astern and drained some water off the now settled fuel and suddenly BOOM! The engine burst into life and we were able to make our way on to a small boatyard where Peter and Leo drained the fuel tank and found a thick grotty sludgey residue of stuff like bilberry preserve and lumps of soggy goo at the bottom of it. No wonder we wouldn't go with stuff like that in the tank. With a clean tank we filled up with good clean diesel and moored near the top of Wigan flight for the night and hoped that from now on all would be plain sailing

It was the usual slog down the flight but we all worked well as a team, with Leo and I doing the locks, Peter handling the boat and Mavis brewing up endless cups of tea. As we only had one anti vandal key I'd cycled down from the lock we were negotiating, to prepare the next lock and undo the safety locks on the gates. Once this was done I cycled back to the lock which was by then full and ready for Peter to enter. Between us Leo and I opened one gate for Peter to take the boat in, shut it again and locked the paddles after lowering them, then opened the bottom gate paddles, wound them up and emptied the lock before opening the gate to let Peter out. Then finally closing the gate after Peter, dropping the paddles and locking the vandal locks and moving on to the next lock What a performance. It took us five hours to get down the flight, on average each lock took fifteen minutes to get through.

Two miles out of Worseley, in the Astley Green area, I was sitting up in the bow with my camcorder. Leo and Peter were astern when about five youths came sauntering along the towpath all loud mouthed and shouting something about 'giving us a lift'. Next thing I heard Peter shouting and the boat suddenly veered at a sharp angle towards the bank. I thought the engine had cut out because we hit the bank with a wallop. I looked back and saw Peter jump off and walk towards the boys shouting angrily at them. Two boys ran off and the other three with dogs pleaded innocent saying "we didn't throw it". One of the lads had thrown a big lump of solid clay that had hit Peter on the back of the head and he was livid. He said that had he been younger he would have run after the two boys that had absconded and given them what for as he could run like the wind then, but those days were over.

Mavis and Leo left us at Preston Brook and we called in to see Gary and Heather but they were both at work so we left a message for them to let them know where we were heading. We only went a mile or so to moor on a familiar stretch between Stockton Heath and Preston Brook. Later, after we had gone to bed, around midnight we heard loud voices, probably youths coming home from the pub we thought. Then there was loud banging on the windows. Peter shouted out at them and we had no more trouble. It would be reassuring to have a phone which was now on order.

We thought a trip into Runcorn would be about our last chance for sometime to try and find a second hand bike for Peter, so we took the boat down the Runcorn Arm where we had been told there was a shop with lots of bikes. We were disappointed as they only had one big mountain bike which wasn't as good as the last two that Peter had had, but knowing it could be weeks or months before we were able to pick one up somewhere else we decided we had better get it. It was £40, with one tyre very bald and a flat back one with a puncture. Apart from that it seemed okay so we paid for it and wasted no time getting back to the boat and off.

The next day was dry and warm so Peter set about repairing the bike and sprucing it up.

He was out astern and had a little upturned box on the towpath which he put one or two things on including his glasses. Well, that was the last place he could recall putting them after he'd lost them. He was able to see most things without them until it came to reading and then he struggled. I wondered if they had fallen into the water when he had picked the box up. There was no knowing, we would just have to wait until they did or didn't turn up.

Earlier in the day a little dog had come along and stopped by us. He had no owner with him and seemed lost, so we made a note of the two phone numbers on his collar, gave him some left over food and he settled down, so I nipped off on my bike and cycled to Moore to a phone box. I dialled one of the numbers and got through to a work place and was told that the dog had run off that morning when the owner had left to go to work and that it wasn't convenient for him to pick the dog up at the moment as he was out on a delivery, so would I please either take the dog down the canal to the two cottages by the aqueduct or hang on to him until the owner could come and get him later. It seemed that the dog wasn't far from home anyway but it was all a bit 'iffy'. When I got back Peter said, "Oh let him go, he'll find his way back" and added, "He stinks". He did stink too, as if he had been rolling in some rotting flesh. He was a bit of a nuisance Peter thought, so I said I'd take him down to where I thought the cottages where he lived were. The girl on the phone had said to just shove him in the garden of either of the cottages. So off I went with 'Toby' on a piece of rope and he loved it, gambolling along. I decided to let him take me to where he lived and off he went down off the canal path to these cottages which I presumed were the right ones. I wondered what would happen if I shoved him into the garden of a wrong cottage. He ran into a large drive with an open barred gate and I went round the side and felt like an intruder. I knocked on the door but there was no answer and I couldn't just leave him as there was only the big open drive gate with a two foot gap beneath it, so I went around to the adjoining cottage which did have a solid side gate, knocked on a door and felt again like a very suspicious character. Well I wasn't getting anywhere so I decided to just leave Toby in the garden, so having done that and shut the gate behind me I trundled back up the lane towards the canal. The next thing I knew, Toby was gambolling around alongside me, so I tied the rope on him once more and took him back. As I looked in the first garden for somewhere to tie him up, I realized that the back gardens were all joined together so when I had put him into the next one he had just run straight round and out the other side. I didn't really like the idea of tying him up in case he became all tangled up in the rope so I resolved myself to the fact that he would just have to come back to the boat with me till his owner came to fetch him. I think it was all good fun and games for Toby and he had me well and truly on a piece of string. I took him back to the boat and he hung around for about an hour then just disappeared, so no doubt he just instinctively knew it was time to go home.

That night when we went to bed, Peter couldn't see to read so I sorted out some old pairs of glasses that I kept for just such an emergency and found a pink rimmed pair he could see with. He looked like Dame Edna!

Peter went wandering off up the towpath the next day and came back with his glasses which he had miraculously found, somewhat chewed up, alongside the towpath.

Toby, while at the boat, in his playfulness had grabbed an old rag off the box that Peter had put his glasses on and run off with it throwing it around and jumping on it. Obviously he had also picked up the glasses in the same way. We were just glad he hadn't dropped them in the long grass or where we would never have found them.

Chapter Sixteen

Snowball or Blobs

With no more problems, thankfully, we made good time down the flight and in a day or so were at Preston Brook where Leo and Mavis departed. We met up again with Gary and Heather and arranged for the boat to be taken out of the water so that we could give the hull a good clean and fresh coat or two of bitumen. The boat was out one day and back into the water the next, all done.

Reaching Middlewich we soon shot off up the three locks to the turn off branch through Wardle lock and another one and out into the nice countryside. At Wardle lock I had a chat to the lady who lived there and who had grown up on the boats. She'd been one of eleven children and her husband had been one of seventeen and they had worked on the boats including later on the Josher boats. She was on Thomas Claytons boats, the oil run from Ellesmere Port. She told me that not long ago she had gone to answer a knock at her back door at about 8pm and found two youths in balaclavas (just the eyes showing) threatening her. One youth was wielding a dagger or butchers knife at her. She told them they could go to hell and grappled with them and they ran off. One tough lady I am sure, with more than a few tales to tell.

We were still painting and doing odd jobs on the boat, it seemed never ending. We'd had more than enough upheavals over the past year, all the work done on the boat, snow and ice, gales and rain and unpleasant moorings with vandalism and theft, illness and hospital treatment, loss of Blobs. We really were ready just to enjoy some pleasant uncomplicated leisurely boating and time to enjoy our hobbies again and the best part of life on a boat which of course was during the summer months.

In order to have anything like a perfect life on our narrow boat I think it would have been necessary to make the cats walk the plank or keep them in cages. They seemed to delight in acting out drama scenes late at night, always of course involving us in a dramatic rescue scene. Jessica was expert at becoming stranded on the wrong side of the canal, due to going off and crossing any bridge she came across to explore new territory (the grass is always greener or the mice always browner on the other side). Then instead of retracting her steps she would just trundle along the opposite bank towards the boat and stand looking across at it yowling in distress at being denied access by the expanse of water between her and it. With yet another "I'm stranded" episode being acted out one evening by lady Jessica, we untied the mooring ropes and shoved the bow across the canal and then gently nosed close enough to the far bank for me to climb off and just as I did so and was ready to pick her up, she jumped aboard by herself and there I was stranded in my nightie, just me and a field full of cow pats and Peter bawling at me to "get on" and "quick" Good job he couldn't hear my reply. Never mind 'quick.'

Did he realize the bow was now feet off the uneven and overgrown bank and that the bow angle was far too steep for me to just leap onto like a trapeze artist? He had to come in close again so that I could safely launch myself onto it. A night gown wasn't the most suitable of outfit to be wearing on such an occasion.

On quiet stretches of canal towpaths the cats loved nothing better than to accompany us on walks and would trot along with us, in and out of the hedgerows, bounding about, chasing each other and stopping to listen and watch for creatures they could prey upon. They were very comical and also inquisitive to see what we also stopped to look at too and liked to be involved in exploring anything we came across of interest. They would follow us for miles if we let them, just like dogs, but of course unlike dogs they weren't trained to obey commands or be put on leads for safety so we couldn't allow them to follow us around all the time but it was nice when they could come with us. We'd sit down under a tree in the sun and they would play or come and sit down with us. I am sure cats that live in the countryside have better lives than town cats. Moggo of course assumed he was 'king of the jungle' and asserted his male ego over Jessica and Yetti, just mere females. We had a lot of doubts about any prospect of him and Jesse getting along together. Jesse was, by all accounts, king of the castle around the farm at Bugbrooke and would probably not take too kindly to some whipper snapper of a specimen who didn't know if he was a cat or a dog. There would be fireworks we were sure. In fact we had resigned ourselves to the fact that Jesse might not be interested at all in our return and us or the boat and after so long would not want to know us. We would not force him to come with us but just see what reaction we received and take it from there. I had lots of heartaches over him and was very excited at the thought of seeing him again, but I felt so painfully guilty too.

We sat astern one evening reflecting on this and that as the sun set in a crimson sky of fire with ever changing colours like a kaleidoscope as it continued to sink lower and lower in the sky. I had never seen so many wonderful sunsets in my life as I did during these years on the canal. They were really awesome. So much of this life was awesome too in many ways and had to be experienced to be appreciated At times, the boat almost seemed to become an integrated part of the landscape and surroundings in a way that a house could never be. We moved in tune with the natural world when we were out in the countryside miles from anywhere inhabited by humans. It was a very soul satisfying feeling, a contentment with the '**now**' of all things happening in harmony. A time when you could say you had so much more of the true values of life by having so much less of material baggage. **Less** really was **more** for us. What did it matter if a chair was old and worn as long as it was comfortable to sit on. What did it matter if you didn't have gadgets, hair dryers, washing machines and couldn't get a TV picture on your tiny 14inch or so screen. None of it was a big deal, as long as we had water we could wash with, fuel to keep warm with and food to eat and most importantly of all, each other to share this wonderful life with.

As early as 3.30 am one morning we heard a cuckoo calling but it was a bit too early to be heralding the dawn for us more owl like natured beings. We were now on the Shropshire canal and allowed ourselves to become luxuriously reclusive along a nice quiet deserted stretch of towpath where much of the path did not exist and therefore made it impassable. It was perfect, no one man or beast to intrude upon our peaceful retreat. We had nice views over our garden of miles of lush fields and trees and a little stream running along the bottom of the nearest field. Black and white cows grazed in the meadows all around and one very formidable looking bull in another field across the canal. It was reassuring to have the canal between him and us, especially knowing how curious cattle were of cats.

I don't know what we found to talk and laugh about, but we always did though of course we weren't always nattering the hind legs off donkeys. We spent lots of quiet quality time doing our hobbies, reading or just sitting out together enjoying our surroundings and each others company, talking about this and that, events of the moment and interacting with the cats, whose antics never ceased to entertain us.

Our peace and quiet was shattered when we moved on to Nantwich. I left Peter watching the cricket and nipped ashore on my bike for some stores. On my return Peter had some bad news. A holiday boat just starting out on its holiday had come out of the boatyard, through the bridge and smacked right into our stern at a fair old rate of knots. The chap steering was a nervous wreck, shouting apologies to Peter and moored up ahead so as to come back to see what damage he'd done. He offered Peter cash and said he'd never been on a boat before. The back wheel of Peter's mountain bike caught the brunt of the collision and was absolutely buckled beyond repair. The chap willingly agreed to pay the bill for putting it right or for a new wheel if necessary. Peter had only had the bike three weeks after his previous one was stolen off the boat and now we would have the inconvenience of finding a repair shop and getting it there. We didn't really want any further delays on our agenda but having a bike was a priority. We still had forty miles of canal and twenty seven locks to navigate before reaching Autherley junction where we would then join the Staffordshire and Worcestershire canal.

Peter's arthritis had eased off with the warmer weather and at long last his knee was less swollen. A course of Volterol tablets had seemed to help. After we had both been sitting for any length of time our joints were often stiff and painful and to see us get going was like watching a scene out of 'Zombies of the Dead'

More holiday boats were on the loose and they were more dangerous when the weather turned windy. A big crash astern one day and all manner of boats crashing into us as a boat travelled down the canal sideways in the wind, hitting everything it passed. The woman steering the boat was trying to avoid collisions by fending off moored boats with her foot while two men pranced about up on the roof of the boat with boat poles. I hardly dared to look for fear the woman would get her foot crushed or the 'joisting' crew would end up clobbering each other or fall off into the water. The boat finally moored up and the woman came along to apologise and assess any damage that might have been done. The only damage done was to our nerves.

As a rest from ongoing painting jobs we took a stroll along a disused railway line, all three cats following us. It was a magical time of the year for me with so many plants flowering. There were tall colourful pink and purple 'fairy bells' better known as 'foxgloves' with bees buzzing about them. We sat on a bank, carpeted with soft yellow ladys bedstraw, intermingled with patches of mat-forming dowdier yellow crosswort. The latter is named not for it's bad temper as it suggests but because of it's un-stalked leaves which are arranged up the stem in whorls of four (cross like) as are the little clusters of four petalled flowers above the leaves. While looking along the bank we found tiny wild strawberries which although they were so small their flavour was as, or more delicious than any larger garden variety.

It was nice to sit and soak up the warm sun and beauty of the day around us. Peter lay back and looked up into the sky. He could hear the sky larks high pitched trilling song from way up high but could not see them.

Bowers of delicate June roses with their soft baby skin pink petals hung gracefully from the Dog rose bushes and their sweet perfume permeated the air. Honeysuckle or woodbine, was coming into flower with its trumpet like clusters of flowers which Pepys remarked on as being 'bugles' and which he said 'would blow scent instead of sound.' It was a scent as sweet as the nectar which was hidden deep at the end of each flowering tube.

As lovely as it was to stay put and enjoy the nice weather, we had a schedule to keep to, not just the rendezvous with Jesse, but my friend Shirley's daughter was getting married in a week or two's time and we had arranged for my son to pick me up on his way there, so we were aiming to meet up at a suitable mooring within a few miles of the M6 motorway.

We had recharged our batteries for a change from those in the boat and we now felt ready to get to grips with the twenty two locks now between us just south of Hack Green and Market Drayton. It was always a bit easier going down locks than going up them and the locks were set in such lovely countryside it was enjoyable just taking our time and watching swans, moorhens, Canada geese and ducks with their young. One duck was paired up with a rather fancy looking drake. He certainly wasn't a mallard and looking in our bird book he was similar in appearance to a Mandarin but his markings didn't quite tally up. So we took a photo of him so as to look him up in a library sometime. We wondered what the offspring of this strange alliance would look like.

We managed a total of twenty locks in the space of about eight miles, most of which were at Audlem and Adderley. Then it was with relief that we had more than twenty rural miles of lock free canal from Cheswardine to the junction to enjoy. Peter took 3 asprin and went off to bed in a cheerful mood singing "I'm H-A-P-P-Y". Life was amazingly good.

We thought we had made a wise decision once reaching Autherley junction, not to travel through the twenty or so locks into the industrial areas of Wolverton and the Black country's maze of canal systems. We decided to opt for the more rural route down the Staffs and Worcs canal towards Stourport and the River Severn which would be a very new experience for us. However before we did that we needed to back track and go in the opposite direction towards Gt Hayward and travel ten to fifteen miles to somewhere near Penkridge and a junction off the M6 to find a good mooring for a few days while I went down to Luton for the wedding.

Once onto the Staff and Worcs canal we had hoped to find a place without having to travel too far, but with extremely high corrugated metal piling banks, busy road bridges and railway lines, it was far too dangerous for the cats for us to contemplate mooring. If the worst came to the worst and we had to moor up then we would have no choice but to keep them in till we moved on. We didn't really like to do this after they had been shut in all day while we travelled. It was almost 9 pm and we were not hopeful of finding any rough stone or natural banks but our luck changed and about two miles past Coven we found a perfect spot and quickly tied up and let the 'tigers' free. Also the big game hunter as before long came the cry of "Pheaso on the starboard bow – action stations". I hardly had time to blink before Peter was back aboard with a nice fat cock pheasant tucked away out of sight in his jacket. When Peter got around to plucking it Yetti, Moggo and Jessica sat spectating but Moggo didn't want to be watching. He fancied eating it instead and attempted to snatch it a few times. His eyes went the size of saucers and his whole countenance turned wild, like a miniature puma. He nearly ended up in the bag that Peter was plucking all the feathers into.

We had made good time and still had a few days before I would be leaving for the wedding so, after establishing that we would moor at Acton Trussel the day before I had to leave, we explored the canal as far as Gt Hayward Junction where the Staff and Worcs joined the Trent and Mersey. Just before the junction the canal entered a very wide expanse of water called Tixall Wide and became more like a lake than a canal.

At Gt Hayward there was a cabin cruiser called 'My Way' with an expectant mum aboard in the form of a nifty little moorhen nesting astern on the boat between the rudder and stem of the Z-drive. She was sitting there all proud on seven eggs.

'Ours II' passed and we exchanged cheery waves. They were on their way back to Leighton Buzzard. We got chatting to a couple Gordon and Jan on a boat called 'Cloud Cuckoo Land'. What a wonderful name and how magical that we could all live on such fantastically named boats. One of my favourite ones had been given the name of 'Me-and-er'. Such names gave clues to the nature of their owners for sure. I mean to say with a name like 'Boozing and Cruising' what did that tell you?

We had such marvellous days and one day reflecting on such a day I said to Peter.

"If there is such a place as heaven or paradise, I don't want to go because I'm already there." That surely summed up us and our life.

Midsummer's day, my birthday and just the fact that I was born on such a significant day was more than enough to make me happy. Sons Michael and Mark arrived to take me down to Luton and I dashed around preparing a meal and getting my things ready while catching up on news. Suddenly the breeze whipped up, spots of rain became a deluge, stuff up on the roof began clattering about. Michael went up to see if anything had blown off and in the space of 10 seconds or so was soaked to the skin which we all thought was hilarious. The rain and wind took on the speed and sound of an express train, starboard side on, the force of it blurred all visibility with a white rain and wind, a fog like atmosphere. Then there was a crash amid the howling and screeching wind, loud cracks and crashes and a tree, a large willow was uprooted and fell across the canal just a few yards up from our bow, in the very spot where we had first attempted to moor. The severity of it all then struck home and I was very frightened. A boat had only just passed by and must have been stopped in its tracks and pinned on the opposite bank by the wind. The trees alongside were leaning dangerously, their trunks straining over to their limit and giving the impression that they were actually falling on us. The papers described it all as "a freak electrical storm which threw many areas into chaos after a day of sweltering heat".

We had had a narrow escape and considered ourselves very lucky. The freak storm passed as quickly as it had struck and we climbed thankfully ashore to see an even bigger tree which had fallen just yards further down the towpath completely blocking the canal and only a yard or so off our friends' Geordie Girls stern. So they would have been counting their blessings too. As the fallen trees were blocking the towpath we had to push the boat across the canal and scramble off over a cabin cruiser moored there, before we were able to make our way to the cul-de-sac where Michael had parked his van. There was no van to be seen. Almost unbelievably it was hidden from view by a massive fallen beech tree of some 60 or 70ft tall, about 100 tons of tree. Luckily, a lamp post, was all that it had fallen on and that lay squashed and hidden under all the branches. It could so easily have been Michael's van which was parked just a matter of five or six yards from where it had fallen down. The ground was strewn with branches from trees that had been snapped off and scattered. Michael's van parked in the cul-de-sac was cut off by the tree with no way of getting it out, so we were in a dilemma as to what to do next and how long it would be before we could start on our journey to Luton. People were milling about all quite shocked at the sudden devastation around and one chap informed us that it would all be cleared enough for us to get our van out in about an hour. So the lads went off to get a drink in the Moat House and I went along on the opposite to the towpath side of the canal bank to see if I could see Peter and let him know what was happening. There was no sign of the boat or Peter where he had been moored so I continued to make my way along and past some private moorings but there was still no sign of them. Peter must have moved on around the corner, so I had no choice but to hoist my skirt up and wade around the edge of a boggy cornfield with high overgrown foliage and hidden ruts. My legs were sopping wet and my shoes were squelching with water. Then I saw our boat and standing across the canal opposite it I started yelling 'P-E-T-E.' But all in vain. So I tried a few 'YOO HOOs' but they also fell on deaf ears and got no response from Peter. But all three cats had come out and were standing staring at me as if I had lost the plot. So near yet so far, I couldn't stand there all day waiting for Peter to show up, so I found some small stones and threw them, hoping I'd miss the windows but the first one hit a window and bounced off into the water. If I'd been trying to hit a window I never would have in a million years. The next two stones fell short of the boat and a fourth hit the boat and the fifth brought Peter out thinking someone was firing an air gun at the cats. I shouted the latest news about the tree saga across to him and he said he'd make his way up to the van and see us and pick up the bow saw at the same time. I told him to bring me a dry skirt.

Well, that wasn't all that happened as I was shouting across the canal trying to draw attention to Peter. As I stood there yelling, a boat passed and I half hoped they might stop and draw Peter's attention to me. I shouted to the couple on the stern that the towpath was blocked and I was trying to contact my husband on that boat, pointing across to it. Well, trying to hear what anyone was trying to say to you when standing on the stern of a narrow boat with its engine banging away noisily, was like trying to converse in a disco. They thought I was either deranged or telling them the canal was blocked which they already knew. The latter that is, not that I was deranged. However, they noticed the boat and the cats on it and slowed down their boat to ask "Did you lose a cat last autumn, about August"?

"Yes" I said thinking he'd found poor old Blobs drowned in the canal or something just as awful.

"A white one"? they asked.

"Yes with ginger patches". I replied not believing what I was hearing. Then the bombshell came!

"He's at the bottom lock being looked after by the lock keeper."

I was absolutely dumbstruck, so was Peter. We seemed to be leaving a trail of reincarnated cats all over the country. My head was in a spin with so much happening all at once. Poor old Blobs it would be marvellous if he was still alive. I hoped he was but I wouldn't be convinced till I spoke to the lock keeper. It must, I thought, be the nice chap at the bottom lock called Pat who I'd spoken to after Blobs went missing. We couldn't do much at the time

We set off for Luton, somewhat delayed and the whole journey was one big thunderstorm with terrific lightning, like watching a fantastic firework display. Somewhere in the Midlands a boater on a narrow boat was struck by lightning and was now in hospital.

On arriving at our destination the hotel had no car park but had arrangements for its patrons to park in the multi storey opposite. However, the van was too tall to get in. We couldn't find any suitable parking and no one could recommend any especially on a Saturday night. We ended up visiting relations and family down for the wedding and coming to some arrangement whereby the van was parked safely and we were given a lift back to the hotel.

The big day started dull but brightened up and was a perfect day in all respect. I filmed much of the event and had a weekend to remember with so many friends and family present.

Back at Acton Trussel I phoned BW in Wigan and soon had the phone number of Pat and his wife and phoned them. They said they had Blobs or a similar looking cat who they had taken in last Aug/Sept time. I arranged to send them a photo of Blobs and to wait for them to confirm it was him or not before we arranged a trip up and said I'd ring again in a few days. They had renamed the cat 'Snowball'. I could only find a photo of Blobs showing his head and hoped that would be good enough, but within a few days of sending it I phoned and Pat said that he could not be sure whether it was him or not so he was going to send us a photo of him to save us going all that way in vain. Some of the things he said about Blobs just didn't add up, but we still felt optimistic that it was him. But they said 'Snowball' was a real mouser and Blobs was never ever that. After a good route around on the boat I did manage to find a full body shot photo of Blobs, and got it in the post as soon as possible.

It was the month of the 'insects', flies of all shapes and sizes all invading any bare flesh they could find. An ugly brute of such was trying to eat me alive while I was painting on the side of the boat but its bites were tame compared to the nettles I kept kneeling on, in and by. In the boat there must have been two million diddley sized ones and if they decided to bite we'd be eaten alive. At night time they congregated in dancing clouds around the lights, spiralling and tumbling out of control. Peter wafted his socks at them and they were soon all tranquilized.

Peter was nice and comfortable fishing off the stern one evening and half asleep when a hen pheasant suddenly shot across over his head like a scud missile. It was only a few feet over Peter's head and was on its way across the canal to roost in the trees where it probably roosted every night. Well, he nearly fell off his chair and just got settled again when another, the cock bird, squawking and clucking whizzed over flying just as low. It was obviously the evening 'flight path' for them. If Peter had raised his landing net in the air as they had flown over he would probably have caught one.

We hadn't any fresh news about Blobs or a photo of 'Snowball' although ours had been received but the couple still weren't sure about the identity of the cat they had. So I wrote to my family to see if one of them could go to Wigan and see for themselves if it was Blobs or not. Meanwhile we would just have to stay put a bit longer, which meant Peter could get some more fishing in. He decided we'd move a short distance to a nice fishing spot and as he jumped ashore to moor up a big black cow came out of the undergrowth from behind the willow trees and onto the towpath and mooed at him. Peter jumped back onboard. He was definitely not the matador type. The animal ambled off up the path and disappeared. Later on Peter was quietly fishing and glanced over his shoulder to see another cow with a white head starring at him from the towpath. It had a short run with its head down at Yetti, so Peter got brave and at a safe distance did a cow herder's "gooourn wi yer". The moo crashed all down the bank into the undergrowth and lumbered its way laboriously along the barbed wire fence until it was past us and the boat then ambled back up onto the towpath where it continued to wander on mooing loudly.,

Michelle phoned with the sad news that Snowball the cat wasn't Blobs after all. She had been to Wigan to see it and to someone who didn't know Blobs it could have looked similar. But as far as markings or character, the cat was nothing like our old Blobs. We were disappointed but such was life.

Moggo delayed us setting off by about an hour and a man came along the towpath, stopped and mumbled to himself, "Oh, where is he"? He proceeded to call what we presumed must be his dog and then stood by our boat and stated that, "If he sees the cats he'll kill them you know." I couldn't believe anyone could be so blatantly arrogant. I frantically jumped off the boat. Jessica had run onto the boat so was alright but Moggo and Yetti were out sitting on the path oblivious to what was on its way. I retrieved Yetti but Moggo ran through the hedge into the field.

"He's a lurcher you know," continued the man, almost proudly, " he'll kill cats,"

"If that's the case why don't you put him on a lead you bloody idiot?" said Peter angrily. It was an hour before we managed to get Moggo in as he'd gone across the field to sleep in a hedge that attracted him. We had to scramble on all fours through a hedge, under barbed wire, cross the field and search and call before he just came strolling out and quite happily let me pick him up and cuddle to me, till he saw Peter who he must have seen as 'the gaoler' while he saw me as the 'munchy rewarder'.

We weren't the only ones who worried about our cats and inconsiderate dog owners as later on our travels we spoke to a lock keeper who had notices all round the locks asking people to 'put dogs on a lead.' He told us that one day an Alsatian dog had run into his garden and killed one of his cats which at the time had been laying there peacefully asleep. He had a dog himself which he took out on a lead and which only ran free in his garden.

I was on a diet but Peter seemed to be losing the weight instead of me. It was most annoying.

Peter's hearing was getting worse or he needed a new hearing aid, or maybe should have had two. It was funny at times when he'd mistaken what I'd said. I was looking for a plate in the cupboard one day and told Peter

"The back of the cupboard is out". To which he exclaimed "You've put the cabbage out!!!?" Another remark I made about the mooring peg (spike) missing when I said "The spike's gone". And he replied in horror. "What! my bikes gone!!?" I don't think he could have survived another bike theft.

An elderly chap, of about 77 I would guess was fishing one day and Peter went to speak to him and noticed that he had gashed his arm. He was, he said, just beginning to regain his strength after spending four years in hospital, seventeen months of which time he'd been confined to a bed and had gone from weighing fifteen stone to about seven stone. He had fallen dangerously ill after visiting the dentists for a filling and contracted a rare and killer disease caught through unsterilized utensils. A young woman of 28 also a patient had caught it too and had, unfortunately died. He was very happy to be sitting by the canal fishing but added that he wasn't really supposed to be out unattended as he was very unsteady on his feet because he had lost a lot of feeling in them.

We did some serious travelling and three weeks into July were approaching Stourport and looking forward to navigating part of the River Severn. We cycled into the town for some stores and the traffic coming towards us was horrendous, unbelievable and so much of it. No wonder, as we were going the wrong way in a one way system.

Once we'd locked down into the river, watched by many sightseers, we felt very small on such a wide expanse of water compared to the narrow canals. There were some very expensive and snazzy looking cabin cruisers. River banks lacked the mooring up facilities which mattered more if you had a feline crew to worry about. We didn't want to hang about wasting time as the locks at Diglis basin closed at 7.30pm We made it in time and were soon off the river and onto the Worcester and Birmingham canal where we pushed on up six locks hoping to get away from the urban area and vicinities of housing estates which we knew from previous experience did not make ideal moorings. We were more than ready for a rest. The canal was very narrow and shallow with badly eroded banks and much of the towpath side was inaccessible to boats because of thick barriers of six to eight foot high reeds. So on and on we went looking for a suitable countrified mooring. Dusk was moving in on us and, as 9.30 pm approached, more locks loomed up in front of us. Ahead of us on a bridge was a group of youths so we prepared ourselves for the usual verbal and sign language abuse. As expected, they pulled faces, made gestures and cheeky comments and threw gravel at us and if that wasn't enough one or two also spat at us. How I would have loved to have given them all a 'thick ear'

Approaching what we decided must be our last lock before it became too dark to see where we were, especially in unknown territory, Peter announced that the stretch above the lock "looked good" and promptly went off to empty the lock so I could take the boat in. Once it was empty he opened the bottom gates and I went in. He shut the gates and I waited for him to go to the top gates and flood the lock, but they were padlocked for the night, something we had not come across before, so it was obviously a rough area. We had no choice but to reverse out of the lock and moor up by a large industrial estate for the night. The cats were all meowing to go out as they had been confined inside all day but we played safe and kept them in. We were up early the next morning when the lock keeper came to unlock the gates and tell us a few tales of horror when he stopped to have a chat with us. He said that his house had been broken into and burgled umpteen times. Once the culprits were caught and he was awarded £78 but five years later he was still waiting and had not seen a penny of it due to the 'ability to pay' ruling The lock had to be padlocked because vandals or idiots more likely had flooded the housing estate and the previous year flooded the factory which was closed down for many weeks because of it. So it was necessary to lock both paddles and at two other locks just one paddle was left operable so that there was less risk of flooding.

We didn't hang around and plodded on up more locks to Tibberton and thought we'd found a good place to stop but there was a railway line parallel to the towpath so that put paid to that idea. We knew that if we didn't stop soon we would be on top of the forty odd locks to Stoke Prior and Tardebigge, so we sneaked in by a farm bridge where the towpath was poor. The cats all ran ashore with legs crossed. We weren't enjoying our travels up this canal but that changed once we moved on to the beautiful countryside along the Tardebigge locks. However, there were so many of them we had little chance to fully appreciate the scenery or to stop. We started going up the locks quite late at 5pm with another boat pushing on our tail all the way up. The top paddles had two- man spindles but for one to open on their own it was most difficult and in my case the only way I could manage was to do an inch or so at a time by positioning the windless ready to push down on an inch, take it off and replace it in the same position and keep doing this until the water started to slowly fill the lock, and the pressure on the paddle eased. So Peter did all the top paddles while I took the boat in each lock, got off when the lock was full, dropped the paddles, opened the gate, took the boat out, stopped to close the gates while Peter went on in front to prepare the next lock. They seemed to go on forever. At 9 pm we at last arrived at the top lock then went on to do another and a short tunnel which took us up to 9.45pm by which time we just had to tuck the boat into the bank just short of a farm bridge for the night and put planks out to the banks before it became too dark.

Travelling on and through the 2,726 yard long Kings Norton tunnel and more locks, we were of the opinion that this canal had not been worth the slog. We had a plague of flying ants on the roof so lit the fire hoping we might smoke them off. At the end of July it was a breath of fresh air to reach the Grand Union canal. Since leaving the River Severn we had travelled 60 miles and gone through 120 locks. Summer was dashing on relentlessly and so were we with our next challenge in front of us in the shape of Hatton Flight 'candlestick locks' which the paddle gear resembled. Halfway down the locks there was a woman standing at an empty one and she said to Peter

"You're not going to flood this lock are you?"

Peter could see no sign of her boat at the next lock down so asked "Where's your boat?"

"Three locks down" was her reply and "I'm going ahead to get them ready and this one is ready."

Peter wasn't having any of that three locks away malarkey and told her that she shouldn't and couldn't be doing that and that by the time her boat reached this one we'd have already been in and out of it. Some people were the limit.

We were soon on familiar territory between Napton and Braunston

Yetti had red paws and left a trail of footprints through the boat after she had jumped up on the bow where I had been painting.

We had news from our friends in Canada that they would be visiting the UK sometime in early September for three weeks and would make a point of visiting us. So nearer the time we would find a suitable mooring, probably down near Cosgrove, for them to visit us.

At long last we were just days from Bugbrooke and Jesse. We were further delayed with top lock restrictions due to water shortages. Most locks were now only open from 9 am – 4 pm and boaters all had the same idea, to be up and off early into the locks which resulted in considerable congestion.

I had a good old ding dong with Peter one day after he traipsed mud all through the boat. He'd been tramping around a wood assessing the pheaso situation. The sooner we managed to get some cushion flooring down on the floor the better as bits and pieces of carpet were not at all practical.

Chapter Seventeen

Mission Jesse

As we neared Bugbrooke I started to feel excited and apprehensive at seeing Jesse and hoped he was still in fine fettle and wondered if he would remember us? It was 6 pm before we moored up in the same spot where we had been when we lost him We wandered across the little farm bridge into the fields, searching with our eyes for any sign of him, scanning the farm buildings that had been his home for nearly two years now and expecting to see him. My eyes played tricks on me, every black shadow or shape became a black cat. 'There he is under that farm implement, can you see him Peter?' It was only a small black wheel. We walked back across the fields and down the towpath towards the farm and Anchor house, both situated across the canal at bridge 43. Train after train thundered past the buildings and as we neared the bridge we saw how busy with traffic it was and it crossed my mind that it was a miracle Jesse had survived. As we walked along I called out his name how I used to. Suddenly, Peter shouted excitedly. 'There he is' and there across the canal between the cottage and canalside brick barn, walking along the edge of the stone quayside looking across at us and responding to my call was Jesse. My heart missed a few beats and we were absolutely elated. We then saw Mr Reid in the garden and announced ourselves and asked if it would be alright if we went around. Of course it was alright and we made our way up onto the very busy road bridge where traffic was stopped at the level crossing. I gazed at it with a mixture of horror and amazement, knowing how shy of traffic and noise Jesse had always been and how we always worried about the cats being near roads. Around the back of the cottage we at last met our kind 'foster parents' Ruth and George and their son and of course dear Jesse who was making a fuss of George. I called him and he looked but made no move towards me and for a moment my heart dropped and I thought, 'He doesn't remember me.' I stooped down low, sat on my haunches and called him to me again and brought out some pieces of stewing steak from my pocket that I'd bought for him. That did the trick. He wasn't shy then and made short work of the meat and then made one big fuss, rubbing round me while I stroked and fussed him, then joy upon joy he did a big roly over for me then fussed around George again and then Peter, then back to me. George and Ruth were quite surprised and said that so very few people ever got near him and we ourselves knew that he was very shy of people and always avoided strangers. We knew that it had taken months for Jesse to get this close to people after he had been stranded in the area. We were indebted to them and Mary and Doug who first gained his confidence and fed him and for all the kindness and care they'd shown to him.

We decided not to force anything on Jesse, but these type of situations were always unpredictable and never went according to plan, so we didn't really have a plan at that moment. We decided to just play it by ear. We thought that if we stayed moored not too far away Jesse might gradually get to know us and the boat again. So we made our way back through all the big farm buildings, some with sheep in, some stacked high with bales of hay. Jesse followed us and we walked slowly, calling to him and stopping to make a reassuring fuss of him. Sometimes he seemed unsure or wary as noises distracted him and once he disappeared into one of the buildings but came out again when I called him. Trains continued to roar past frequently and a loud motorway ran among the buildings. At times Jesse seemed apprehensive and uneasy but still he followed as we opened a gate leading into one of the sheep grazing fields that led down towards the canal where the boat was moored but on the opposite side to the field.. Still he followed me, fussing when I stopped to stroke him but sometimes seemed reluctant and unsure whether to go any further and glanced back and around him as if he felt threatened out in the open field. We climbed a fence into the next field and Jesse came along too but wasn't eager to leave the little stream area and cover of a bush or two but he came a bit further then stopped. He looked back then looked at me and seemed confused at his predicament. I didn't know what to do either, how could I leave him when he had followed me so far? Abandon him again? Yet, he obviously now knew the surroundings but the boat would be a different kettle of fish for him after so long away from it. My heart ached as I tried to make the right decision. Right or wrongly I could not leave him, so I picked him up as he would not follow us any further of his own accord. I held him close to me and carried him across the cattle bridge, and with difficulty climbed two fences. Peter had gone ahead to get back to the boat and shut the other cats all except Yetti, astern. We brought him in and suddenly he was alienated, leaped up onto the small shelf in the fore cabin, and his eyes took on a wildness like caged big cats have in zoos and he hissed and growled at his unfamiliar surroundings and at us if we tried to stroke him. In time he lapsed into settling down to having a snooze and wash himself between bouts of spitting and growling. We decided after dinner to take him back to the field but after dinner we had a change of plan and thought the too-ing and fro-ing from farm to boat would not be the best plan so we decided to give him a quiet night astern with us away from the other cats which would be the most difficult part of the resettlement procedure.

Jesse was little changed in appearance, a good healthy looking coat, a bit of a saggy belly now but eyes as bright as black diamonds. One of his back legs had distinctive brown shades on it which seemed odd but I think was due to him getting older. He was about eight or nine years now. Well he continued to growl, spit and be wild eyed one minute and the next would affectionately rub his face on my hand when I stroked him. His two front fangs were equally as long and lethal looking as Moggos and I didn't dare think about what would happen when they had to confront one another. Fur would surely fly in all directions. As the night wore on, he finally came off the bedroom shelf and settled down to sleep on my bunk on my woolly jumper and later positioned himself on my legs, till they became numb from having to lay in one position as I didn't want to move and disturb him. He went across to Peter's bunk and slept for awhile and was still sleeping there at noon the following day but also still hissing and growling at any undue or too much disturbance directed at him so we were having to try and apply a bit of cat psychology or think 'cat' so we could cause him as little stress as possible. We had now decided for sure that if we wanted him back on the boat with us it was going to achieve nothing but unnecessary and drawn out trauma by taking him back to the farm side of the canal or letting him out so he could 'run' which at the present time we were sure he would do. Then we would have to keep going back to square one and all through the process of trying to coax him back aboard again. Our consciences told us that the sooner we rehomed him with us the better it would be. We would have to go and see Ruth and George and let them know what we had decided.

Jesse settled most when we isolated him in the stern bedroom but we knew that before much longer we would have to put him or the others up for'd so we could run the engine which we knew if we left Jesse where he was it might frighten him, although he had been used to it when he lived on the boat before. We couldn't risk getting flat batteries again.

One afternoon we walked across the farm fields to the farm to see if Doug, the farmer was around We saw his youngest son Ben in one of the grain sheds unloading a truck of grain and he was very pleasant and said his dad was around somewhere. As we reached the farm entrance a land rover turned into it and stopped. Immediately I knew it must be Doug. Yes?, he said, looking enquiringly at Peter and I with a warm friendly welcoming face which broke into a smile of delighted amazement once we told him who we were. Suddenly we were excitedly exchanging details of all the happenings concerning the events leading up to the loss of Jesse and Doug discovering him and gradually getting him into his confidence.

When he first saw us standing in his drive, he hadn't a clue who we were or what we wanted so when I told him he was almost speechless with surprise and repeatedly exclaimed "Never" and "Well I never." He enthusiastically shook hand with us, grinned happily at me and cheekily said "give us a kiss." Then he looked at Peter with a twinkle in his eye and said "That's if you don't mind of course." He was a delightful character.

"You must come and have a cup of tea with us" he said then added that he just had to go and see his son and feed the chickens then he'd join us.

"Go on round to the bungalow over the level crossing, my wife Mary will be so pleased to see you.,"

Well, Mary certainly was and we immediately warmed to her and she invited us in, and not long after we were joined by Doug and they made us feel at home and were nice to talk to. They were now retired but still doing plenty of work on the farmland on which they used to have four farms. They had five grown up sons and daughters and thirteen grand children. Not so long ago, Doug had been rushed to hospital and had to have major surgery and he was now doing very well considering. What struck us most of all was his deep caring and compassionate nature towards animals, even foxes. We were chatting about foxes and I asked him if he would kill one, expecting him to say yes.

"No" he said "everything has its place". He went on to tell us about a sheep who trapped its head in a feeder and strangled itself. They left it awhile as it was heavy and awkward to remove and on returning awhile later there were three foxes having a good feed on it.

Doug also had a sheep who had a blind lamb which she tended to almost knowing it could not see. She would wait for it as it followed along behind her, touching her with its nose. One day it fell into the canal and the mother was calling to it but it couldn't get out. Doug arrived and looked for something to assist it out of the water. He threw part of a gate in the water but it was no good. He knew that the lamb wouldn't last much longer in the water so he waded in and the water flooded over the tops of his wellies, and high up his legs but he managed to reach the lamb and drag it out. He had had a sad blow recently when one of his dogs was killed on the road. He had a much loved old sheep dog which he called 'Wal-Wal', which was short for something, but I can't remember what.

We must have stayed talking for over two hours and when we left Doug insisted on taking us back in the landrover, saying to me, while nodding towards Peter "You'll av-ter sit on 'is knee" Mary gave us half a dozen nice big free range eggs and we invited them to call in and see us for tea sometime.

Jesse was quite happy, settled down in the stern cabin and had eaten lots of cod, pilchards, and chicken. He wasn't a bit bothered about the engine running or boat noises. It was just cat smells and sounds that upset him. He made a fuss of us but was still wary if he heard the other cats then he would spit and growl, so we weren't really feeling very enthusiastic about introducing them to each other but felt sure Jessica and Yetti would keep their place, but Moggo, never!!

We continued to keep him confined in the boat cabin for a few days and then decided to leave the interior doors open one night when we were all in and see what happened. I dreaded to think what the consequences might be. Depending on the reaction we thought the following day we might shut the three cats in the fore part of the boat and open the stern doors where Jesse would be and risk him going out and staying around near the boat but at the same time having some freedom and to see if he would return to the boat voluntarily. We hoped the years he'd spent on the boat with us previously would awaken those instinctive memories enough for him to want to, but we also thought that if there was a deciding factor against such a move, that it would be because of Moggo's presence. Jesse would not want to be second in the 'top cat' pecking order.

That night after we opened the cabin door into the rest of the boat quarters, Jesse came out of the cabin and walked stealthily through the kitchen into the lounge, growling quietly and then it was B-E-D-L-A-M as Bedlam had never been before. Moggo exploded off the locker seat where he had beeen stretched out asleep and the subsequent row was like an alarm centre of sirens wailing. It was all over in seconds as Jesse went aft and I intercepted Moggo and sent him in the opposite direction. Jessica had reacted like a banshee in pursuit of the action, her hackles and Moggo's rigid like a flat starched pleat on their backs. So, segregation it had to be once more.

We discussed the situation with Doug when he came across the field later on with 'Wal wal' to see how Jesse was getting on. For a moment he thought Jessica was Jesse when he saw her outside. He had had a busy day and his tractors were busy bringing the grain trailers in from the fields. It looked like being a good harvest for him. We told him we were going to Gayton junction the next day to take on water but would be returning to continue settling Jesse back aboard which wasn't the problem as he was completely at home with it all. Moggo was Jesse's only problem and that was hindering the process. On returning back to our same mooring we let the three terrors out and kept Jesse in but he would not come out of the stern cabin into the front cabin, he just sat by the cabin door. Later on we shut the three cats in the front and opened the stern door and Jesse went out onto the path and had a good sniff around before following me towards the cattle bridge and doing roly-overs on the way. I turned to go back and was encouraged when Jesse also turned. But after a few paces he stopped, sat up on his haunches and sniffed the air towards the farm, then stopped again to sniff some grass and growled. I suppose it was all a territorial thing. He went through the hedge and padded around the field but then seemed to be motivated to go down along the hedge and then into the field, perhaps looking for a suitable place for his toilet. Anyway, Peter appeared some way in front of him and Jesse didn't recognise him so turned and came back to me. So I picked him up and took him back to the boat. He purred and made a fuss and settled down to sleep. Jesse and I had been very close and special companions before I ever met Peter. Later on Peter went in to the cabin to fuss him and he had a little play then spat when he saw Yetti

Jesse took over the stern cabin, and loved it when we opened the doors for him to wander out and about as long as the others were shut in. He kept jumping on and off the boat one day and then walked down the narrow gunwale, stopped to look in the front cabin window before jumping off onto the bank then ran back astern and jumped on again, tail up in the air and lots of roly overs and fussing before going off into the field, where he made his way down the hedge and ignored my calls to him. He must by now have known every inch of this area. We decided that before much longer we had to allow Jesse to come and go as he pleased and also that the other cats would have to be allowed the same freedom. We hoped that Jesse would stay and fight his corner and not go off back to Anchor farm.

Doug came across in his landrover, beeping across the canal, his sheep all baaing around him. He parked opposite the boat and called across to us saying "Thought you'd gorn.

Wife came across yesterday and said you were gorn." He had seen George and George thought that Jesse had gone for good now with us, but Doug said he wasn't so sure about that and that the proof would be tonight when we let him out unsupervised and left our back doors open for him. It was Jesse's choice, us and the boat (cats and all) or them and the farm.

So at about 9 pm after getting the other cats in to allow Jesse a 'free to himself' night, we opened the stern doors and I went out with him, along the path. He had a good sniff around and followed me towards the little farm bridge where I left him engrossed on the path. I went back to the boat for a few hours, then went out on deck and called him and rapped on the metal hatch with a fork, a noisy way of calling to him that he had been accustomed to. I went to bed, with a few misgivings, mainly whether we'd ever see Jesse again. At about ll.30pm there was a noise astern and there was Jesse, back of his own accord. I felt elated and my bond with Jesse became even deeper at that moment. He settled down and slept on my bed till dawn and we let him out again hoping he'd be back again later. Morning came and no Jesse however much I called him and rapped on the hatch with a fork, but the wind was blowing strong and he might not have heard me, but then again the wind was coming from the direction of the farm and no doubt bringing all the familiar smells with it.

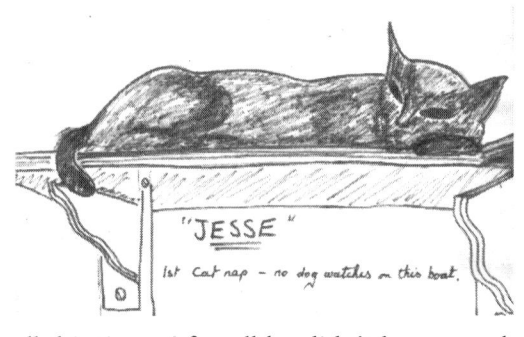

There was no sign of Jesse all the next day and by 7pm there was still no sign of Jesse. I was gutted really as he had seemed to want to live with us again. Perhaps he did but also wanted to have his other territory and company of those who had befriended him all this time. After all he didn't know we had intentions of leaving the area. Well, around 8 pm Mary and Doug arrived in the land rover to give their sheep some feed stuff, then made their way around to see us. At the same time, George and his son arrived to tell us that Jesse had come back to the cottage but at what time they didn't know as he could have been asleep in one of the barns all day and just visited them at the usual feeding time when they returned from work. Well with us all present we had a meeting on the latest Jesse situation and what best plan of action we should take. George wasn't feeding him now so as to encourage him to stay on the boat with us which was one measure in our favour that might persuade Jesse the best place for him was with us. Peter and I followed them across the field when they left and met up with them again by the yard gate. We called Jesse all the way and at the farm gate he came running out towards me, hesitated a bit here and there then started falling into heaps rolling around and fussing about. Doug said to Peter that it was a lovely sight to see and that "Now I've seen it with my own eyes I believe it." He was so very happy that Jesse should react to me like that after two years. Me too! We walked back across the fields calling to Jesse and he followed more keenly than he had the first

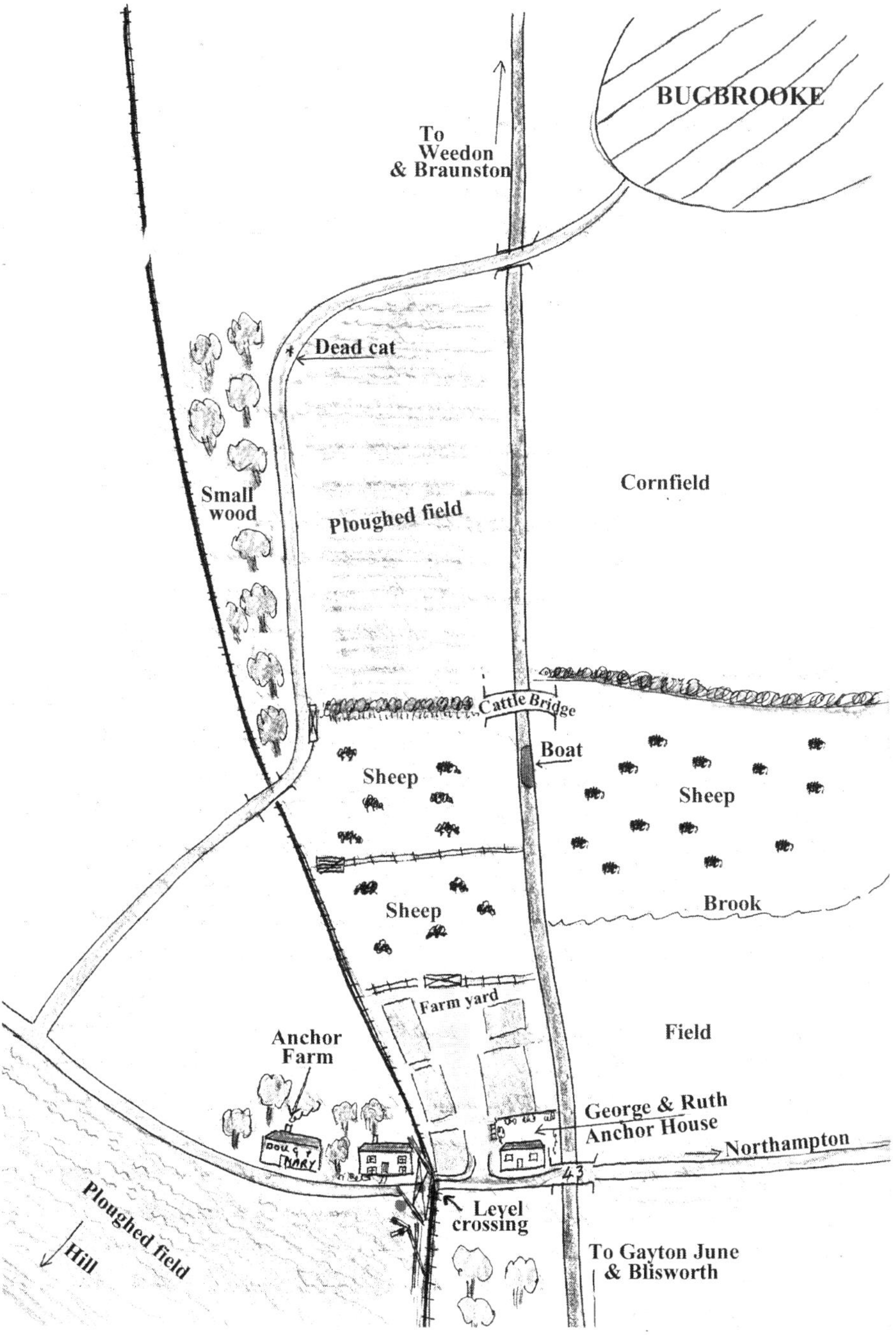
BUGBROOKE
To
Weedon
& Braunston
Dead cat
Cornfield
Small
wood
Ploughed field
Cattle Bridge
Boat
Sheep
Sheep
Sheep
Brook
Farm yard
Field
Anchor
Farm
George & Ruth
Anchor House
Northampton
43
Leyel
crossing
Ploughed field
Hill
To Gayton June
& Blisworth

time and did not stop and hesitate as he had done before. I fed him cod and chicken and he was hungry and ate the lot. He was still growling at the others but they weren't taking much notice of him and all the interior doors were left open so that they could mix or not, if they wished. However we kept Jesse in with us all that night and he was happy enough and more relaxed. We were glad we had opted for this way of re uniting him with us. Any other way would have been far too traumatic, stressful and more than likely very unsuccessful.

That night, Yetti came into my bed and curled up under the covers with me. After awhile she went and sat up on the stern door step, not a bit bothered about Jesse apart from giving him one little growl. He wasn't bothered either. Then Moggo came in walked along the floor and Jesse growled from the bed and he ran off. He had a peek from the safety of the kitchen now and then and didn't do any growling. Jessica gave Jesse a black look and they exchanged further black looks from a distance. Jesse was going out more now but wouldn't come back to the boat if any of the cats were near. He just kept out of the way down the hedge. It was great that he was coming back and not going over to the farm anymore and before long he was going out of the cat flap like a dose of salts which really surprised us. It had taken all but Moggo weeks to learn how to use it. Jesse loved being out at night. I hoped we were doing the right thing taking him off on the boat with us as perhaps it was better for a cat to have a more established home and familiar territory than so many different ones to sort out all the time.

Jesse and Moggo were having regular set toos when there would be much wailing, hissing and growling, but they were males and would sort the cat hierarchy order out before too much longer we hoped.

We were distracted from cat behaviour by a couple of walkers who informed us that there was a cow in the canal further down and people were trying to get it out. One chap had gone into the water and was putting ropes round it, and had to go right under the water to enable him to do so. We hoped they would manage to get it out alright.

Mary came along with Jesse's collar and said it looked as though he'd had a skirmish with something as the soil and foliage where she had found it was all disturbed. Who knows, but we also learned that sometimes cats would get their front leg caught up in a collar especially if it was a bit loose. Maybe that had happened to Jesse and he had had to struggle to free himself. We didn't like the idea of collars getting caught up on barbed wire either or any other sharp obstacle which was possible and could result in the cat even getting strangled as it twisted around trying to free itself. But if we didn't put collars on and they went missing or someone saw them and thought they were strays that could be dangerous too. So we always opted for collars with lengths of elastic incorporated into them which gave them a better chance of freeing themselves if they did get caught up in them.

We had an unexpected visit from Gerald, his son Adam and girlfriend and Adam's mum Mary and we had a merry little gathering and catch up of news. It was late when they left and there was no sign of Moggo or Jesse. It was unusual for Moggo not to come bounding out from wherever he was when he was called. We went out to look for them, thinking it likely that one or the other of them were blocking the other off in a confrontation. We found Moggo first, he was shut in the stern locker seat but no Jesse. So we decided to walk across to the farm and down to the canal bridge and back along the towpath. Before we got that far Peter pointed ahead to the busy road and Jesse on the other side of it. He started to cross the road towards us and my heart was in my mouth hoping that a car wouldn't come whizzing along. It was a relief when with tail up he safely reached us but I decided there and then that enough was enough, shore leave would be cancelled. While he could have all this familiar territory and us he would obviously continue to spend his time between the farm and us, so we needed to leave soon so that his only home was with us. I felt sure that if we didn't he would end up the same as the dead cat we had picked up two years ago on the road at Bugbrooke thinking it was him.

With our good friends at the farm in mind we took a trip into Northampton on the bus to look for a little gift or two. In and out of every store we searched high and low for a nice black cat ornament. We must have looked in every shop in Northampton and only came across one black cat but it was too ugly. We wanted one that resembled Jesse a bit but there were wooden ones, jade ones, black and white ones, ginger ones, tabby ones, brass ones, multi coloured ones and even stone ones but NO black ones to be found. Had we been looking for any other colour, black ones would no doubt have been everywhere. I had one last dash around while Peter sat and waited in the market place, but nothing. We had to give up when the shops shut and did a quick grocery shop in a supermarket before making our way to the bus station. The last bus had gone at 6.10pm and it was now 6.17pm so we had just missed it. I enquired if there were any buses that went near or within a few miles of Bugbrooke but there weren't, so the only other alternative we had was to get a taxi. We found one and enquired how much the fare would be and the driver said £5 or £6, so off we went. The driver didn't seem to know of Bugbrooke too well so I said that once we got there I would direct him to where we needed to go. We shot off up a dual carriage way, past the Bugbrooke turn off.

"You've gone past the turn." I said

"Oh, you said you were going to direct me" he replied rather arrogantly.

""WHEN we reached Bugbrooke I said I would. You said you knew your way there?"

I wasn't letting him pass the buck to me that easily.

"Oh we can get to it if we carry on this way". He replied.

The meter seemed to be rapidly clocking up 10p every two or three seconds and we were still no nearer to our destination.

"We're at Nether Heyford now" I exclaimed. "That's past Bugbrooke!"

We could have done without a guided tour of Northamptonshire.

I re addressed the subject of the agreed fare as suggested at the office and he said good humouredly that we'd arrange something when we got to Bugbrooke. When, that was any ones guess. The meter kept ticking over, £7, £7.50, £8, £8.50 and ended up at £8.80 when at long last we recognized we were in Bugbrooke. After negotiations he settled for £7.

The boat battery was flat when we arrived back so we had to charge that before we could make our way back to our mooring near the farm. As we drew near we saw another boat moored in the same spot almost but we had to stop and moor nearby as we had yet to call in on our friends to say goodbye. We had to continue to run the engine to make sure the batteries were topped up. Just as we finished mooring up a chap popped his head out of his side doors to look at us. I said to Peter that I would just nip across to the farm to give our little presents to our friends, but before I got down the path, the chap came out of his boat, with his face set like concrete looking most annoyed he blurted out, "How long are you going to be running your engine?" and "We've come out here to find a place for some peace and quiet and you moor up right behind us and run your engine!"

We would never have normally done this but in this case our circumstances were so that it was necessary. We could understand the chap being annoyed but he didn't give us chance to explain our position and his attitude was very rude. Peter had to walk away as he said he felt like dropping him into the canal. I quietly tried to explain the situation, why we were mooring, the cat saga and our flat battery problem but he wasn't interested or listening and kept butting in before I had chance to explain anything. I repeatedly asked him to just "listen and hear me out." But how did you talk to someone who had 'tunnel vision' and was just tuned in to themselves and their importance above everyone else?

"I'm not interested in your cat," he added and just at that moment Moggo decided to sus him out and jumped down onto his boat, landing at his feet. He shooed him off and in annoyance disappeared down into his boat.

"You'll get nowhere with the likes of him" said Peter. "Who does he think he is, does he think I'm running my engine because I like the sound of it or that I'm going to sit here with a flat battery, no lights, water pump or tele just so he can have some peace and quiet?"

Peter came across the fields with me to say goodbye to our friends and give them a few little gifts including one of Peter's walking sticks that he'd made with a goose head handle. Doug had seen the goose head stick when visiting us and put a request in for 'the duck one' and said "she (me) won,t get past 'ere till she's been to see me and brought that goose or duck stick wi' 'er."

"We're leaving because your hedges are no good for making walking sticks." I said jokingly. He laughed, with his eyes full of mischief as usual but he was tired this evening. He said they had had a busy day drilling (sewing grass seed).

It was dark when we returned and passing by the other boat we noticed that the noise from our engine was barely audible, just a gentle purr.

September and it was time to finally leave and head on south. Moggo had met his match with Jesse and would slink past him keeping a very low profile and looking wide eyed and petrified in case Jesse pounced on him. So Jesse had established his place among this pride of boat cats. He was without a doubt the Captain of the cat crew.